ORM  IS
IUS

THOROUGHLY!

Seven decades in the sport
of Kings and Crooks

First published by Ormond Ferraris with Charl Pretorius, 2022

Copyright © 2022 Ormond Ferraris and Charl Pretorius

ISBN: 979-8-3662-9051-7

Copy editor: Thalia Pretorius

Cover Design and Interior Formatting by Gregg Davies Media
(www.greggdavies.com)

All rights reserved

The moral right of the author has been asserted. No part of this publication may be reproduced, distributed, or transmitted in any form or by any means, including photocopying, recording, or other electronic or mechanical methods, without the prior written permission of the author, except in the case of brief quotations embodied in critical reviews and certain other non-commercial uses permitted by copyright law.

To Maureen, I miss you more with each passing day.

INTRODUCTION

I am writing from my son David's property on the Keurbooms River near Plettenberg Bay, where I am visiting for a few weeks to relax, spend time with my family and to reflect on what the next period of my life may bring. Having turned 90 recently, I suspect I'll be taking things easy. I may even drop a rod in the river to see what I can pull from the waters.

Being here at Keurboom reminds me of a short holiday I enjoyed with my family in 1939, when my mother had saved just enough money to allow us to travel from Johannesburg to Plettenberg Bay in my father's 1936 Plymouth. I recall walking down a lane flanked by bluegum trees, and meeting a kind old gentleman next to the river. He drove a dented Vauxhall and I sat on his car's roof every day while he put bait on his hooks and told fascinating fishermen's tales. I walked along the same lane to the river recently, his spot was still there.

I was approached in October 2020 to share my many decades of life as a trainer, something I wasn't particularly keen on since I really only spent most of that time around horses. I reckoned there wouldn't be

INTRODUCTION

much to tell. I trained for more than 70 years, some wonderful horses came into my care and I won many races, but that was it.

However, I was pressed to go right back to where it all began, to jot down some thoughts. Believe me, I retired without a vault of money, but I am privileged to have retained a vault full of memories. When I started dusting them off, many a tale of joy and woe revealed themselves anew. Having agreed that they would bring value to readers, I decided to press on.

If I had to pick a central theme that runs through this work it will be the stunning and consistent lows and highs that racing brings to a career. Alongside this, numerous accounts of good luck and bad; incidents so bizarre they beggar belief; unbearable tragedies; a succession of fallouts with wealthy patrons and not a small dose of racing's bitter and ugly politics.

I have to say, at the outset, that I described the many horses and individuals I came across, and my interaction with them, as accurately as possible. I was asked about specific, documented incidents and I answered those and other questions posed to the best of my ability. One of them was, 'Do you regret anything you did or said in your career as a trainer', and the answer was a firm 'No!' If I can have it all over, chances are I will do and say exactly the same again.

I have never denied having had a bad temper in my younger years. I was like a strict schoolmaster around my horses, staff and patrons, but this disciplined approach served me well because it showed in my racing results. I didn't see life as a popularity contest and was considered by many to be a grumpy old man who lacked people skills. But that was because my horses always came first. I never spent my afternoons playing golf or entertaining friends in a pub. My days started at 4 am and ended at 6 pm when my horses were all healthy, well fed and happy. Owners paid me to do a job, I did it thoroughly and there was no need for any of them, ever, to tell me how to do it. When they tried,

INTRODUCTION

I gave them a piece of my mind and sometimes things got ugly. I am also proud of the fact that none of my runners tested 'positive' for prohibited substances in my entire career.

I'd like to point out that I bear absolutely no grudges against any individuals mentioned in this book. You will probably agree that I have reached a stage of my life where there is no point having axes to grind. I want to spend my twilight years in peace and harmony. What happened 20, 30 or 40 years ago is over and done. The stories you will read on these pages form an inseparable part of my life reflected in a biography, and are as factual as I recall them to be.

The last few years have been good to me. Before I retired in 2019, I had the truly amazing opportunity to support my grandson Luke Ferraris with a few good rides, among them his first two career winners at the Vaal on 24 April 2018. I later got to see him make rapid progress and ride G1 winners including the Cape Met. I am so thankful that I can still watch him riding in Hong Kong. Following Luke brings me much joy still, keeps me going as I wind down, and helps me to stay in good health.

I am very proud too, of having started the Trainers Benevolent Fund in the 1970s and managing it until just recently when I handed over to Jeff Shill. We have helped many, many retired trainers and wives of trainers who passed on, with a financial contribution every month, and we have a good amount of money in the bank to keep the fund going. Racing is a game like no other. I've seen dozens of top-class trainers and jockeys, many famous individuals, pass away without a brass penny to their names. In most cases, we had to pay for their funerals. Having worked with and appreciated the talents of everyone we have assisted, it was an honour for me to keep the Fund in operation for over 50 years.

When we re-examined and edited this book I enjoyed seeing it all come together and I agree now that mine will go down in history as a

INTRODUCTION

significant contribution to the sport of racing. I am deeply worried, like most others, about the state of the South African industry today, the ongoing personal fights and agendas dragging everyone down. I remain disturbed about what brought us to the tipping point. There have been some encouraging developments in the Cape and in Johannesburg it seems like matters are being addressed, but to be honest I am not wholly positive about our future in a land going backward fast.

I am deeply thankful, however, for having lived through the golden decades of racing and being able to participate at the highest level for so long, working with the most magnificent creatures on this earth. I believe you'll share a laugh and a tear, perhaps, reading about my adventures, and I thank you for doing so.

Yours in love for the thoroughbred.

Ormond Ferraris

November 2022

ACKNOWLEDGMENTS

I'd like to pay tribute to Kim Remington and Leigh Clayden who have been wonderfully supportive of me before and after the passing of their mother Maureen, my dear wife, in 2003. Thank you also to Clive Barnard, who bought Rooispruit Farm from me and has become a good friend; and Dickie Roberts, who never really received the accolades he deserved as a riding master, but proved his good character and horsemanship over and over as Stud Manager and caretaker at Rooispruit.

I wish to thank the individuals who made this book possible, starting with Natalie Bergh and Jay August who gave of their time tracking down some hard-to-find research material, and Jehan Malherbe for making the ARO database available. Chesty Wolfaardt, JC Photos, HF Kenny and the Form Organisation found and produced photos of many of the horses mentioned. The Cape Photo Lab developed some old film for us. David and Paul Ferraris, Sharon Kotzen and Weichong Marwing helped to fill in some of the forgotten details and Charl Pretorius put it all together. Lastly, a big thank you to Advocate Nigel Riley for originating and funding this project. Cheers to all of you!

FOREWORD
ALEC HOGG

The arrival of my pre-publication copy of Thoroughly sparked a degree of trepidation.

For four decades, reading has been at the core of my personal and professional existence. Far too many books, probably 90% of those published, are a waste of time. This worthless quotient rises still further with autobiographies – the author's own life story.

More than a few relationships have been destroyed by honest feedback to authors. And as Ormond Ferraris would expect nothing less that brutal honesty, I feared the worst.

Overlay this with the subject being a very private man, one who has always counted his words before releasing them. And this project was unlikely material for a page-turner.

I need not have worried.

With the expert assistance of talented wordsmith Charl Pretorius, the end-product is a gem. From how to pick a yearling, a scuffle with a jockey and a warning off, through to Distinctly's July, from the reason he was forced to abandon the Cape to why he tossed it all in, there is much to savour.

Admitted, I was unable to linger as long as I wanted, racing through the pages like a Ferrari runner at the business end of the Oaks. Then again, the real judge of any book is the number of times it is revisited. Which in my case will be many.

Thoroughly opens a long-closed window to extraordinary life. For those of us who know and love the man, it is classic Ormond Ferraris, offered without apology or embellishment. Because that's his way. He has always told it as he sees it. Most often correctly.

There is much in the pages which follow that paints an accurate picture of this unparalleled horseman whose love for the thoroughbred, whose principles and integrity, will live long after he has left us.

His track record proves him to have been an excellent judge of horseflesh, among the best to set foot in one of SA's sales rings. Not as evident, though, is an unerring ability to judge human beings.

Bear that in mind as you absorb the stories and insights that follow. To illustrate, indulge me with one of my own stories.

For years, whether joining his first string for pre-dawn work, a coffee in his Turffontein office or on memorable trips to breeding farms, Ormond and I fenced over differing opinions about the SA racing industry's dominant owner, Steinhoff CEO Markus Jooste.

Ormond referred to the man as "Joostie", dismissing propaganda that claimed he was the country's most successful business-builder. He saw the celebrated entrepreneur as someone without honour. One who pursued his own narrow interests and to hell with the way it affected the horses.

He was deeply suspicious of Jooste's acclaimed business prowess which transformed his small company into a global giant - and its

FOREWORD

CEO into the dominant South African owner and house guest at the most prestigious racing establishments, including Ireland's fabled Coolmore.

Ormond wasn't swayed in this conviction, even though the world's biggest banks, the most respected investment analysts, the clutch of accounting experts on Steinhoff's directorate and even Big Four auditor firm Deloitte publicly backed the billionaire.

At his peak, such was Jooste's grip on SA racing that pretty much every trainer had a set of black green and gold silks hanging in their cupboards. These well known colours almost made it into the Turffontein mancave. But not quite.

After much nagging from my side, Ormond eventually relented and agreed to train a horse for him, provided I race it in partnership with Jooste. When the poor beast arrived, its chosen trainer was apoplectic, sending the float straight back to where it came from. The incident gets a brief mention in this book.

The story which hasn't been told is how Ormond saw the arrival of this "deformed" animal as confirmation of everything he believed about "Joostie". In the months and years since, he spared no opportunity of reminding me of it. Repeating his warning that this man was not to be trusted.

It was an unerringly accurate insight, as the rest of humanity only discovered much later when, in December 2017, Jooste was unmasked as the engineer of South Africa's biggest ever corporate fraud. A con job that cost investors hundreds of billions of rand.

Then again, in a long and colourful career, Ormond knows better than most that racing is an enterprise which has always attracted society's princes and knaves. The best and the worst of humanity.

Determining who fits where, is not always easy. Once again, Ormond Arthur Ferraris is an exception. For anyone who has met the man, there can be no doubt into which category he falls. Ever.

Alec Hogg

Founder of Moneyweb and Biznews

CHAPTER 1

I first saw the light of day on Thursday 31 March, 1932 in a farming settlement called Wolwehoek in the Northern Orange Free State. I was the youngest of two children following Ethne, my sister, by two years. My father was a Post Office technician who, at the time, worked on the old 'party' telephone lines in the District Heilbron. My mother was a teacher.

Wolwehoek's claim to fame was its housing of a concentration camp, set up by the British Empire in the Second Boer War between 1900 and 1902 specifically for the black trackers and farm workers who had fought alongside the Boers. It was also a prominent railway stop, but the ruins of the old railway station are all that remain in the region today.

We were in between World Wars and in the middle of a worldwide depression, but there was a lot going on at the time. I was born on the day Henry Ford launched the Ford Motor Company's first V8 engine in Dearborne, Michigan, and a day after Amelia Earhart became the first woman to fly solo across the Atlantic.

According to Google, I belong to 'The Silent Generation', so named because many of its members found it wise not to speak out. I guess that those individuals who were witness to, and perhaps party to, the human rights atrocities committed around the world, lived in fear of being called out after the wars were over.

The Great Depression in the United States in the early 1930s led to a slump in world trade and had a pronounced economic and political effect on South Africa, as it did on most nations at the time. The demand for South African agricultural and mineral exports fell drastically, and communities in farm areas and in cities were affected. The poor way outnumbered the rich, and thousands died of hunger.

Over 300,000 South African men fought with the Allied Forces in East and North Africa and Italy from 1939 to 1945, but no battles took place on our own soil. Our people were predominantly affected by the world economic downturn that had started a few years before WWII.

South Africa's saving grace was our large and advanced gold mining industry and our gold resources. The price of gold rose as investors sought a haven from the dead financial securities market. Gold and diamonds are what brought my grandfather, Bernardo Ferraris, to South Africa from his place of birth in Northern Italy at the age of 15. He arrived on a boat in Cape Town, migrated to Kimberley and was among the thousands of fortune-seekers during the Gold Rush. This was a wild and adventurous period of time that started in the 1870s and despite the wars with the British continued well into the 1900s.

Bernardo, the keen diamond prospector, was an active Italian in his downtime too. He fathered 10 boys, including my own father, Ernest Ferraris, as well as two girls. They were all born in the mining town of Kimberley.

My mother Jose, a Kimberley girl herself, was trained at the Teachers College in town in the 1920s and I can recall some of her stories about the early years of the Depression. In her time as a young educator she was first assigned to a school in Leeudoringstad, in the old Transvaal colony and in her care, she said, were the poorest of children. They came to school without shoes or jerseys, even in the middle of winter, and many were underfed. She returned to Kimberley and married my father.

My uncle, Umberto Ferraris, the eldest of Bernardo's children, fought for the Allied Forces in South West Africa in WWI. During his service in 1914, whilst out on the front lines, he volunteered to go down a dangerous well to fetch water with the knowledge that a German mine had been planted on the side of the well. He received a Military Cross for Bravery.

My short history lesson would have given you some background to the world of my youth, and I'll put the timeline into more perspective.

Due to my father's Post Office duties, our family had to move first from Kimberley to Wolwehoek in 1931, and then to Potchefstroom in the old Transvaal Province in 1938. My father drove a 1936 Plymouth, it had a spare wheel fixed to the back of the car and we were proud of it. My sister and I had already attended a number of schools, but we were a happy bunch as my dad was doing well at his job and my mother had found another teaching position in our new town.

Rumours of war, and the actual outbreak of the Second World War in September 1939 brought fear and worries to all. When Britain declared war on Germany on September 3, 1939, South Africa's United Party split. Although South Africa was still a British territory, General JBM Hertzog wanted us to remain neutral, but Jan Smuts opted for joining the British war effort. Smuts became the Prime Minister, and South Africa declared war on Germany.

About 334,000 men volunteered for full-time service in the South African Army during the war. They joined the war on the Allies side and fought major battles in North Africa, Ethiopia, Madagascar and Italy.

The war had a huge social and economic effect on South Africa. Gold and mining remained our biggest industry in the country, but with the need for supplies, manufacturing had begun to expand significantly. Places like Johannesburg and Pretoria were bustling with activity.

My father's technical skills were in demand in the big and growing city of Johannesburg. We moved from Potchefstroom to the so-called 'City of Gold' at the end of 1939. We moved into a rented house in Hillbrow before we settled in the south of the city, in the suburb of Forest Hill, where we were surrounded by a host of small training establishments on the roads bordering Turffontein Racecourse.

CHAPTER 2

Johannesburg in the 1940s was a sprawling place. The old Victorian character of the city began to change, as many historical landmarks of old Johannesburg fell prey to land economics.

The northern areas around Parktown and Illovo were developed to house wealthy entrepreneurial, financial and upper management classes. There were enormous mansions numbering 20 rooms or more, seemingly built with little consideration to expense. Many of these houses were occupied by highly qualified mining specialists, head-hunted from America and England with promises of lucrative salaries and comfortable living conditions.

The City Council made attempts to develop similar suburbs south of the mine belt, such as Turffontein, Rosettenville and La Rochelle, but they failed to attract the high-income groups they desired. These areas soon developed a distinct working class flavour.

There were big building operations in Johannesburg's city centre but on the southern side, where we'd moved in, the city retained its old-fashioned character with small merchant shops, general dealers and cafés, served first by horse-drawn trams and later by an electrical tramway system that connected workers from the south with the central business districts.

Turffontein was to South Africa what the town of Newmarket is to England - centred around horses and the trainers, jockeys, grooms and farriers who worked with them. In 1940, there would have been about 30 trainers with houses and stables near the race track in Turffontein's neighbouring suburbs of Forest Hill, Rosettenville and Booysens. Each trainer had a house with stables and an empty stand next to it which served as a paddock. Most had only 10 to 15 stables, the bigger trainers housed a maximum of 30 horses.

My only contact with horseracing was a few newspaper reports about Lenin, the superstar of the era who'd beaten everything in sight in races like the SA Nursery, the Benoni Guineas, the SA Derby and the Summer Handicap. In the latter part of his career, he was stabled at Turffontein and trained by Willy Murphy.

My mother often spoke about her brother, Arthur Victor, who was a jockey riding in Kimberley, Port Elizabeth and Cape Town. He'd completed his apprenticeship under a trainer named Harry Bradley, but could only ride about 30 or 40 horses every year because of weight problems.

Every day, I saw jockeys on horses walking near our new family home in Napier Street and some of them looked on the heavy side too, like I'd pictured uncle Arthur. Jockeys were supposed to be small guys. "No," said my father, smiling. "They are the horse grooms and normally a bit bigger than the jockeys. They look after the horses in their stables and take them down to the track in the morning to exercise and get fit for races."

There were a number of trainers just around the block from us, in Holt Street. Two names I remember were Howard Ginsberg and Les Rathbone, successful horseman who'd be among my colleagues in later years. Sometimes I walked alongside the grooms and horses to their yards and others for a casual look inside the stables and paddocks. Other youngsters from the neighbourhood were interested too. There was always a commotion around the big thoroughbreds and most trainers allowed children to pat or hug the laid-back ones before they were put back into their barns. It is safe to say that Turffontein in the 1940s was a place where horses were loved and appreciated by the entire community. The place smelled of 'horse'!

My mother got herself a good teaching job at the End Street Convent in downtown Johannesburg. The Convent later became St Theresa's School, was moved to Parktown, and is one of the oldest existing schools in Johannesburg. Ethne was educated at the Convent, while I was sent to Marist Brothers in Koch Street, a few blocks up the road near Park Station in the city centre.

I took the tram to my school in Koch Street, perhaps never a lad destined for academic greatness due to a mild lack of interest. I did not know it in those early years at school, but I'd been bitten by a bug and acquired an ailment for which the only known remedy was a life-long education in horsemanship.

CHAPTER 3

I was a quiet young chap and didn't make many friends at school. I don't remember too much aside from learning all the basics from our teachers and going through the motions. I didn't dislike being there, but I wasn't exactly mad about sitting in classrooms all day, either. My mind became occupied with horses. There was just a nudge at first, followed by stronger impulses as I got a little older.

One boy, Mike McLean, shared my enthusiasm. We were about 12 or 13 years old, I think, in Standard 6, and he became my first good mate. Mike lived with his family on a smallholding near the Rand Airport in Germiston, just up the road from the Gosforth Park Racecourse, and they owned 10 riding horses.

Visiting Mike at their home on Saturdays held the vague prospect of sneaking a peek at horses racing at Gosforth Park. But the track was partly secluded behind tall trees and didn't have a low wire fence and a roadside view like certain parts of its Turffontein equivalent.

At that stage, however, I was more intrigued by horses than by racing itself. I wanted to get on horseback to try my hand at riding. I soon got my opportunity when Mike showed me around their plot and introduced me to the hacks they had stabled there.

The name of the first horse I touched here escapes me, but Mike put a saddle on one and saddled another for himself. He showed me how to mount the horse, how to hold the reins and how to make it go left or right. We went for rides around the farm and I fell off a few times, but within a few weeks I was good enough to gallop my horse as fast as it could go on a long stretch of land parallel to the airport's landing strip.

In due course we started challenging each other to race next to the runway, which gave me a chance to feel like a professional jockey. I experimented with the length of the stirrup irons, lifted my backside from the saddle and pushed my rides out to go faster. Mike did, too, and our races became more intense. It was a whole lot of fun as we won races in turn. Those became some of the best days of my young life.

Back home, my visits to racing stables in our neighbourhood became more frequent. I spent most of my time off from school befriending grooms and eventually managed to sit on a few thoroughbreds. Other keen young lads from the area who knew the basics of riding were also allowed into the paddocks. There were some friendly trainers who didn't mind us trotting the quiet horses around at certain times, as long as someone kept an eye on us.

Aged 16, with big dreams, I'd more or less made up my mind. I wanted to be a jockey. I discovered that the other guys coming around the paddocks had the same ambitions but I felt I was one up on them. My many afternoons racing on the McLean farm had made me a capable rider.

It was time to put my plans into action.

CHAPTER 4

One of the leading trainers of the era was George Weale. He was known for winning the Durban July with Longstop (1921) and Glen Albyn (1928), and for his exploits with horses like Colesberg, winner of the 1920 Triple Crown (Benoni Guineas, SA Derby and SA St Leger), Superficial, Fair Bay, Gay Lady and Slip Knot, who won the 1944 Johannesburg Winter Handicap and Summer Cup in the same year. Weale was based at a stable complex in Nelson Road, on the other side of the Kliprivier Motorway, owned by the wealthy financier and goldmining entrepreneur, Norbert Erleigh.

A horseman of distinction, Weale had also trained for other prominent, high-profile people from South Africa and abroad. They included the diamond tycoon Sir Abe Bailey, one of the so-called 'Randlords' knighted for his services to the British Empire, and one of the wealthiest men in the world in 1930. Other patrons were Solly Joel, who took over the massive Barnato Diamond Company when its notorious founder Barney Barnato died; and the Honourable Hugh Windom, a High Court Judge.

Following an argument with Erleigh in the mid-1940s, Weale moved to a new premises in Ferreira Street, about 10 blocks away from the racecourse where he had a house, 15 stables and an adjacent paddock. That will sound like a small string for a top trainer, but they were only allowed a maximum of 30 horses each. The horse population was spread among the many small trainers domiciled in the jurisdiction, as noted earlier.

Weale was the most respected trainer in the Turffontein village. He was a gentleman on top of being a true horseman, a kind soul with time for everyone. He'd missed out on training his former patron Erleigh's champion sprinter, Gambut, to trainer Jackie Gorton, but the old man continued to churn out winner after winner. Gambut, incidentally, was exported to the UK in 1947 where he raced successfully before a return to South Africa in 1950, where he won again, aged eight!

My mother, Jose, attended the same church as Weale's wife, Yola. Both were ardent Catholics and became good friends. My mom knew that I was dead set on becoming a jockey and, you guessed it, I was soon introduced to the Weales. I started spending more and more time in Ferreira Street.

This was 1949. I had just finished school and my experience with the McLean horses proved to be invaluable. Riding came naturally to me. There was no Jockey Academy like there is today. Young lads who were considered promising enough would serve their apprenticeships with a trainer, living on the premises, learning to ride and working in the respective training yards.

I wasn't indentured as George Weale's official apprentice - at the time I wish I had been - but he taught me what I needed to know about balancing myself in the saddle, closing my knees with toes pointed in, and to be easy on the whip. He gave me a few opportunities to ride some of his well-tempered runners in work. I was good at it, later started riding the stronger ones, and my ambition grew because I was light, not too tall and seemed to have a rapport with horses.

Weale was watching me, quietly. He wanted his horses to run at a certain pace and he used a stopwatch to make sure that his work riders got the fractions right. If we tried to ease up a little going around the bend, where he couldn't see us, or if we made the gallop a bit faster than required, Weale knew. He wasn't fooled, and he let us know as much!

I tried to keep my weight down. Every morning my father prepared sandwiches for me to eat at lunch, but I gave it to our gardener on the way out. I ate just a little bit each day, motivating myself to stay light by thinking of my first ride in a race, and the silks I'd be wearing.

In due course, however, Weale gave my hopes a dent when he said one day: "I know you are keen son, you ride very well. But you're going to be too tall and too heavy."

My parents reminded me that my uncle, Arthur Victor, had to battle for every ride because he was too heavy and his constant wasting had caused him to suffer health problems along with financial heartaches. They were worried about me. We spoke about other career possibilities and they tried to help.

My father found me a job at Lezards Auctioneers in Fox Street, Johannesburg. They were auctioneers of antique furniture, stinkwood furniture, oil paintings and all sorts of valuable things. I enjoyed it, because I learnt a lot in the short time I was there.

I clearly remember being fascinated in this time by the work of Irma Stern, who painted landscapes and portraits in saturated colours and became hugely popular. Lezards sold many of her paintings. Investors from all over secured them for 10 - 15,000 Guineas in 1950 and I wish I had made a plan to get one, too. One of her paintings, Bahora Girl, sold for R34-million at a London auction in 2011. They are still in demand and worth a lot of money today.

Another memory that sticks out was taking my sister, Ethne, to the newly founded His Majesty's Theatre in Commissioner Street. She was an exceptional ballet dancer and I recall waiting in the parked car for her, for hours, while she rehearsed for live ballet shows and musicals.

Ethne made ballet her career, a refined person with a love for the arts. But the Ferraris family was only made for one fine artist. This guy was not going to be an auctioneer, and I wasn't cut out for sales either.

I received an offer from Burchmore Auctioneers, who sold cars and property and horses and everything else. Herbert Greenwood offered me double the salary I received at Lezards to join JC Burchmores, but my head was still with George Weale's stables in Ferreira Street. I felt I was old enough, at 18, to make an important career decision.

CHAPTER 5

In 1950, the first signs of political upheaval were noticeable when the Transvaal Indian Congress (TIC) initiated what they termed the 'Decade of Defiance', against the white Nationalist Party. In the same year, Nelson Mandela became president of African National Congress Youth League (ANCYL).

In the world of thoroughbred breeding, The Birch Brothers of Vogel Vlei Stud had risen to prominence and E.V. Birch's three sons - Sydney, Ted and Walter - each assumed control of a separate farm, all of which operated under the Vogel Vlei banner, with 120 mares. They imported a succession of high-class stallions that became champion sires: Fairthorn (by Fair Trial), Ranjit (by Fairway), Herculaneum (by Donatello), High Veldt (by Hyperion) and Plum Bold (by Bold Ruler).

Due to import difficulties during the Second World War, and pressure from local breeders after that, the government placed a ban on horses imported for racing purposes. There was also, for economic reasons, a limit on the amount that could be spent annually on imported breeding stock.

On the racing front, Milesia Pride, Good Health, Dizzy II, Mowgli, Black Cap and Gambut, on his return from the UK, were the best performed and most spoken-about horses.

In the suburb of Turffontein, I was at George Weale's barn one day talking to the boss, and my parents had come over for tea with his wife, Yola.

"Ormond," Weale said, "you have to let it go young man, you're not going to be a jockey."

I pleaded: "But I want this, I want to be here, riding. I can do it!"

Weale, in thought, looked around his training yard and rubbed his chin.

"Tell you what. I can actually do with some help. Come work for me as a fellow-trainer. You can be my assistant. I can give you plenty to do. And you can still ride a few in work."

Perhaps that wasn't exactly the answer I'd wanted, but that I could work in the stables around horses every day was enough to ignite a new spark. I liked the suggestion.

My father wasn't keen on Weale's offer and my mother looked concerned, as I knew she would.

"George, what if he doesn't make it? What then? He'll be a bum on the streets. Please, we don't want that to happen, we'd rather send him out to learn a trade," said my father.

Weale replied: "I'm getting old, Ernest, I need help. Ormond will be ideal. He's dedicated, keen as mustard. He will make it!"

I am not sure what I would've done if my parents had put a final and vehement stop to my plans that day, but they didn't. I suspect Mother handled the issue in prayer, and Father simply supported me as he always did.

The Jockey Club's statistics show that there were 242 trainers registered in South Africa in 1950. Of them, 180 were owner-trainers. There were 109 jockeys and 83 apprentices who were housed with trainers around the country.

Before I joined George Weale, there were no assistants registered in racing. I can't officially verify it, but I am near certain that I became the first official Assistant Trainer in the land.

Interesting times lay ahead!

CHAPTER 6

I remember George Weale and my days working for him as if they were yesterday. It's hard to believe that what I see in my mind's eye today, happened more than 70 years ago. I can clearly recall the sound of his voice, the way he spoke, the way he walked and of course the many little things he taught me about horses and horsemanship. I am thankful that I was able to start my career with the guidance of such a fine horseman.

Weale was a pleasant and mild-mannered man. Not once, for example, did I hear him raise his voice at his wife, Yola. If he had a temper, it never surfaced during my few years in his employ. He was not soft on his staff, however, a hard and punctual taskmaster.

I was not to earn a wage, but that never bothered me. Times were hard, jobs were in short supply. I was quite content with my serving of a free apprenticeship under a top trainer, with a view to becoming a trainer myself. The time spent under the tutelage of a master of his craft would prove to be priceless.

Weale's first lesson was one that I passed on to my own assistants many years later, was: "Races are won in the stable, not on the track!"

Lesson 2: "Feed them right!"

Lesson 3: "Get them as fit as possible. Fit horses win races!"

Lesson 4: "Place them in the right races!"

Lesson 5: "Keep your mouth shut at all times. Speak to nobody about our horses. Never give away the stable's secrets!"

At the time trainers and jockeys were not entitled to a share of the stakes won by their horses, not even a small percentage. Trainers received their stabling and training fees from their patrons; jockeys were paid a fee per ride by the Jockey Club. Since owners were paid all the stakes, trainers had to take bets to make ends meet, but only did so after careful preparation of their own runners and consideration of the race opposition.

The most popular bet for a trainer was the Double, betting on a horse from his own stable to win, with the winnings all going onto a horse from another stable to win on the same day. On occasion, doubles were taken on two horses from the same stable, running in different races. The obvious aim was to bet by claiming the best odds available on such doubles. When word got out, the market reacted and bookmakers shortened the odds dramatically.

We were careful not to give out any information. There was no openness with punters, no relationships with them or with journalists trying to access stable talk. We kept things close to our chest and, a few times a year, we reaped the rewards.

What I soaked up in those early years remained with me for the rest of my own training career.

Weale, as noted, was big on stable management, punctuality and routine. He did not tolerate tardiness, negligence or lethargy. He was attentive to detail like no other, meticulous and careful. Mornings, before sunrise, we'd check the horses' leavings, look for obvious niggles and feel for heat in their legs. That didn't mean rushing past every box with a quick look-in, but taking care to study each one with full focus. In time, as good horsemen will attest to, you get to know every horse inside out which makes it easier to see when they're behaving out of character or feeling an injury not yet detected.

We fed them oats, lucerne, bran mealies and carrots in the mornings and evenings and followed the same routine every day. Weale, like most others from the old school, trained 'from the manger'. Every horse has a feeding-to-exercise ratio and the state of fitness of each individual runner is determined, among other factors, by following its eating habits and comparing the quantity of feed eaten up to the quality of its track work and its physical condition.

To explain that perhaps a bit better: To get a horse into prime racing condition you have to adapt the volume of its feed to what it shows you by its physical appearance. We had to add a measure or reduce a measure of feed as horses started approaching their peaks. If they were slightly overweight their feed was reduced, and if they looked too lean, a quantity was added to their daily diets. Thoroughbreds are all different in this respect, they progress at differing rates. Without the luxury of horse scales, one's always watchful eye was the only way to tell whether your runners were top fit and ready to race.

The first string of runners walked out to the track at the first sign of light and the second string followed them a while later. We had a small barn of 15 to 20 horses, but even in the later years when I trained between 30 and 60 at a time, I didn't send a third string out to the track. I am not sure how trainers of today with 100-200 horses and three or four working strings manage to stay in full control.

There are owners and racing fans who joked back then and still joke today about trainers being up at sparrow's fart, but the rise-and-shine routine is an essential aspect of training because so much more quality work can be done when trainers and horses are fresh for their tasks. It makes perfect sense. Putting them through their paces at dawn means you can afford more time with each horse in the stable later in the morning. Also, importantly, they get a chance to rest for longer periods, and there is time for the necessary administrative issues, race planning, entries, or sometimes a walkabout in the barn with a farrier or a stray patron.

I didn't consciously set out to learn every basic aspect of horse care and stable management from George Weale. My early knowledge was acquired in the course of carrying out my duties for him. My skills increased steadily and to a point where Weale, into his 70s, was happy to leave me in charge on my own, for a day or two to start and for longer periods when his body was weakening as his health deteriorated.

I started saddling horses on Weale's behalf on race days. It was a time of great pride and excitement and my parents, bless their caring souls, became staunch in their support. Later, when I trained on my own, my father bought a horse for me almost every year. They raced in his white and orange silks, a set of colours still used today in his memory by my son, David.

In my time as an assistant trainer I also had the pleasure, or misfortune in some cases, of meeting most of the stable's patrons. One of them was Norbert Erleigh, the gold-mining tycoon who was the first in a line of several hugely wealthy individuals I was to bump heads with over the next few decades.

Ironically, I was very fond of Hitch Knot, a smart colt by Weale's Summer Cup winner Slip Knot, originally owned by the very Norbert Erleigh. I bought Hitch Knot for myself at a yearling sale which came about in 1951 following his owner's conviction on a variety of charges stemming from his first arrest in 1947. It was a case that dragged on and into the mid-1950s, when Erleigh's appeal hearing ended what at the time was branded, "the longest, most complicated and most expensive trial in South African history."

Indeed, it's fair to say that, the more the games and manoeuvres of rich men changed from 1950 through to this writing in 2021, the more they stayed the same!

CHAPTER 7

Between 1942 and 1953, high-profile gold-mine entrepreneur Norbert Stephen Erleigh was a major patron in George Weale's yard. Erleigh was making solid progress in racing and phenomenal headway in business. He was a man full of cash and he liked to flash it.

Erleigh had bought Dwarsvlei Farm outside of Middelburg, Northern Cape, from leading breeder Henry Nourse who, at his death in 1942, was one of the leading thoroughbred breeders in the world. Erleigh was intent on expanding his own breeding interests and stocked the farm with more broodmares. Weale and Erleigh had a good run of winners, including their 1944 Summer Cup winner Slip Knot, who would later stand as a stallion based at Dwarsvlei.

They had a few arguments too, and one serious disagreement about Slip Knot, midway through 1945. Erleigh had been told by a race track tout that jockey 'Cocky' Feldman had 'pulled the horse up' to prevent him from winning a prep run for a subsequent feature race, and Weale denied it. At loggerheads, Weale vacated Erleigh's stables in

Nelson Road, Booysens, and moved into his own yard in Ferreira Street.

Erleigh, through his social prominence, literally had some 'friends in high places' and they included the Agha Khan III who was reportedly, on occasion, a guest at his plush Johannesburg residence. In 1946, Erleigh chartered a boat to Dar Es Salaam in Tanzania so that he could watch the Aga Khan being weighed in diamonds on the celebration of his 60th year in power, named as his Diamond Jubilee.

The powerful leader of the Nizari Ismailis was weighed on an elaborate scale at a massive ceremony. His 17,5 stone (about 110kg) was balanced with the weight of real diamonds, placed in secure containers on the scale next to the sizeable Imam. They were donated by his followers, several wealthy friends and associates, and later handed out in portions to different charities.

Erleigh, via an association with South Africa's top player, Bobby Locke, also befriended the legendary US golfer Sam Snead, who won the 1946 British Open. He sponsored a tour for Snead in South Africa and loved the media hype around it.

There was to be poor publicity too. Erleigh's run-ins with the law began in this period and he was in and out of court on a variety of charges relating to his businesses, though his racing interests were not affected. He was in good standing with the Jockey Club and had been awarded Life Long Colours, which prevented the suspension of his privileges and his navy-and-light-blue silks.

Erleigh's high society flitabouts were interrupted when he was arrested in December 1947 and a newspaper report stated: "Norbert Erleigh, colourful South African mining millionaire, with his associate, Joseph Milne, has been arrested after investigations into their New Union Goldfields Company. Erleigh (44) was arrested in the garden of his opulent Johannesburg mansion as he was admiring his rose garden.

Erleigh is renowned for the multiplicity of his business schemes and the abandon with which he throws around £5 notes. They were remanded on £5,000 each."

I had to smile when I came across this report in our research for this writing, because I was once invited to a social function at Erleigh's prestigious home in Inanda, Johannesburg-North, which had a beautiful garden, a big swimming pool, a fleet of limousines and butlers attending to visitors.

What I recall from this single visit to the Erleigh residence was that he played the piano very well. He sat at his Baby Grand, dressed in an elegant dinner jacket, playing tune after tune while waiters served his guests with expensive champagne and oysters on ice.

Between 1947 and 1950 there were any number of investigations into what Erleigh himself had termed, his "gold-mining and industrial empire" comprising over 150 companies, most of them engaged in exploiting gold-mining concessions in the Orange Free State. He and his business partner, Milne, were in and out of court and, one day midway through 1948 he actually contacted Weale from a prison cell to ask if his runners could return to our stable. Weale agreed and welcomed him back.

―――

In April 1950, Erleigh and his then ex-partner, Joseph Milne, were convicted on a combined total of 63 fraud and theft counts. The court said that their New Union Goldfields Ltd., which had once controlled 160 companies valued at some £30 million, "was, in reality, a gambling house."

Again, in reading a report published in Time Magazine, I had to chuckle, because something sounded eerily familiar: "Erleigh and Milne, the court found, had shifted the assets of their various companies back and forth to run up the shares of the different companies, and had pocketed hundreds of thousands of pounds in profits. When the empire collapsed, holders of New Union shares lost £14 million."

Erleigh and Milne were each sentenced to ten years in prison at hard labour, and in addition Erleigh was fined £95,115 and Milne £88,810, with total prison sentences to run 52 years if fines were unpaid. They were the stiffest sentences ever meted out in South Africa for such crimes.

The fines were paid, any kind of hard labour was avoided, and Erleigh was not defeated. He appealed the verdict and published advertisements in the Johannesburg newspapers revealing his new stock promotion, 'Union Gold & Base Metals Corp. Ltd.'

By late 1950, he was back in business and roaming around Johannesburg, doing deals and hosting parties. Horseracing seems to find men like these. Or, do they find horseracing?

CHAPTER 8

Early in 1951, Norbert Erleigh decided to have a dispersal sale of his yearlings. I can't recall whether he was away from home travelling or whether he was in prison again. His wife Olivia took care of the sale which was held at his old Nelson Road stables.

Weale and I attended the sale, which had about 30 lots on offer including a number of our own runners in the catalogue. All but one was sold - Hitch Knot, a son of Slipknot. He was a small yearling with a clubby foot and buyers decided to pass him by.

"Hold it, I like him!" I said to Weale after Hitch Knot had passed unsold. "I like this little horse!"

He said: "Okay, go speak to Mrs Erleigh. Ask her if you can have him. She has to let them all go today."

I approached Olivia Erleigh, an attractive woman in her mid-40s. I offered her 50 Guineas (borrowed from my generous mother), the equivalent of about R50 at the time. To my surprise, she accepted my offer. I had proudly purchased my first horse.

A good spell of luck started here. Being a licensed assistant trainer, it was easier for me to obtain individual owners' privileges, which normally only came after a process that involved lengthy interviews with the Jockey Club Executive who'd also take a good look into your financial affairs. Weale pulled a few strings and I was granted individual colours for one horse. Excited, and after careful consideration, I registered my silks – going for a red body with an emerald sash, yellow sleeves and cap.

Hitch Knot was brought into work as a two-year-old and he came along steadily, showing good work in his morning gallops. We measured him at 14.3 hands, which meant that he was so small he had to start his career in the 'Pony and Galloway' divisions which were available to trainers at time.

After a few sprint preps, we picked a Maiden Plate over 1600m at Gosforth Park for him on 29 November 1953, and Jimmy Dinwoodie was booked for the ride. Hitch Knot got up to win a tight finish and we dealt the bookmakers a tidy blow. He won two more races in 1953, and I was suddenly full of cash having collected the owners' purses and the betting profits.

I was different to other young men of the time in that I was spending all my time in a stable yard instead of a tavern, a bioscope (cinema), a university hostel or a sports field, but the desire to own a car was an item we had in common.

After Hitch Knot had won his third race, I took a bus to Sauer Street in downtown Johannesburg and visited John B. Clarke Motors, an upmarket motor dealer whose range of shiny products I'd seen in newspaper advertisements. I drove away with a 1953 Wolseley, the small version, bought in a cash deal off the showroom floor.

Known as the 'Cop's Car' for its appearance in many police movies of the time, the Wolseley had sleek proportions, a top speed of about

115km p/h and a reach of 60km per hour in about 27 seconds. It was a true 'women magnet', they said, but at the time the fairer sex was the last thing on my mind. I enjoyed driving it around Turffontein and to the races – a 21-year-old announcing himself to the Johannesburg racing fraternity. Life was good!

Midway through 1953 I was more or less fully in control of George Weale's stables. Weale was suffering from ill health, he'd started taking longer breaks from the yard, and my already significant responsibilities were extended. I appreciated the trust, enjoyed good relationships with our patrons and our runners were consistently in the money.

My confidence kept growing and I felt I was ready to give training a go on my own. With Weale's blessing, I applied to obtain my own trainers' licence, but my first attempt was knocked back on the grounds that I didn't have enough experience. About eight months later, around April or May in 1954, I applied again and this time was granted an open trainers' licence.

I'd soaked up a lot of knowledge and experience at Weale's side and, in looking back, I could probably have waited another year or two before going solo. But I was doing what I loved, successful at it and things seemed to fall in place for me. At 22, having already owned a winning racehorse, I believed the sport of racing was conquerable.

Nothing ventured, nothing gained.

CHAPTER 9

I started off in the first quarter of 1954 on a small property in Stanton Street. It had eight stables and a small paddock. There were seven horses, including my own Hitch Knot, and the eighth stable served as a feed room. I'd entered one of the most competitive sports known to man in an era of superb, old-school horsemen and, being a youngster, I had to know my place among the established yards of trainers like George Azzie, Jackie Gorton, Howard Ginsberg, Les Rathbone, Henry Eatwell, Boet Huckell, John Breval and George Graham.

I employed one groom per horse, something that later became impossible due to the cost of labour. Most of our grooms were farm workers from places like Volksrust and Standerton in the southeast Transvaal who migrated to get jobs in the city. Having worked on horse farms, these handlers could all ride well and they were fiercely dedicated. They loved their jobs because they loved horses. After morning work and feeding, they'd spent the rest of the day in the stables at the side of their runners, brushing them off or petting them. Sometimes, I had to call them out of the stables to go home!

The established trainers treated me like a colleague despite my being a horseman of tender years. Most of the stables in the vicinity of Turffontein were occupied by owner-trainers with the permissible minimum of six horses in their care. As I noted in a previous chapter, there were almost as many owner-trainers as there were trainers who had other owners in their yards. We were all focused on the business of training winners and we helped each other, unlike the modern era in which professional jealousy and back-biting is the order of the day.

We had six race tracks on the Highveld – Turffontein, Newmarket, Vaal, Gosforth Park, Benoni and even a small track near Auckland Park. The Gold Rush of the prior decades brought people to the region who were gamblers by nature and, as you can imagine, racing as a legal betting activity was hugely popular.

In our racing-mad Transvaal Province we enjoyed a midweek meeting at the Vaal or Newmarket while the Saturday meetings alternated between the other tracks mentioned. There were three tracks in the Natal Province namely Greyville, Scottsville and Clairwood, with Milnerton, Kenilworth and Durbanville in the Western Cape; Arlington and Fairview in the Eastern Cape Province.

The many small trainers contributed to the size of the fields. Most meetings had at least three races with 20 runners or more. The stands were packed and horses and their connections were celebrated. The first totalisator outlets opened and betting turnovers grew every week. Racing was one of the biggest developing industries in the land.

Two dozen or more bookmakers manned upright cubicles arranged in a circle around the centre of the action in front of the grandstand. The 'men with cigars' priced up every race on their boards, shouted odds at each other, shortened or lengthened the odds, and made hand gestures across the betting ring to show betting moves.

There was never a dull moment. Many punters came to the track to place just a few bets on the day by following the action in the ring. It amused me to watch 10 or more punters run as a group from one bookies' cubicle to another to secure a single extra betting point offered just before the start of each race. These 'stringers' stood in the ring and studied the moves of the most successful punters. They knew the individuals who were placing bets on behalf of trainers. When the big punters made a move with big money, they followed them to place the same bet.

The bookmakers' circle was like an ant's nest in the heart of every racecourse and the single place where punters introduced themselves to fellow punters. Bookmakers got to know their clients and every bit of gossip and the latest hot tips were shared. There was friendship and camaraderie among them, perhaps dozens of small groups of friends. Some had a known identity, like 'The Lebs', 'The Chinamen' or 'The Bag Boys' who shared info at every meeting but kept the best to themselves until the last minute. Small stands with food and drinks and ice cream vendors kept them nourished throughout the day. Race days were bright and laden with activity and on Saturdays there were long queues to get into the different enclosures for which gate fees were charged.

It was a huge thrill to start training in this wonderful time when racing was blossoming. I thoroughly enjoyed every minute of it, though I was at times distracted by racegoers pressing me for information (like they did with all other trainers on the racecourse) and getting too close for comfort. It wasn't my intention to be rude, but I was so absorbed in my handful of runners and my new, independent career that I probably offended some by telling them off when they came to ask for betting advice.

As my string of horses increased and the winners started rolling in, I had no choice but to become hard-headed and pragmatic. There was no time for chit-chat with punters, press people or members of the public. There were owners, too, who made a nuisance of themselves. I came to the racecourse to serve my runners with focus and I hated interference when I was in the process of doing my job.

I came to deal with owners in my own way, which may or may not have been the right way. But that's the way things developed for me and how I was primed to survive when launching this remarkably tough and unique journey.

CHAPTER 10

One of my first patrons was attorney Jack Moodie whose firm, Moodie and Robertson, handled the affairs of the Johannesburg City Council. He raced in the silks of his wife, Brenda, and they sent me two horses, Shenandoah and Storm Ballet.

I'd expected Hitch Knot to be my first winner as a licensed trainer, since I'd won three with him at George Weale's yard and he was still in good form. But as it turned out Jack and Brenda's Maiden colt Shenandoah became the runner to put the stable officially on the board. He came to hand while I was looking for suitable races for Hitch Knot, and broke the ice on Saturday 14 August 1954 in a Maiden Plate worth £300, raced over 1600m at Gosforth Park.

This chapter, incidentally, is being written on Saturday 14 August 2021, exactly 67 years after that glorious afternoon of my first winner and, again, my memory of the occasion is vivid. I'd booked jockey George Masterson, who rode him to instructions. Shenandoah raced handy into the bend, received a shake-up with 300m to go, got to the front and stayed on well to win by a length. He was fit and I deeply enjoyed the fact that his preparation was spot-on. The way he kept going to hold a rival called Roosblom at bay, was encouraging. I'd done everything right.

The last 50m of the race went by as if in slow motion. Shenandoah had matters in control, but in those hazy few seconds to the winning post, the last 10 strides, the race seemed to drag on forever. Until he got there. And then the fleeting moment of pure joy and heart-in-the-mouth excitement was replaced by goose flesh and a sense of pride and relief.

This strange sense of time standing still just before my runners got to the winning line was something I knew would become an addiction, because those brief moments would always contain every bit of hope, planning, care and exercise put into every winner. By the same token, every narrow loser brought the opposite - deep disappointment, a bitter taste in the mouth if the jockey had messed it up, an attempt at regaining composure before unsaddling the runner, and a few days pondering what *could* have been!

I trained 12 winners from my seven individual runners in my first season, using a number of jockeys including Masterson, Benny Little, Johnny McCreedy, Johnny Westwater, Roly Flynn and Bobby Palm.

Little rode my second winner Storm Ballet (also owned by the Moodies), at the Vaal in November 1954 and they followed up again at Gosforth Park in January 1955.

The warrior Hitch Knot started a good run of success and won a strong handicap under Johnny Westwater at Newmarket in February 1955. He followed up twice under Flynn in March 1955 and then landed a further two 2000m handicaps at Gosforth Park, including the £750 Germiston Handicap under Frikkie Eckard.

Prominent owner Mickey Livanos joined me with a smart, leased two-year-old colt called Saint Memo and Alphenic, a lowly handicapper. Saint Memo was by the Caerleon stallion St Seirol, well-bred. He finished a good second for us in a Maiden Juvenile Plate over 1600m before getting on the winning trail with a six-length win in a £750 Juvenile Handicap over 1600m at Turffontein on 30 July 1955, ending the season on a high.

CHAPTER 11

Mickey Livanos was a colourful character who enjoyed a punt, and in Saint Memo he had an opportunity to win some money. This colt was improving every morning he stepped onto the work tracks and his riders returned with glowing reports.

I believed Saint Memo was talented enough to go for a three-year-old classic and Durban's G1 SA Guineas looked an ideal race for him. We weren't given a chance to win by any of the newspaper pundits, but he'd blossomed in the early Johannesburg spring and I thought, "what the devil, let's take a chance."

We drove Saint Memo down in a horse float on Friday, 30 September 1955 and he arrived on the eve of the Greyville contest, having travelled well. Whether I had told Mickey to have a bet or not, he would've put his cash on anyway. He was in the parade ring, and minutes later on the grandstand as the runners cantered down.

Saint Memo was trained by an unknown newcomer who'd only saddled a handful of winners and had never travelled a horse to another racing centre before. There was no market support except for Mickey's bet, which couldn't have been taken seriously in the bookmakers' ring. Our runner remained in the 20-1 range while a 'boom' colt called Commonwealth attracted all the action to start in the red at 8-10.

Commonwealth had won six races in a row and had the services of jockey George Patmore, brilliant at the time and in form. They were expected to win the race with no fuss, but Bobby Palm and Saint Memo took them on at the 300m-mark. A battle ensued with both horses giving their all and both riders flat to the boards.

I put down my binoculars to scream along with the sizeable crowd, urging our runner on over the last 100m. Commonwealth and Saint Memo went head-to-head and at the line Palm got his mount's nose over the line first. We weren't sure until the official result was announced and waiting for it felt like a year, but it was, we'd won, and it was a moment to behold!

―――

The Saint Memo story has an interesting tail to it.

When he returned from Durban, we battled to win another race with him and after a while Livanos decided to cancel the lease. He reckoned Saint Memo was in his place and wouldn't win again soon, but I disagreed and took over the lease from breeder Harry Barnett.

Early in the 1956/57 season, Saint Memo placed a few times, improved again and I managed to win another two with the colt in my own silks before returning him to Barnett, who put him in training again in Durban in 1958, won another race but eventually gave up too and sold the horse on.

One day, in the early part of 1959, I received a phone call from the Jockey Club, who had its Head Office in the old AGEIS building in Loveday Street, not surprisingly situated across the road from the prestigious Rand Club, the private members' retreat for the city's male business tycoons and legal eagles.

In those days, when the Jockey Club summoned you for a visit, it could only be a serious matter, so I almost wet my pants when I was requested to come in to see Captain Stockdale of the Head Executive. I couldn't think of anything I'd done wrong. I'd lined up one or two runners for a bet, using preparation runs in which they were not ready to win, but that was a method employed by most trainers in the course of strengthening runners pointed at a specific future race.

The stipendiary stewards did not have access to big-screen TVs and advanced technology with replays like they have today. They studied the running of every race through binoculars and were masters at spotting little things that transgressed the rules. There were individuals among the stipes of the 1950s who are regarded as legends today – George Dyamond, Jock Sproule and Frank McGrath, to name but three – all well-respected and not to be messed with, ever!

I expected to find perhaps Messrs Dyamond and McGrath there on my arrival, but was received instead by several of the Jockey Club's Head Executive, including Captain Stockdale, Lt-Col Ross-Thompson and Messrs Harry Oppenheimer, Allan Robertson, Dennis Mosenthal, Warwick Bryant and Hennie Visser.

My knees were shaking and I thought, "Did I owe someone money? Did someone report me for something?" One easily makes enemies in this game.

"Ferraris," said Captain Stockdale. "You trained a horse called Saint Memo, right?"

"I did. Yes, sir." *(What in the world?)*

"Can you remember Saint Memo's markings?" came the next question.

There were no passports for every horse like we have today and hence no reference to go to for any official, but I clearly recalled, "Yes, sir, his back foot. He had a white, off-hind foot. Do you have a photo?"

Stockdale said: "No, not at this stage. But tell us, when Saint Memo left your stable, where did he go?"

"I sent him back to Mr Barnett, his breeder, and he raced again in Durban," I told them.

They asked a few more questions and then actually hauled out a big, blown-up photo of Saint Memo.

"Is this him?" enquired Stockdale.

I looked carefully, just to make doubly sure, and it was him, all right, the horse on the photo was Saint Memo.

Then, the Head Executive revealed what this was all about.

"Don't tell anyone, please, but Saint Memo has won a race for one- and-two-time winners in Salisbury, Rhodesia. He raced under the name 'Thamuz'!"

I was shocked. How did this happen?

"He was substituted with Thamuz, a horse who couldn't win a race in East London," I was told.

What had transpired was this: Harry Barnett sold Saint Memo to trainer Dave Marks at Turffontein. Marks, in turn, sold him on to an individual in Rhodesia to race at Bullawayo's Borrowdale Park and the track at Salisbury. All good.

But then, a Maiden runner called Thamuz appeared out of the blue, to race at Salisbury. He was entered by a trainer, Mr Harper, in a race against winners. He was backed to win big money. Thamuz, whose form showed that he had failed to win a race at the country track in South Africa's East London, came home 'smoking a pipe' against his Salisbury rivals.

An investigation followed and, by hook or by crook, it was discovered that the winner was our former G1 star Saint Memo who had raced in this moderate field as 'Thamuz'. The two horses were born with more or less exactly the same markings and the connections had landed their coup by swapping the bad racehorse for the good one on the day, assuming that nobody would notice.

The outcome: Mr Harper and everyone else involved in the scam were warned off for life and prize monies had to be refunded. The amounts wagered, or won, were not established. The real 'Thamuz' was found, but Saint Memo was never seen again. He disappeared when the investigation started.

This, to my knowledge, was the first racing scandal involving a 'Ringer' – one horse swapped for another of similar looks. About 30 years after this, one of my training colleagues, W.F. 'Barney' Barnard, tried to pull off a similar stunt at the Vaal Racecourse but was caught in a case that received mainstream publicity.

As Mr Harper and, later, and Barney Barnard, would discover – a racing saying goes, "There are snitches in Heaven. You tell nobody, nothing!"

CHAPTER 12

Aside from our wins with Saint Memo, 1956 and 1957 were two slow years. I moved to a property in Holt Street owned and rented to me by A.V. Lindbergh, whose family had started the Central News Agency (CNA) at the turn of the century and were hugely successful with their venture.

Lindbergh at the time was Chairman of Turffontein. He'd also owned a stud farm near Makwassie in the old Western Transvaal where he stood a successful stallion called Stormy Weather. My new training facility was bigger, I could stable up to 16 horses but averaged 11 or 12 in the barn. The stable only really started firing again in 1958, when I sent out 15 winners, mostly thanks to the support of my own family.

My father, Ernest, raced a very nice colt called Storm Quiver, by the very Stormy Weather. We campaigned him over five seasons and he won eight times with 35 places, ridden in turn by Charlie Barends, George Masterson and Duncan Alexander, who partnered him to a win the £600 Provincial Handicap at the Vaal in November 1959.

I'd built up good relationships with George, Duncan and Benny Little, who rode for me regularly, while I tried to book Charlie and the champion jockey Tiger Wright as often as possible on their visits to the Highveld from Durban.

My cousin Dr Arthur Victor (son of jockey Arthur Victor and a practising eye specialist in Kimberley), became one of my best supporters. His first success came with Battle Venture, a smart colt by Battle Hymn who posted nine wins and 24 places between 1958 and 1960.

A few other patrons came along including Alec Morris, who ran his business from Sauer Street in Johannesburg and owned Upper Ten (Gambut), a five-time winner who got on well with Little, and Hellcat (Murrayfield) who won for Charlie. Owner J.H. Visagie brought me a colt called Rooipyl, by Master Alex, a six-time winner who loved to run for George.

Also back in the game and on board was our former acquaintance Norbert Erleigh, the mining mogul, who had apparently ended his many run-ins with the law and was back in a new, booming business called Union Gold & Base Metals Corp. Ltd., managed from offices not far from my stables in Holt Street.

Erleigh had a nice new string of runners, including some young ones and we raced several of the progeny of his former star Gambut who went to stud at Dwarsvlei, the farm he'd bought from Henry Nourse a few years earlier. Also in his group of runners was Stage Struck (Thunderhead II), a colt who won a few for us in the late 1950s before moving on to Port Elizabeth where he won the EP Merchants in 1963.

I'd found a very nice filly called Effort (Murrayfield) on Gert Strydom's farm, Rossmead. She was a 'cheapie' who started racing for owner Donald White, a Scotsman from the Meyerton area in the Vaal Triangle. She kicked off with a five-length win in a Maiden Juvenile Plate in October 1958 and then ran fourth in the Nursery. When she won again early in 1959, White, an unpredictable man, felt that her 'odds were too short', that he was unable to have placed a good bet on her and hence wanted out.

Norbert Erleigh offered to relieve White of his burden and bought Effort for a bargain price. She won three more races on the trot and Erleigh was a 'happy chappy', so much so that he started visiting my stables, and my house, on occasion. He was a strange man, I knew that, but I found him even more peculiar when he started arriving for our appointments with women at his side, none of whom were his wife, Olivia.

Erleigh was never on time. When he said to be expected at 4 pm, he'd arrive at 5.30 pm; and I was kept waiting. When he and his entourage eventually arrived, he'd pace up and down from one end of my office to the other. He never sat down in my lounge at my adjacent home, either. He walked from one end to the other whilst scratching the top of one hand, which was always red and flaky and made me wonder if he had a skin disease.

The pacing, feverishly scratching Erleigh was an individual unlike the gentlemanly character I saw playing the piano in his beautiful mansion a few years earlier. His female companions were awkward too. They reeked of cheap perfume and had applied just a little too much lipstick. I was overly aware of that spicy smell that seemed to linger every time they left. I hoped that my mother, who was just a few blocks away, wouldn't visit and suspect me of keeping that kind of company in the house!

Thankfully, my relationship with Erleigh came to an abrupt end one morning midway through 1959. With the streets around Turffontein getting busier as working families moved into the neighbourhood and businesses sprung up everywhere, our horses walking to and from the racecourse enjoyed increasingly more company.

An impatient man in a truck was trying his best to get around my walking string when he drove into the back of a young horse. When I confronted him, he was drunk and spoke a version of Portuguese that nobody could understand. The horse, owned by Erleigh and named 'The Dude', was injured and I had to place a call to the restless businessman.

I'd bought this colt myself, he was a beautiful specimen and I was upset and disappointed. To this day, I haven't forgotten Erleigh's words when I explained to him what had happened. After a moment's silence, he shouted, "Ferraris, what have you done? This is utter neglect, utter neglect I tell you!"

For a moment, things appeared to go black around me and I just lost it. I drove from my stables to Erleigh's Mining House in downtown Johannesburg to confront him. There was a lady at reception who made an attempt to cool me down and call him to the front, but I jumped over the counter and barged into his office.

With his colleagues around us, no punches were traded, but I grabbed Erleigh by his shirt and screamed at him, "I want you out of my stables. Come and get your horses now and get out!" *(Rather brave for a 27-year-old!)*. Things happened fast and I cannot recall whether he said anything in response, but Erleigh took serious note of my request. A few hours later his horses were removed from my premises, there were 12 of them, which left me just a handful to race with.

The year ended badly too. George Weale, who had taken a vacation to Durban to rest and improve his health, passed away shortly after his return, in December 1959. I am forever thankful for his generosity, his kind disposition, the chance he afforded a fervent teenager to work and learn by his side, and for teaching me principles of horsemanship that stood the test of time and provided the cornerstones of my career.

CHAPTER 13

The 1960s was a time when the youth of the world got restless. There was free love and 'flower power', hippies, psychedelic drugs and social mayhem around the world. The Beatles rocked, Elvis Presley rolled and we witnessed changes in the political climate, including Vietnam War protests, the sexual revolution, civil rights and indeed the Sharpeville Massacre of March, 1960, one of the first violent demonstrations against Apartheid in South Africa.

The popular culture of this era and the politics passed me by. Racing is an all-consuming industry which demands full focus. I was so committed to establish myself that the lures and shenanigans of the youth and the political developments were miles away from my mind.

The racing industry was still in a phase of steady growth. Harry and Bridget Oppenheimer had started to lay the foundations of what would become their great South African racing and breeding legacy. They'd bought Mauritzfontein Farm in Kimberley in 1945 and in 1951 imported their first stallion, Janus, who had been a top-class racehorse in France. Janus was the sire of their smashing horse Tiger Fish (winner of the Durban July Handicap 1959). He also sired Baccarat and Dame de Coeur, who were back-to-back winners of the Oaks (1962-63).

In 1959, Mauritzfontein imported Wilwyn who, incidentally, was the first horse ever to be flown into South Africa. Four years later he was crowned South Africa's Champion Sire, as a result of his top-class progeny, King Willow, Smash And Grab and Uncle Ben. He became a fantastic broodmare sire and his daughters produced, among others, Sentinel, Hidden Magic, Faro and Canyon Creek. Wilwyn's son, Col. Pickering, is also the broodmare sire of the famous Horse Chestnut.

It was never easy to compete against the mighty Oppenheimer racing operation, but we had to take our chances when they came or plan alternative races for our runners who weren't able to compete against the many big guns who raced in the Oppenheimers' black-and-yellow silks. Their runners were originally trained by Tim Furness and later by the incumbent John Breval, who won no fewer than 11 Oaks with daughters of Wilwyn and their next stallion, Free Ride.

While Breval and George Azzie were ruling the roost with their variety of stars, I enjoyed a pretty good spell among the lesser lights between 1960 and 1967. I saddled an average of 15 winners per season from a string that was never bigger than 16 runners per term.

The year 1960 kicked off with mixed emotions and a handicap win, on New Year's Day, by Kathy Winsor (Lincoln Imp), an eight-year-old mare leased by George Weale and ridden by 'Shorty' De La Rey. Weale's death, not long before this race, had upset the Turffontein community and while this was perhaps a suitable send-off for the popular trainer, I took time to get over it.

Kathy Winsor won in Weale's black silks with a red sash and cap. I promptly decided to cancel my own emerald, yellow and red silks and to race, forthwith, in Weale's silks. They were registered in my name and carried to well over 100 wins by my own runners over the next 55 years.

Kathy Winsor was returned to her owner Meyer Lewis, then Chairman of Turffontein and partner in H. Lewis & Co. Produce in Johannesburg. He was a gentleman, one of my better patrons in the '60s and we had several winners, including Svengali (Lincoln Imp) and Beaujolais (Red Wine). Kathy Winsor was again successful in February 1960 and concluded her career as a nine-time winner.

My first winner in the old Weale silks, now my own, came in February 1961 courtesy of a grey filly called Queer Sprite, by Queer Street. She was a cheap filly I'd bought from Gert Strydom's Karoo Farm, Rossmead. She won three races and was just touched off by the top colt Pompey in the 1961 SA Nursery, but she was really small and she found the competition tough as she grew older.

The year 1961 also presented my girlfriend, Norma Perrier, who was an executive secretary from Johannesburg I'd met at the races. Norma was at the top of her profession. She was so good at what she did that she won the Miss Secretary of Southern Africa Contest and was flown to the United States as a part of her prize.

Norma and I were married midway through 1961 and we had three boys. Alan was the first to arrive in 1962 followed by David in 1963 and Paul in 1965. They were all fond of horses, like their father, and while only David later pursued an active career in training, they've all made me proud with their achievements later in their lives.

CHAPTER 14

My son, David, reminded me the other day of how we'd battled financially in the late 1960s. He recalled that there was never enough money for luxuries and that the roof of our house next to the stables in Stanton Street was always leaking. Grandpa Ernest and Grandma Jose had to help out on occasion to get things fixed.

David recalled, too, that we were a happy little family all the same. This reminded me of the support given to us by my own parents and family, and brought back a few good memories.

Ernest and Jose, who lived just a few blocks away, loved to have us over for breakfast, and not just at the weekends. They adored the boys. The smart Ernest, never without a tie around his neck, even on weekends, put his apron on and the kids liked to watch as he turned the eggs or splashed some cooking oil over the bacon. In their neat little garden, the boys played with 'Chummy' the dog while Grandma Jose, the boss, kept an eye on Grandpa's handing out of sweets. They called him, 'Pops'.

Every family has treasured memories and days that pass by far too quickly. I'm glad that today, almost 60 years later, most of mine are not rubbed out and I am able to indulge in some special recollections. In a horseman's life, time wasted is time lost. I think that I appreciate those golden moments more today than I did back then.

My cousin, Dr Arthur Victor, had become so successful as an eye specialist that he was able to develop a thriving sheep farm in Kimberley, and he kept supporting the yard. We went to the National Sale and bought a good horse for him called Heraldry, by Sybil's Nephew, who became my first really good stayer.

For some perspective, let me note here that the champion of this era was the extraordinary Colorado King (Grand Rapids) trained by Syd Laird. He won everything in sight, including the Cape Guineas, the Cape Derby and the Durban July and was exported to the United States, where he won a further six times.

While it was almost impossible to challenge the major stables and their expensive, well-bred runners at this point, we were content with the crumbs off the table and, in hindsight, it was a period in which I had to learn to place my own runners very carefully in order to be competitive. In time, I became good at this.

Heraldry was another example of a small horse with a big heart. He started off winning a Nursery Plate for us in June 1960 and in the same year finished third in the Benoni Diamond Guineas, a good effort for a horse that needed more ground as he showed that he possessed class and ability.

Heraldry partnered early with jockey George Masterson, they won a few, and then struck up well with 'Shorty' De La Rey, a polished little rider whose name did him justice. De La Rey was a lightweight among the lightweights, so he suited the small-framed Heraldry and they won their races in eye-catching fashion. One day in October 1961,

Heraldry won a handicap over 2400m by 10 lengths, the margin could have been 15 lengths if Shorty had so desired.

While he was still furnishing, we'd earmarked Heraldry for the 1962 Johannesburg Goldfields Handicap over 2800m at Turffontein, the equivalent of today's Gold Bowl, and we planned his races accordingly. In June 1962, he started his build-up with another runaway win for Shorty De La Rey in a 2400m contest at Newmarket, but was then beaten under a length by his old rival, Glide, in the Woolavington Stayers over 3200m at the end of October.

The defeat by Glide didn't really worry us, because I was bringing Heraldry to his peak and on 26 December 1962, we put big bets down on him to win the Goldfields Handicap. The favourite was Jackie Butler's accomplished stayer, Ontario (Janus), a big gelding who'd already won a few significant stayers' contests including the Rhodesian Derby (then a prestigious race). But Duncan Alexander rode the race of his life and Heraldry got his head down after a ding-dong battle with Butler's runner.

I can't remember the exact amount, but Arthur and I won plenty of money on Heraldry that day. My own joy was amplified by the fact that I'd prepared a runner, over a period of time, to win a specific race. Everything fell perfectly into place and the gamble was landed. This was a feat I managed to repeat with other runners many times in the years to follow, but, make no mistake, we were also beaten when we expected to win, perhaps just as many times!

On the strength of his Goldfields win, we took Heraldry through the Autumn Handicap at Turffontein to have a tilt at the 1963 G1 Gold Cup in Durban, our major stayers' prize. But as good as he was, our game gelding was not quite up to the standard of the winner Jerez (Dramatic II), who beat us into midfield in a strong renewal featuring the likes of Kerason, Larome, Whitechapel and Ontario.

Heraldry was sold on to a Rhodesian trainer in 1964. He raced for eight seasons in total, winning eight races and placing 28 times, and will always hold a special place in my heart.

CHAPTER 15

Racing people invariably make most of their friends in racing circles, because individuals who work outside of this complicated industry often fail to understand its mechanics and the 'talk' that goes with it. If I were to ask readers of this book how many times they've been asked "…but is racing a crooked sport?", I'd probably get a full-house with their hands up!

One can't really explain the fabric of this industry and its workers to outsiders and this is why one's best friendships (and worst enemies) are forged within this closely-knit community.

In the 1960s, I met an attorney named Paddy Hinton, a professional and knowledgeable man who'd become my closest friend for the next three decades. Paddy worked in Johannesburg and had made racing his hobby. He loved horses and betting on them. Paddy attended most meetings, got to know the stewards, trainers and jockeys and before long landed himself a job as part-time race caller for radio broadcasts.

The main man in the commentary box was the seasoned professional 'Wolfie' Wolfaardt, who called races in his native Afrikaans, but when the demand grew for English, Paddy was there to fulfil the role. He'd take time off, midweek, and spend his Saturdays on the Transvaal courses assisting 'Wolfie' and presenting his share of races in English.

In the circles we moved in, everyone knew everyone, news and rumours spread fast and awkward situations and disagreements were spawned by the nature of our work and our unique interactions with each other.

Paddy was there to turn to, following an altercation between myself and jockey George Masterson in the car park at Turffontein on the morning of Thursday, 30 May, 1963. I'd come from the work tracks when I saw George sitting in his car and, since I wanted to have a word with him, approached him and he rolled down the car's window.

I was annoyed with George. Our professional relationship was not what it used to be and he hadn't been riding for me anymore. I had a small stable and, battling along with not many runners, I wanted the best available jockeys when my horses came to race. George was not the rider he was when we joined forces in the 1950s. He was getting weak, making mistakes and losing races he should have won. I couldn't afford this anymore.

After I'd started booking other jockeys, I was told that George was slinging off about me behind my back, telling people that I didn't know what I was doing, that my horses didn't look well and that I was losing races because I trained my runners the wrong way.

"George," I said at the car. "I want you to stop talking nonsense about me. Face it, you're not what you were. I've been feeding you for a while, but I haven't got anything left to feed you with! Now will you please leave me alone and shut the hell up about me?"

George looked at me for a moment, turned red and then opened his car door, jumped out and took a wild swing at me. I stepped back and avoided the punch, then returned a blow that must've landed well, because the jockey fell over in an instant. Unfortunately, he hit his head on the tarmac and appeared unconscious for a while.

I looked around, shouted for help and first to come to my aid was jockey Vic McMurtry, who got George to get up, helped him into his car and drove him to South Rand Hospital, where he was diagnosed with a concussion. The Star Newspaper reported George saying that he did not remember receiving a blow and that he woke up in hospital.

In the days after the incident there were some jokes about me being odds-on to take the world boxing title away from the reigning champion Floyd Patterson before Sonny Liston could do so. George had been released from hospital and was recovering, but things were about to turn nasty.

George was said to have been keen for 'revenge' and his emotions had been stirred by his good friend Dr Vincent Boy, a dentist from Rosettenville and councillor for Turffontein. Vincent was a big fellow and a well-known community member who'd raced a filly called Panakush with me in 1961, but never seemed happy in the stable.

Vincent was at his loudest when he dropped by my stables after work sometimes and drank every beer I had in my fridge – he could wolf down a dozen lagers in a single early evening and almost stuck me in the poorhouse. He liked to have a bet, too. I have little doubt that he was disgruntled when George's rides for the yard dried up and his source of betting information was throttled.

It didn't come as a major surprise to me, when the matter was reported to the Jockey Club and I got called in. The stipendiary stewards, led by George Dyamond, opened an inquiry. I was frantically questioned by a group of angry and irritated men and, to my shock, the stipes found me guilty of behaviour unbecoming a trainer and recommended that I be suspended from racing and banned from all race meetings – effectively warning me off!

I consulted Paddy Hinton. This had become a serious matter that was about to affect my own and my family's well-being. I was keen to appeal the Jockey Club's finding and I wanted him to represent me. Paddy was in a difficult position, however. His relationship with Racing's Executive Board and the stipes, including Jockey Club Chairman Warwick Bryant and Secretary Hennie Visser, extended to personal friendships. He was in a corner.

It was Visser who actually came to my rescue. "I will help," he said. "I know a good advocate who will take care of this." A day later, he called to say that Advocate J.D. Jerling had agreed to represent me. This was good news, because Jerling was a no-nonsense man with a big reputation. He was nick-named 'Rooibaard' for his red beard and fiery conduct in courtrooms.

George Masterson, meanwhile, had also filed a criminal charge of assault against me. Advocate Jerling advised me to file a counter civil claim for assault and defamation, and in my appeal to the local executive of the Jockey Club we stated that any action taken against me could be construed as contempt of court and that the matter was therefore *sub judice*.

Trainers of today will chuckle at the following response from Jockey Club Chairman, Warwick Bryant, published in The Star and in relation to my appeal: *"I am not aware of all the details of the case, but I can tell you this: The findings of a court of law will definitely not influence the Head Executive when it deals with disciplinary cases. We operate according to the rules of racing and our word is final, unless someone takes us to court, which is quite often."*

The Jockey Club: Judge, Jury, Executioner. The more things change, the more they stay the same!

Despite Bryant's indication that the Executive would oppose my appeal tooth and nail, they did not uphold the recommendation of the Jockey Club to suspend me from racing. Perhaps Paddy Hinton had put in a good word for me, in the quiet, after all. Maybe the Executive was scared of coming up against Advocate 'Rooibaard'. I'd never know. But in the end I was fined £100 and the matter was closed.

CHAPTER 16

To the best of my memory, George Masterson's criminal case against me finally reached the Johannesburg Magistrate's Court in June 1964, more than a year after the incident.

After a year of worrying and seeing my name dragged through the mud, I was asked to appear before Judge F. Drieselman, and Advocate 'Rooibaard' was in attendance, in my corner.

George's team had a surprise in store. They presented an alleged eyewitness, Mr Prince Mbele, who testified that he was riding a horse through the Turffontein car park on the morning of the incident when he saw me repeatedly hitting the jockey and dragging him about.

This was an utterly absurd and, under cross-examination, Mbele gave several different versions. The amused magistrate found that the witness had lied. He warned Mbele to leave the court as soon as possible, threatening him with a fine and a six month jail term for perjury.

That was it. I was found not guilty of assault and was a free man. I remained shaken, however, and my good name was tainted because the incident was reported in full in the official South African Jockey

Club Calendar. The outcome of the court case, however, never received a square inch of coverage in the same publication.

I never spoke to George Masterson again. He rode for a few more years and retired. That was a generation of top riders, but I'm not sure if George was flush after he'd hung up his boots. Jockeys only started receiving their cut of stakes in the 1970s, which means that the likes of Charlie Barends, 'Tiger' Wright, 'Shorty' De La Rey, Johnny Westwater, Percy Cayeux, Johnny McCreedy and Benny Little didn't have a penny to fall back on in retirement. While jockeys had pensions and injury funds put into place a few decades later, the fate of poverty continues to befall trainers in today's economic climate. Horseracing is as cruel as it can be wonderful.

I launched the Owners and Trainers Benevolent Fund in the 1970s to assist people who gave their lives to the game and had nothing to show for it in their advanced years. This was a cause I managed until recently, when I called in Jeff Shill of the Tawny Syndicate to assist me with its administration. More about this later.

The Masterson brawl, the Jockey Club's hanging me out to dry and the court case, had left me disillusioned. If it wasn't for a horse called Pipe Band I would have turned things up when the Jockey Club tried to warn me off in 1963.

Pipe Band was owned by H.A. Mckenzie, a wealthy cattle farmer with a massive ranch outside Vryburg on the outskirts of the Western Transvaal. He was a nice bloke, a big punter and told me that Pipe Band had cost him plenty of money in lost wagers. A son of English stallion Buzunzu, he came to me as a Maiden from Durban, where he had a big reputation in the stable of Terry Ryan, but was simply unable to produce his track work on the racecourse.

Pipe Band had raced eight times without success and I wasn't expecting much when I started training him. Horses that work well at home and fail to run well when they get to the track are not uncommon, but I put this one through his paces to see what the fuss was about. Pipe Band delivered the kind of work I'd seldom seen, he was a terrific galloper and, for the life of me, I couldn't understand why he hadn't yet won a race. He was beating the best runners in my stable without much effort.

On the evidence provided, I knew that this was the type of horse that can shock you with failure, no matter what he'd shown in work. But, like a new consumer's product, I had him well tried and tested before we brought him to the market. I saw nothing in the way of Pipe Band and his first win. To get the best odds possible on our Maiden, we entered him for a D Division Handicap at Newmarket early in November, 1963.

I realised that Terry Ryan would've felt as excited as I was when he sent Pipe Band out expecting to win, and I hoped that, this time, the gelding would do what I knew he was capable of. Even just once. I engaged the under-the-radar lightweight rider Robbie Thompson and told Mckenzie to have a bet.

Having been through this before, Mckenzie was a nervous man when he arrived on course that day. I was tense too, there were butterflies in my stomach when Pipe Band cantered down. I saw the owner pacing up and down in the bookmakers' ring placing bets. Too late now, I thought, no time for turning back. I'd also put a lump of cash on the horse, every cent I could scrape together.

Pipe Band reached the start and milled around, all relaxed, but back on the grandstand, sweat was dripping from under my hat and rolling down my cheeks. What followed were some of those memorable moments when racing lifts you to another level. Pipe Band started well, got into a good position and swept clear to win by a distance, unchallenged.

The sense of huge relief, coupled with a shot of adrenaline and pure joy is something just one sport can provide, and we were all smiles. Mckenzie said he'd placed bets at 7-1 and better and that he'd made a small fortune. He was as happy as I'd ever seen a racehorse owner. I won a bundle, too!

CHAPTER 17

I'm stating the obvious when I say that betting strikes can become addictive, but, however good you are, the sport of horseracing has never been conquered by a punter and never will be. If you're not meticulous and disciplined, racing will take you down in the blink of an eye.

Every old-school trainer will tell you not to train at all if you're going to train with the sole purpose of betting. The two just don't go together. One influences the other and inconsistent results are guaranteed. While it's arguably impossible to go through a career training good horses and being presented with big betting opportunities without placing bets, you'll be on a hiding to nothing if betting becomes your master.

In the year-and-a-half after the court case, I was a troubled man. Perhaps I was unconsciously trying to be someone on a strong rebound from a setback, and after our money made on Pipe Band, I fell into a spell of heavy gambling. Betting profits are swiftly consumed, however and, while Pipe Band continued to win his way through the divisions in 1964 and 1965, he never started at long odds again. I was trying my best to line up a few others in attempts to cash in on more, 'easy' strikes.

I fell deeper in a hole with every attempted betting coup. My runners were getting beaten and some of them frustratingly lost on the line, including my own fillies Lambeth Way (Filipepi) and Xanadu (Fair Reward II), who kept finishing second and third. They were driving me to distraction.

A really good little horse called Roman (Herculaneum) came along. He was owned by Simon Freedman and was a class act who could sprint and stay. He got us through 1965 and into 1966 with a few good wins, but my descent into misery hadn't stopped and my moods were starting to affect my family.

Things happen as they do, and in February 1966 I received a call from my cousin, Dr Arthur Victor, the Kimberley eye specialist. He would have seen my results and probably heard from my concerned mother that I was suffering an unfortunate spell.

"Come to Kimberley, you and the family can stay on my farm and all will be well. We'll teach you all there is to know, I think you will enjoy it and the pressure will be off."

Arthur, over the years, had grown his sheep farm outside of Kimberley to a significant concern with 500 head of sheep and his offer was intriguing enough to present to my wife, Norma. Arthur never planned to lure me away from racing, he was only interested in relieving our stress and his call came at an opportune time.

Being in this unusual and awkward frame of mind, upset with racing and the world, I convinced Norma right there and then: We were turning up racing, saying goodbye to Johannesburg and moving to Kimberley with our three young boys to become sheep farmers!

My patrons were taken aback. They thought I was joking when I told them I was handing in my licence and that they had to make plans to move their horses. I think most of them realised it was a spur-of-the-moment decision taken in a somewhat emotional state, but because I was a man in a hurry to get out, they didn't want to stand in my way.

I believed that my main owners, H.A. Mckenzie, George Thompson, Simon Freedman and Mickey Livanos would be well served by fellow Turffontein trainer Roy Unsworth, a good horseman who had battled, like I did, to get a consistently profitable business going with a small string. I advised them such. Pipe Band and Roman were among my runners who moved over to Unsworth's yard, a few blocks away.

I refused to listen to a few colleagues who were trying to convince me to stay. I was hard-headed, intent on venturing into a new career. I managed to keep my emotions in check by focusing on what I believed would be a more relaxed, country lifestyle with beautiful sunsets, no frustrating, nasty clients to deal with and a steady income.

Being an animal lover with a basic knowledge of farming, I believed that I'd have little trouble in assuming the duties of a sheep farmer like feeding, shearing wool, giving medication, maintaining the farm buildings and fences, monitoring the flock for any signs of illness or disease, assisting with births, and managing waste.

I'd soon discover just how wrong I was!

CHAPTER 18

Sheep are economical converters of grass into meat and wool. The foundation stock is relatively cheap and the flock can be multiplied rapidly. It's a good business if you're off the mark and on your feet, and you enjoy farming.

There's another side to farming sheep, too, as I discovered soon after arriving on Dr Arthur Victor's farm on the Modder Rivier Road, outside of Kimberley, in March 1966. Sheep suffer endemic lameness, miscarriage, infestation and infection. They're hard to peg down if you want to look at their hooves. And they bleat a lot, like humans who complain incessantly.

Arthur did everything he could to make us comfortable and to help us settle in, but we arrived in the Northern Cape during an intense drought, it was as cold as I've ever experienced and the farmhouse was old, run-down and needed attention. My many early winter mornings at Turffontein took some getting used to, but this was something on another level!

Learning the ropes of day-to-day sheep farming was relatively easy. Arthur and the band of farm workers helped me along, but I had some trouble communicating with the Afrikaans folk, who probably didn't enjoy the fact that there was a new boss who tried to run their farm like a racing yard.

Having two toddlers and a young boy in his nappies in our cold new home wasn't ideal. Aside from all the farming activities, Norma and I had to keep an eye on Alan and David, who were investigating all the plants and insects on the property, while little Paul was crying away.

I'd brought a mare called Pacarana to the farm, and stabled a few others to ride, but within a few weeks I started missing my racehorses, my morning routines and the sport of racing itself.

My sister, Ethne, her husband Brendan Geoghegan and their lad, Kieron, came to visit us early in June, 1966. Again, I wonder if my good old mother had mentioned that we needed some encouragement and in fact she would've been right. It was nice to see some of family members and let off some steam.

In the week of their arrival, I discovered the pitfalls of dipping sheep. Sheep dips contain hazardous substances. I knew sheep handlers were most at risk from absorption through the skin and tried to take precautions, but I absorbed some of the poison and my hands and arms broke out in a very sore, red rash that wouldn't react to ordinary balms and got progressively worse and more painful.

I was taken to hospital and bandaged up, I looked like a mummy that had risen from a tomb, with bandages from the tips of my fingers all the way up to my elbows. I was unable to do any physical work for several days and, in a foul mood swearing at sheep and the world, I asked my 10-year-old nephew Kieron to help me with some of the daily duties, including driving the farm truck, feeding and catching limping sheep who had hoof infections.

I probably pushed the youngster a bit hard, but he proved to be as tough as nails and tried his very best to do everything I asked of him. Kieron learnt all there was to know in a week or two and we formed a good team, the mummy and the boy – so good that Kieron asked to stay on the farm for the remainder of his school holiday when his parents had to drive back to Johannesburg.

Kieron was also the first to know of my plans to return to Johannesburg. He reminded me recently that, when we dropped him off at the airport midway through June in 1966, I told him, 'Fly well, boy, I will see you soon back at the stables!'

The drive back from the airport took us past Mauritzfontein Stud, where I'd once waved to Harry and Bridget Oppenheimer at the entrance to their farm. As I recall, they waved back. Ironically, I would train a Triple Crown winner for Mrs O, more than 50 years later!

I didn't contemplate whether my swift return would be embarrassing in the eyes of the racing community or whether I'd find any horses to start training again. It was still bitterly cold in Kimberley when we packed up quicker than we'd unpacked six months earlier, thanked Arthur for his kindness, said goodbye to the farm workers and set off on the journey back to Johannesburg.

———

Most of the runners I'd sent off to Roy Unsworth were returned to me when I was back on duty. A.V. Lindbergh had sold his Holt Street property, and I found a premises with stables adjacent to where I'd started 20 years prior to this in Stanton Street, across the road from the Turffontein Post Office.

Roy had won several races with my old string and was probably annoyed that he had to lose them, but my former patrons were happy to come back without a nudge from me. When they heard I was back in town they were on the phone, asking to return.

My six months as a sheep farmer undoubtedly removed any doubts I had about my career and I dedicated myself to my horses once more, with personal lessons learnt and applied. My renewed vigour brought results. The period between 1967 and 1969 yielded 60 winners at a good average of 20 per season from only 15 horses in the barn.

My stable established itself as a firm competitor in this era of truly wonderful horses. The great Hawaii appeared on the scene for trainer George Azzie, a sensational thoroughbred who swept away all in his path and was exported to the US. The members of the top league around Hawaii were not to be frowned at. There were runners like the popular star, Sea Cottage, also Cuff Link, Chimboora, William Penn, Peter Beware, Jollify, Home Guard, Damask, Jolly Drummer, Magic Mirror and the super filly Renounce. I can extend this list with stories attached, but we only have so much space and I have more of my own experiences to share.

Suffice to say that the late 1960s was an incredible time to be alive. Today's social media, Artificial Intelligence (AI) and private trips to space are mesmerising the citizens of the world, but imagine the joy, amazement (and fear) of our years back then with the Vietnam War, Man On The Moon, the assassination of Martin Luther King Jr. and the exploits of the Beatles dominating world news. Back home there was the ever-brewing political melting pot; Dr Chris Barnard performed the first heart transplant; we liked to visit roadhouses for milkshakes and cheese burgers, took the kids to drive-in theatres and listened to the original LM Radio.

I couldn't yet compete with the top trainers of the era, but there were cherries to pick among the lesser races and Saint Hyacinth (Hyacinth) got me going in 1968 with wins in the Derby Trial and the KZN

Breeders. Leased by Lou Goldberg from breeder Harry Barnett, he won eight races in total.

I won the 1968 Gosforth Park Fillies and Mares Stakes with Safe Return, a smart filly by Noble Chieftain owned by Dr G. Maas, a German medical professional. Jock Brown sent me a horse called Herald's Choice, also on lease from Barnett. He blossomed and won 13 career wins in this term.

Simon Freedman's Roman was a top little stayer by Herculaneum whose wins included the Johannesburg Autumn Handicap under jockey James Maree. Alf Peerman's Mystic Song (Mystery IX), kept up the momentum with five wins. Peerman ran a massive wholesale butchery business, and assisted me with finance when I moved my operation to Newmarket.

My old acquaintance, 'Trickey' Mickey Livanos, owned an excellent trio of runners in the sprinters Thetford (Marsolve) and Gizeh (Ambigious) – who won about 15 races between them, and Mustafa, a two-time winner.

Mickey, as I told you, loved a punt, and any number of them came off handsomely. But midway through April 1969, I received a call from him touching base about Thetford, who was beaten in the 1969 Merchants Handicap earlier in April when we fancied him to win.

"Ormond," he said, "…uhm, you know… Thetford…"

I knew where this was going, but heard him out.

"We… uhm… you know, I think… maybe we should give Roy Unsworth a try with him…?"

I happened to see Mickey and Roy in deep conversation behind the holding stables at Turffontein a few days before this call - just by chance - so I was not surprised.

"Mickey," I replied. "You can take Thetford. Please send a float this afternoon. In fact, send three floats. I want you to load Gizeh and Mustafa as well. Do it today, and get out of my stable!"

I was sorry to lose three regular earners, but my fuse with unappreciative owners was as short as ever.

With some confidence, and perhaps even a measure of arrogance, the stable shot into the 1969/70 season like Apollo 11 had shot into space. This would be the best season of my first 15 years of training.

CHAPTER 19

Before we go into the 1970s, I'd like to focus on auction sales and two questions I've been asked more often than I can remember: "How do you pick horses to buy for your stable? What exactly do you look at?"

Success at the racetrack is probably a 60-40 affair – 60% percent selecting them and 40% training them. I'll give you a few pointers that may help – starting with the fact that there are no shortcuts. You can't cut corners. You have to do your homework at every sale. I've looked at thousands, probably tens of thousands of horses over the years, and I've been successful in picking many good ones, but there have been disappointments too.

You don't just 'find' good horses without doing spadework. There are rare stories of owners buying horses because of their nice names, or big ears, or flowing manes but, believe you me, try that and you'll be down and out as a horse picker before you know it!

There are two aspects in relation to spending time doing your homework at sales, over and over, year after year. You get to compare all the individuals at any given sale to each other, which makes it somewhat easier to sort the wheat from the chaff; and after a few years of active engagement around the sales barns you get to know which attributes of a horse 'work' for you personally.

Let me explain this if you're not with me: When you buy often, within a few years you'll be able to look at your own record of runners bought. You'll be able to tell which ones were good and which ones turned out not so good. Over time, your mind starts forming a picture of the individual traits in yearlings you selected that went on to become bad, good, or top horses. You'll go back to every new sale with a bit more experience, and then a bit more after that, and in time you'll become a decent judge of horseflesh.

You will also learn that you can never predict with full confidence that you've picked a star. You'll only know that when your purchase gets to the track, and you'll be frustratingly wrong more often than not. But dedication and time around horses will guarantee you a better strike rate of selecting the good ones. If you persist, ask questions and are willing to learn, you can become good at this, and you'll have a better than average chance of picking a few plums from every year's sales crop.

Okay, so here's something you can remember forever, my little pearl of wisdom to horse selectors. Well, I guess not mine alone, really, but something I've worked by, always: 'Look Down First!' Memorise that. 'Look Down First!' Then, look up to the rest of the horse.

If you were to look at a horse from the knee down and then consider the strains and stresses of racing, you'd believe it to be a miracle that so many survive. The feet are absolutely essential in the displacement of weight – if they are deformed or slightly out of line, it means that pressure will be transferred to other parts of the leg when the horse starts to run.

Barring my first horse Hitch Knot, I can't recall training top racers who had faults as yearlings, or had faults that I forgave when I picked them. From the early days of Heraldry, through to Distinctly, Wagga Wagga and Pretty Border, to Crown Pearl, St Just, Fine Regent and Travel North, to the later days of Tracy's Element, Summer Line, Cholula, Sabina Park and others, they were faultless as young horses.

It's hard to find the perfect horse, but the feet are the best place to start with every horse you look at. A yearling's feet have to be cared for, from the word go. Often, either out of ignorance or a wrong farrier diagnosis, they arrive at the sales with the odds stacked against them

So, I say again, the horse must have good feet, and straight legs. Those are vital, especially for the hard tracks on the Highveld. Think about any athlete. If an athlete has sore or deformed feet, he or she will battle to walk, let alone run.

Some have club feet, they turn in. Poor feet often surface in joint or leg injuries on the training track or in a race. The yearling's legs must be straight, without even the slightest deviation. If you accept weaknesses early, they'll also present themselves as problems later.

It's difficult to say what makes a great horse, but those with big hearts, courage and the will to win, go a long way. I lean towards speed stallions. Mrs Lindbergh, A.V. Lindbergh's wife, always said, "Blood will tell," and I never forgot that. You have to look for strong dam lines, and the quality must be in the first and second dam, not too far back because then it becomes dormant. Black type in the first and second dam is an important factor to consider.

I never chose particularly big yearlings, it's as though they've almost reached their maximum growth, and there's little scope for improvement once they grow older and start training. Try to avoid stubborn horses. It's a flaw you can see straight away, so why start off with a troublesome animal?

I like the obvious attributes like most other horsemen, including a good girth, which indicates good lung capacity; a good chest, not narrow; a good shoulder, strong hindquarters which propel them forward; and good hocks. Avoid the ones with sickle-hocks.

Some horses appear to have 'bold' eyes and some have nicer looking heads, but that goes more to personal preference and I don't regard a horse's eyes or its face as major factors when I look at them, overall. I had a horse called King Of Jazz in the early 1980s, to name but one. He had what most would call an ugly face, he looked like a bank robber with his strange white facial markings, but he could run like hell. Overarching, Graham Beck's great racer, was a strange looking mare, she always appeared to be pregnant, not the best looker, but her feet and legs were fine. She had hindquarters like a brick outhouse and few could gallop with her!

I must concede that today's horse pickers have an additional hampering factor to contend with. Horses of today are soft, many are mollycoddled, pampered for their commercial value. They arrive at the sales with weak legs and don't stand up to training. They're kept in smaller camps because of rising costs. Most breeders can't afford to let them run freely because even a minor knock on the knee can leave a bump that will affect the sales price.

I was always a Karoo man for horses, a place where breeders like the Birch Brothers were renowned for raising the young horses tough in a rough environment. Their horses, and most other Karoo-breds, stood up to training. But the Karoo has long fallen out of fashion, most of their wonderful blood lines have run their course, and fewer and fewer come to the sales these days.

Best of luck to all starting the journey of horse selecting, and those already on the rocky path!

CHAPTER 20

In the late 60s and 70s, several businesses and industries deserted Johannesburg's Central Business District for various reasons, including rising rental costs, and the neighbouring Turffontein's population expanded.

Soon, 'Turffies' was no more a sleepy horseracing village. Working class families from surrounding industries whose breadwinners worked for printers, motor dealers, engineering shops, furnishers and various manufacturers moved into our suburb and one result of this was that the traffic got progressively worse.

The Turffontein Tramway had been discontinued in 1961, and by 1969 our grooms had to compete more and more with the growing number of cars in the area. It was no longer safe for us to walk our horses to the racecourse and back for training sessions, and to the races on Saturdays. Aside from the holding stables for visiting runners, stabling at the racecourse was non-existent so we couldn't keep the racers there.

When I returned from my Kimberley adventure, I had enquiries from owners who were keen to join my yard, but with only 15 stables on my Stanton Street premises, and the flow of traffic getting worse, I had to make a plan to move my operation to a bigger, better and safer place.

The horse village around Newmarket racecourse was growing steadily and 'Newmarket' had become the buzz word. Trainer George Azzie was the first to move. He made the Alberton suburb his home as early as 1955, and a few others had followed over the years. Most trainers had a five-acre plot and some trained privately for single patrons, like John Breval, who was in charge of the Oppenheimer string. Breval and Azzie, especially, enjoyed spectacular results from their Newmarket stables.

Newmarket had become what Turffontein had been in its early years – horse-friendly, peaceful and quiet with all the roads named after English tracks and racing landmarks, including Epsom, Ascot and Derby Roads. Most of the streets in the area were secluded and private, with a subway under the main road next to racecourse that connected the training village with the training tracks so horses could walk along with no traffic around them.

Where there is a will, there is a way. Hearing of my plans, my patron Alf Peerman, the wealthy businessman, offered to tide me over with a loan to buy a property in Newmarket, and we received further assistance from another patron Frank Ecksteen, who was a bookmaker and Chairman of SA Perm, the building society with its office in Krugersdorp. Banks gave home loans, but were hesitant in granting funds for the building of stables. *(Yes – Frank and I had punted a few winners together, but he was a kind man who would have helped me, all the same!)*

I wanted to compete with the best, so we spared no costs and everything was factored into the bond over a five-acre property we found at the bottom end of Doncaster Road, Newmarket. We built a beautiful house, 30 stables with tack rooms, a feed room, paddocks and grooms' quarters. I chased the builders every day and work, they did. We moved into our new premises in the first quarter of June, 1970, with high hopes, nice horses and a number of old friendships rekindled.

We named our establishment, 'The Curragh' and our neighbours in Doncaster Road were seasoned horsemen. We had Jimmy Polley on one side and Jim Brady on the other, with Eric Stranger and Henry Eatwell nearby and George Azzie just around the corner in Epsom Road. Not long after we moved in, Roy Unsworth took up boxes in racing executive Jeff Moffatt's property at the entrance to Doncaster Road and Maurice Passmore also brought his small string along from Turffontein.

Maurice was a really top, old-school trainer and mentioning his name reminds me of how he refused to use a veterinarian, unless there was something critically wrong with a horse in his yard. Most of us weren't keen on vets those days as it were. I also stayed largely away from them throughout my career, but Maurice set the example. His principle was, if you look after them with great care and attention, horses will be healthy and sound throughout their careers.

Racing has changed since then. Horses are softer, as I noted previously, there are more race days and fewer horses to race, so they are exposed to a tougher environment and rigorous routines. Today, the veterinarians rule racing yards. Vets get called in when a horse pulls back his left ear instead of his right. The doctors get to visit daily for all sorts of ailments we would've treated ourselves back in the day. The veterinary fees are often exorbitant and aggravating to most owners.

―――

A Jockeys Academy was established at Gosforth Park. They took in a number of young jockeys every year, and at times they were sent out from their hostel to spend some time with trainers, living in our homes, helping the grooms at the stables and riding as much work as they could so we could improve their skills and teach them about race riding. At the training tracks they also learnt from the senior jockeys who were willing to help.

I'd been using the most experienced jockeys available, including Johnny McCreedy (the best hands I've ever seen on a rider), the veteran Duncan Alexander, the superb Gerald Turner, champion jockey at the time, and Raymond Rhodes, the talented and level-headed jockey of the moment. He'd made a big name for himself in the 1960s on George Azzie's top horses, including Durban July winner Numeral, and the phenomenal Hawaii. Raymond had also started an association with up-and-coming Durban-based trainer, David Payne.

When McCreedy moved to Durban with his trainer, Brian Cherry (a good friend), I came to rely more on Raymond and we became friends to the extent that he bought a beautiful house across the road from us in Doncaster Road. Raymond and his wife Liz moved in with their daughter Penny. They were a lovely couple and we enjoyed dinners together and even went to the movies after weekend race meetings. I think it was Raymond who nick-named me 'Archie' – I'm not sure why, maybe he found me comical at times or thought that my nose was too big. That nickname stuck.

Penny had two ponies on their property, she shared our love for horses. She was close to my boys, a good little friend to them until we moved away from Newmarket a couple of years later. Raymond lives with Penny near Cape Town today. I am told he is in reasonable health and both he and Penny are in good spirits.

My first apprentice at Newmarket was Tommy van der Linde, a good rider who had weight problems even as a youngster, but he was valuable as a work rider and assisting at the stables. Another young apprentice came along in the form of 15-year-old Tobie van Booma, a troubled teenager. Tobie was a Hollander by birth, grumpy and sulky most of the time and a lad who needed a hard hand and discipline. He was not easy to work with when he started with me and was even worse in his later years. I am not sure whether Tobie suffered from depression – this wasn't a commonly treated illness like it is today - or whether he'd had stressful times as a boy growing up. He was volatile at the best of times – brazen and happy one day, dark and bothered the next.

But despite Tobie's problems he was an apprentice with much promise because he was intelligent, strong, with good hands and a sense of pace. I took a liking to him, actually had a soft spot for the young Dutchman and tried my best to help him over the following two decades. He started in my garden, mowing the lawns with Alan, David and Paul at The Curragh, progressed to helping the grooms around the barn and then started riding my horses. In the years to come, we enjoyed various spells of hot form, and we had more winners as a combination than most.

In 1970, we established the Transvaal Owners and Trainers Association (OTA), chaired by Tony Ruffel and including myself, Maurice Passmore, Pat Wright, Alf Peerman and secretary, Jack Patience. The electric tote came into operation, more bets were handled and tote turnovers were increased. We also started the Benevolent Fund for retired owners and trainers in need of assistance. This was always close to my heart and I was to take over its administration a decade or so later.

Late in 1970, the International Olympic Committee expelled South Africa from the International Olympic Movement as a result of South Africa's stand on Apartheid in sport. The political scenario in our country was approaching boiling point. Elsewhere, the Watergate scandal dominated the news, and the Beatles announced they were disbanding.

At The Curragh, we were only vaguely aware of what was happening outside the town of Alberton. We'd started working on perfecting the art of training winners, and were getting really good at it!

CHAPTER 21

Apprentice Tommy van der Linde had a nice way with horses and he'd struck up a good relationship with a colt called Benitch, a son of Kingbenitch, an underrated stallion. This one got the ball rolling for us in 1970, winning four races. He was a good contributor to our 70/71 seasonal tally of 39 winners, my best season ever by a long way. The winners came as a result of having access to 15 extra stables, several new, young runners and the excellent training environment at Newmarket.

Another runner to the fore was Dictator (Port Merion), a lovely grey sprinter owned by my wife Norma and Frank Ecksteen. Dictator got on well with Raymond Rhodes and Tex Lerena and won three races that season. Incidentally, Dictator finished just a length off George Azzie's future star Elevation when they made their debuts in a Maiden Juvenile Plate won by Last Laugh in April, 1971. Dictator is a horse I have fond memories of. He won 12 races in South Africa in total and, when he'd reached his mark here in 1974, we took him to Rhodesia where he won a handicap at Borrowdale Park under Billy Harvey. We sold Dictator on to a local owner, and he won again.

My friend Paddy Hinton, the attorney-come-race-caller, decided to get active in buying horses and he acquired a filly called Malagasy, a daughter of Bullrush. Hinton didn't want to race in his own silks at first, so he leased Malagasy to my wife, Norma. Malagasy turned out to be a really useful race filly who won eight races between 1970 and 1974.

I am not sure why Paddy chose to race runners in Norma's silks when he started out as an owner. As I wrote earlier, he was friendly with the big wigs of the Jockey Club – perhaps he felt that racing his horses in his own colours would be one step too 'personal' and that it would cause him embarrassment after my run-ins with the Jockey Club in 1967. But he changed his mind and we were to form a major, ongoing partnership just a few years later.

While Paddy, the diplomat, was playing his cards safe, Norma was leading Malagasy into the winner's enclosures. His own wife Maura didn't really enjoy horseracing at first, but it grew on her and over time she became almost as enthusiastic as her husband. The three of us started visiting stud farms, we attended the various auctions together and formed a bond as good friends.

Malagasy was progressive and she improved after her Maiden win. An interesting fact from her career is that she beat her male contemporary, Riboville, Azzie's 1974 Durban July hero, to win the Gosforth Park Two-Year-Old Plate over 1600m in March 1972. I wasn't winning the majors just yet, but the log-leading trainers had taken notice that I wasn't going to be satisfied with only the crumbs off the table. Malagasy also won the H.B. Christian Memorial in May 1972, and the Gosforth Park Fillies and Mares WFA in 1974.

Paddy, on the quiet, was striking property deals that would reward him handsomely. He was practicing law in the North of Johannesburg and, as a man in the know, became aware of several dormant stands in this exclusive, sought-after area of town. They belonged to a number of

English war veterans, who were not interested in developing the property they'd bought cheaply whilst stationed in the area.

Paddy jumped on a plane to England armed with names, addresses and some cash. He looked up these property owners personally, offered to buy their stands in Johannesburg and returned with a file full of deeds of sale. With South Africa getting bad publicity overseas, the 'Tommies' were only too happy to part with their erven, and Paddy soon owned acres of valuable land on Jan Smuts Avenue around the Johannesburg Zoo, and further north in the new, developing areas of Sandton and Wynberg.

When Paddy and I enjoyed drinks at the time, I joked with him. "Paddy," I said, "The Boers are going to track you down. The Tommies bought their land from under their noses all those years ago and now it's in your hands. You'd better watch out!" He laughed, and tried to buy some more.

This was a profitable period for everyone, and with the winners rolling in I managed to repay my loans from Alf Peerman and Frank Ecksteen's SA Perm within just a few years. Frank's success in the stable continued with several runners including Silver Link (Kingbenitch), who won five races and made the final field of the 1971 Jockeys International at Scottsville, where he was ridden by English jockey Geoff Lewis and finished downfield behind Fernando Toro's mount, In Full Flight. He also raced in the 1972 SA Derby but was no match for the star colt, Elevation.

Another high-profile businessman in the yard at this time was Oliver Baring, a young tycoon from the prominent Barings family in the United Kingdom who joined the executive board of the Oppenheimers' Anglo American/De Beers Group. He was a jovial and good-natured chap. I met him a few times when he visited South Africa. He raced a filly with me called Princess Pearl (High Powered II), who won five races. Oliver was too involved in business to nurture a love for horseracing and he didn't show further interest, but I read recently that he is still actively involved in managing mining and banking corporations, pushing 80 years of age.

Jack O'Sullivan, Hinton and I took a trip to Ireland around this time to find a stallion prospect for South Africa. We were looking to inject speed into our local blood lines and we came across Mirraglo (Miralgo), an exciting six-time winning sprinter in Europe. He was bought from Sir Hugh Nugent for an amount equivalent to R50,000, and shipped to Cape Town from Liverpool.

We needed Mirraglo to win a race in South Africa, but he was disappointing in his first few starts. I got him to a peak for his fourth start, the Listed Germiston Cup over 1000m. He was a beautiful, flashy chestnut and he cantered down to the start so well that day, I recall punters streaming to the bookmakers like a school of fish to back him. Mirraglo won by a short head under Tobie van Booma and we retired him immediately to Boet Oosthuizen's Stud near Wolmaransstad, Western Transvaal.

One more horse we were asked to put on the map as a stallion was Fats Waller (Sing Sing), who was imported by the Van der Walt family of Gelykfontein Stud in the Karoo. I remember Fats Waller for his peculiar habit of curling his bedding around and dragging it into his manger every day. He could run a bit, too, we gave him just a few runs and he won a good race for us in top company under Tex Lerena before retiring to stud.

J.P. Ratledge, a prominent figure in mining at the then South West Africa's Tsumeb Mines, sent me a horse called Boat Commander, bred from the stallion Ship's Bell in the Namib Desert. Boat Commander won the Joseph Dorfmann Memorial Stakes over 1200m at the Vaal in April, 1973. Two months later, in June 1973, we raided Greyville and Raymond Rhodes rode a good race to win the Strelitzia Stakes on

Mainliner, a filly by Spaniard's Mount owned by Bob McBay, a mover and shaker from the American company, Prudential Life.

Breeder H.A. Mackenzie was still going strong. We'd found him an English-bred stallion called The Ashes (Whistler) and raced some of this sire's progeny including Rags Of Glory, who won a few races on the Highveld before continuing his career in the Eastern Cape. Mackenzie's best runner in this period was Oaks contender On Wings (Wilwyn), a consistent staying filly who won six races and placed 14 times.

Another notable runner was Pilsener, winner of the 1972 Johannesburg Spring Handicap under another up-and-coming apprentice, Michael Cavé. He was a son of Kimberley Kid, a good sire from a small stud who produced a host of winners from small crops.

With another stable record of 49 winners in 1971/2 and a further 39 in 1972/3, I was just a few short of the 350-winner mark with my first July runner on the way, but there was a notable racing scandal in 1973 I want to touch on before we move on to the mid and late 1970s.

CHAPTER 22

My stable apprentice Tobie van Booma was a youngster with personal problems. In our association of almost 30 years, I never got to the bottom of what exactly it was that troubled Tobie as an individual, but from the start I kept a close eye on the talented Dutchman and did what I could to help him progress and make a success of his career.

Tobie was only 17 years old, early in his apprenticeship, when he was involved in a widely publicised racing scandal involving himself, senior champion jockey Gerald Turner and a racehorse called Swallow Tail (ironically by a stallion called Embarrassment), trained by Peter Blythe.

For some background, let me tell you that Tobie idolised Gerald, the best jockey at the time and considered by many on par, if not better than Michael Roberts, Martin Schoeman and Raymond Rhodes. Tobie was Gerald's 'kit boy' at the races. He studied Gerald's style and tried his hardest to emulate him in the saddle. Gerald would often give the youngster R10 or R20 for his help.

We got in touch with Blythe, today a leading breeder at Clifton Stud and one of the men closest to the events that transpired at the race meeting on Saturday, 7 July 1973 at Gosforth Park. His recollection sheds light on what exactly happened that day.

Blythe wrote:

"In the 1970s, I was an owner-trainer based at the Vaal. I had a small string, but we kept the fires burning with winners and I just loved the game. I tried my best to get my runners in the right races and I made sure that they were as fit and well as they could be when we had chances to win.

"I liked Tobie van Booma. He was a good, strong apprentice who was showing he had the mettle as a teenager and he'd ridden a few for me, including Swallow Tail, who was beaten by just a neck in a 2000m race at the Vaal by a horse ridden by Gerald Turner. This was about 10 days prior to the incident. Swallow Tail made the pace, he was game and Tobie tried hard. Turner and his mount caught them right on the line.

"I was happy with the run, because Swallow Tail was running close to his best ability and I decided to enter him again in a race over 2000m at Gosforth Park the following week. It was all systems go, I was happy to put Tobie up again and I believed that we'd win this race. The field looked of more or less the same strength and we were drawn on the fence in barrier one, advantageous on the tight Germiston circuit.

"I thought it strange that John Thomas, a fellow-trainer at the Vaal, came to me after morning gallops on the Tuesday before the race and said, 'Peter, don't back your horse on Sunday. Save your cash. Owen Sims has a horse in the race that will win. Themeda is a 'oner'. *('Oner', pronounced 'wunner' is racing slang for a horse that has been set up to win by one jockey with the knowledge of his rival jockeys in the same race).*

"I just smiled and John went his way. Racing is never been short of rumours, tales and gossip, but they were often started by conspiracy-minded punters and were mostly just hot air. On form, with our draw advantage and in consideration of Swallow Tail's well-being, I believed more than ever that we'd win.

"On the race day, Swallow Tail saddled well and he looked in good shape. He was ready. He started walking around the parade ring with the other runners as we awaited the jockeys. But when they walked out and Tobie approached me for instructions, I had a sense there was something wrong. He couldn't look me in the eye and seemed evasive. I asked him to ride Swallow Tail like the last time – get him up handy from that good draw, or set the pace if needed. He was very fit and would be able to keep his lead. Tobie nodded his head in agreement, but looked away. He was keen to mount, and I gave him a leg up on our runner.

"Swallow Tail cantered down with his head in his chest and I felt confident, though he was drifting in the betting market as money came for a few others, mostly for Turner's ride, Themeda. The few minutes before the start of every race is always tense. Through my binoculars, I watched Swallow Tail milling around at the start. He entered the Number One gate, the others loaded and they were off!

"Given Swallow Tail's preparation, his way of racing and my instructions I expected to see his silks leading, or prominent among the leaders, but to my surprise Tobie was dropping back through the field to last, so much so that he was a few lengths behind the second-last horse! I thought my eyes were deceiving me, but I heard the race caller confirming that Swallow Tail was out of his ground. The Star reported a few days later that, 'Swallow Tail was so far out of his ground that he disappears from view in a Jockey Club film of the race' and, when my horse entered the home run wide, I finally realised that there was 'graft' in this race. My runner had been the subject of the plot!

"You'll be asking what happened to Themeda and yes, he was well-placed throughout and came to the front under Turner with 200m to go to win going away, landing the gamble. To make the blow worse, John Thomas came running up to me, shouting, 'I told you, I told you!'. I've never been one to react, I tried to keep my composure as the runners returned to the unsaddling paddock.

"To my surprise, Chief Stipendiary Steward, Mike Tillett, was waiting for me down in the ring and he said, 'Peter, what happened here, what's going on? What were your instructions to Van Booma?'

"I wanted him up there with the pace from his draw, I don't know what happened," I replied, feeling, I guess, betrayed and disappointed.

"Tobie was looking everywhere but at us when he brought Swallow Tail back for unsaddling, and Tillett was onto him, immediately. 'Your instructions were to get the horse in a handy position, why did you drop so far back,' asked an irate Tillett.

"Tobie was unsure of himself, he looked shaky and mumbled out a few excuses, eventually settling on, 'My horse didn't want to run, he refused to gallop the way he's galloped before.'

"Tillett was enraged. 'Van Booma, you… and you, Mr Blythe, I will see you at the Jockey Club on Tuesday. Make sure you are there!'

"There were no further words between Tobie and I. He never rode for me again and, as it happened, I never made our Tuesday meeting at the Jockey Club because by then the story had blown up, the crookery was revealed and Tobie and Gerald Turner were the ones forthwith investigated.

"While Tobie initially denied wrongdoing, the truth eventually came out via his boss, Ormond Ferraris, who didn't believe his version and eventually got him to admit what had happened: Turner had asked him to hold Swallow Tail back, he agreed and was paid R200 for his effort, or lack of therof. The money was paid over in the car park after the race meeting.

"There were rumours afterwards that big-hitting punter Hymie Tucker had backed Themeda on Turner's behalf and that they made bagfuls of money, but I have no doubt that both jockeys would have been hugely disappointed in themselves, in the aftermath. Tobie was called, a 'self-confessed liar', whilst he and Turner never managed to live down the incident. Both made a success of their later careers and both were popular, but the 'crook' tag hung around their necks for many years.

"Two notes to end with: I engaged apprentice Allan Fleet on Swallow Tail a few weeks later in an 1800m race at Newmaket, he rode to instructions and they won by half a length. When I gave up training a year or so later, Swallow Tail ended up in the yard of Mrs Jean Barnard (later Heming). One day, at the Vaal, the horse was declared to run against Themeda again and racing journalist David Mollett wrote in a headlined article of the long-awaited rematch between the pair. Jean won the race with Swallow Tail that afternoon. Themeda finished unplaced."

I wasn't at the races the day the Swallow Tail incident happened, only got to know about it a day later, like most others. I immediately questioned Tobie about it and he denied any wrongdoing, but I could see he was uncomfortable. Considering his friendly association with Gerald Turner, I was suspicious. I called Tobie's father first, and later asked a high-ranking police friend from Booysens Police to question him.

At first Tobie, told the colonel his original story, but later he broke down and admitted to being paid R200 by Turner to 'pull up' Swallow Tail.

When investigations had concluded, Tobie was banned from riding for six months and Turner was warned off for life, but following court cases he had his ban set aside by the Appeal Court in 1975. He was back in the saddle roughly a year after his banning.

I wonder, in hindsight, whether honesty was the best policy. Perhaps I should just have kept quiet – like many in the racing fraternity told me to do. Then, Tobie may not have been victimised the way he was. He showed me a newspaper article one day where someone was asking for him to be 'removed from the racetrack for keeps'. He'd also suffered abuse from punters at Bloemfontein, who threatened that 'Turner is going to get you!' and that had upset him severely.

But Tobie had the potential to become a great jockey and it was necessary for him to accept the consequences of his actions. We worked on his confidence again and to his credit he picked up the pieces, focused on his job and rode more winners for me than I can remember. In the latter part of his career, he also won the Mauritian Jockeys' Title in one of the strictest jurisdictions in the world and, though I speak under correction, with Mike Tillett presiding over the Stipes Board.

Tobie never criticised Turner. He was quoted in a Rand Daily Mail article as saying: "Gerald was my great friend and he taught me almost everything I know about riding. He is still my hero!"

The Rand Daily Mail's racing editor was one David Mollett, an import from Britain who had annoyed me to no end with his support for Turner in his popular morning columns. I got so pissed off with Mollett that I tried to have him sent back to his land of birth. Once again, I called in the help of my police friend at Booysens, but there wasn't much we could do. 'Molly' is still with us after all these years – not as old as I am – but he seems to be catching up fast!

For the sake of interest, and it is rather funny, I am including in this chapter a response from Mollett and his own memories of the time. He writes, below:

"I clearly recall Ormond Ferraris' unhappiness with my reporting on the Turner/Van Booma scandal. The thing is, I knew, everyone knew that they were guilty, but Gerald and I were joined at the hip at the time. He was one of the greatest riders I'd ever seen, we became friends. He was always easy to deal with as a pressman.

"Gerald wasn't shy of tipping me, and he was very good at that. One day, he told me to bet on a 16-1 shot he was riding at the Vaal. It was the last leg of the Jackpot. I backed the horse and won the Jackpot a few times for a return of over R30,000, a small fortune in those days.

"I used the cash to go on an extended holiday with my friend Frankie Barnard. We attended the Cheltenham meeting in the UK, went on to Munich and Copenhagen, where I fell in love with a pretty girl from Amsterdam. We flew back to Munich for a few days and then back to Copenhagen again, where I wanted to see my dream girl with a proposal of marriage, only to discover her on the hand of another man!

"So Gerald had been good to me, that was a holiday I won't forget, but while I supported his case in the courts, it was never my intention to make him look innocent. I was upset by the Jockey Club's constant interference with the courts and they deserved harsh criticism. He was warned off, then got his 20-year banning reduced to three years and then, got slapped with 20 years again until his Supreme Court appeal was successful.

"I was at Turffontein one day when Bruce Chalmers came running up to me. He was a clerk for bookmaker Bill Ferguson and he told me to find a lawyer fast, because he'd heard that a Booysens police colonel was on his way to arrest me and deport me back to England. The colonel was a good friend to Mr Ferraris, well connected in diplomatic circles, and evidently on the warpath.

"I followed Bruce's advice, made my way off the course, saw an attorney and for the next few weeks got a fright every time my doorbell rang or when someone came to the reception at my office and asked to see me. But nothing ever happened. I don't think the colonel had enough influence to get me on a plane out of South Africa, and eventually things died down.

"During the course of all of this, I was walking on thin ice at the Rand Daily Mail, where editor Raymond Louw warned me, 'Molly, you're out on a limb for Turner. If he loses his appeal, you're out of a job!'

"The day Gerald won his appeal, I was overjoyed. I drove to the old Jan Smuts Airport to meet Gerald on his way back from the court in Bloemfontein. We hugged like best friends, I offered to buy him a 'sharpy' for the road home. I said, 'GT, now we'll do your story for the Daily Mail. We can talk freely and you can state your case, I can't wait to write it!'

"Gerald's face got serious as we entangled from the embrace and he said: 'Shit Molly, I've already sold my story to the Sunday Times!'

"We didn't speak for years after that - Gerald, Mr Ferraris and I - but I did establish a cordial relationship with the trainer about 25 years later, in 1999, when I became an on-course presenter for the old IGN racing service and he was forced to speak to me live, on air. We've had drinks in a group with other racing personalities, on a few occasions since."

CHAPTER 23

When I went to the National Sale at the old Milner Park Showgrounds near Braamfontein in 1973, I was lucky to find the single horse I wanted from that year's big catalogue. He was a colt by High Veldt from Instinctive by Sybil's Nephew, drafted into the Birch Brothers consignment of 40 horses.

Distinctly was a beautiful, mild-tempered specimen, his only flaw was that he was on the small side, and perhaps the smallest of the renowned breeders' offerings that year. But I'd rather have them too small than too big as yearlings and with all the other boxes ticked, we were happy to get this handsome little bay with the gentle demeanour for R10,250.

The purchase slip was signed by Harry Suckermann who, along with Bennie Peznik and David Kopping were the owners of Johannesburg's Motor Town, a major car dealer – but when he was ready to race, the partnership in Distinctly was registered to Bennie and I.

We had no spelling farms in those days like the trend is today. When new runners or yearlings came to us, we had to move our older, nonperforming horses out of the yard or retire them. Distinctly was moved from the sales complex to my Newmarket stables right away, and even as a youngster he was popular with everyone because he was generally calm and relaxed and enjoyed interaction. He was easy to train and showed us quickly that he was going to be well above average on the racetrack.

We decided to give Distinctly a few pipe-openers to start him off. He first stepped out in an 800m dash for juveniles on 10 October 1973, the old Kruger Day race meeting at Turffontein. Our jockey was Chard Smith, who'd just come out of time as an apprentice alongside his twin brother, Bradford. Distinctly was outpaced, as expected. He finished about 15 lengths behind Eddie Agopian's colt, Ronico.

Roughly a month later, on 14 November, we engaged Jim Polley's former apprentice, Deon Spies, also out of his time and in search of opportunities, to ride Distinctly in a Juvenile Plate over 800m at Newmarket. This was another leg-stretch which saw him finish 10 lengths off John Jacobs' later accomplished sprinter, Grimalkin. We put Spies up again 10 days later in a race over 1000m at the Vaal and Distinctly finished in midfield again in a race also won by the up-and-coming Grimalkin.

Distinctly came back stronger every time, improved several lengths with every training session. To bring him to a peak for a 1200m race, we entered him once more for a 1000m contest at the Vaal, where Martin Schoeman gave him a feel and they ran third to Roy Curling's mount, Snow Goose, beaten by just a few lengths.

By this time, Raymond Rhodes and Tobie van Booma were riding Distinctly in most of his gallops at home and they were competing for getting on next. Rhodes was as good as ever; Van Booma took a while to regain his confidence after the Gerald Turner affair, but he continued to work hard and eventually he was back on song and started getting among the winners again.

We gave Distinctly a short break from racing before entering him for a 1200m Juvenile at the Vaal on 20 February 1974. I decided on Rhodes, the senior rider, and we expected our colt to win. We backed him *(not sure if I got the best price after Raymond's punters got stuck in!)*, he went off 7-10 favourite and they absolutely doddled the race, putting the second horse to the sword by eight lengths.

This first win gave us much confidence for the road ahead and Van Booma got his chance next. Distinctly was entered for a Juvenile Plate over 1300m on the tight Gosforth Park track, scheduled for 9 March, 1974. He drew well, near the inside in Box 3, and this gave us an advantage at the track. Distinctly raced away smartly to beat the Oppenheimer-owned favourite, Col Pickering, who was drawn wide and took second place. Van Booma rode a good race.

Distinctly had now confirmed that our high regard for him was not misplaced, and I put Rhodes up again for the colt's hat-trick attempt in his first try over 1600m in a Two-Year-Old Plate at Gosforth Park on 16 March. Alec Uzent had a 'talking horse' called Amber Ace in the race, he was the 15-10 favourite while Col Pickering was at 22-10. Punters reckoned that the Oppenheimer-owned runner would beat us, just a week later, over the extra 400m. Due to the confidence in the top two, Distinctly was allowed to start at a surprisingly generous 8-1 and we helped ourselves. He swept clear impressively, again, winning by 2,25-lengths from Border Legend with Col Pickering five lengths adrift.

Our main objectives during Distinctly's three-year-old career were to win the prestigious Dingaans and the SA Derby at Turffontein.

He enjoyed a rest at the end of his two-year-old spell and we brought him back slowly via a few prep runs. These included the Bull Brand

International Jockeys Stakes at Scottsville in November 1974, where the capable Argentinian Fernando Toro's name was drawn to ride him in a strong field that included Willie Carson on Border Legend, Secretariat's rider Ron Turcotte on Ambiance, Henry Samani on Archangel, Michael Hole on Elevation and Lester Piggott on Snow Goose.

The surprise winner of this race was Caption, a colt ridden by Garth Puller, who held on at the line to beat Toro on Distinctly, who tried hard but was starting to signal a need for a bit more ground. He went into the Dingaans in December 1974 at level weights with our old rival Col Pickering but again appeared to find the mile too short. We were perhaps mildly disappointed in his fifth place, beaten five lengths.

We had Distinctly near the top of his game for the Derby on 22 March, 1975 at Turffontein. With Raymond Rhodes injured, we put Tobie van Booma back on. Our apprentice weighed only 42kg at the time and Distinctly had to race with plenty of dead weight at 56kg and while we didn't foresee that to be a problem, a rain storm had changed the track condition from good to 'holding'.

The meeting was saved by some sun after lunch and the 13-horse Derby field went down to post. Distinctly was backed to favourite at 18-10, with Col Pickering at 7-2.

Van Booma rode another good race. Distinctly bowled along about 10 lengths off the pace set by Flying Jim, who went five lengths clear but faded when they came into the turn. Distinctly made up steady ground, had to wait for a gap to open between runners but Van Booma kept his cool, moved at the right time and they won going away by two lengths from Col Pickering and Milkwood.

On the strength of this commanding win, my first tilt at the Rothmans Durban July was starting to become a reality. Distinctly was a horse that was easy to ride. His jockeys were able to place him anywhere in a race, he had the stamina for Greyville's 2200m and a nice turn of foot to go with it.

In May 1975, I entered him for the big race and my dream was taking shape. Being a Grade 1 Derby winner, Distinctly had already done enough to make the final line-up for the race and all we had to do was to keep him ticking over for the first Saturday in July.

Distinctly was set to carry 47,5kg in South Africa's flagship race and with Raymond Rhodes unable to make the weight, I had to pick one of several good lightweight riders of the time. But they were in demand all round and I quickly ran out of options.

Michael Cavé would have been my number one choice, but he was riding mainly for Roy Unsworth at the time and the trainer had forbidden him to accept any mounts from my yard. Roy was upset because of my support for Tobie van Booma after the incident with Gerald Turner. Gerald was married to Lindy Coetzee, sister of Roy's wife Carol. I guess he'd expected me to keep quiet and let it play out.

The likes of Stephen Jupp and Marty Schoeman were initially available but within weeks their services were taken and so, in staying loyal, I decided to stick with Van Booma, who was unbeaten on Distinctly and riding very well.

The colt's preparation was absolutely spot on. He was tuned to the minute and we all gained confidence in the weeks prior to the race, so much so that we booked a travelling party of owners and supporters as well as Distinctly on a flight to Durban on Friday, 4 July, 1975, a day before the race.

To my best knowledge, this was the first time ever a 'July' contender would be flown to Durban from another centre and aside from being expensive, getting our horse into the aeroplane was a noisy affair and not near as streamlined as it is today. We had to reverse our truck with the float carrying Distinctly into the cargo area of the plane. There were deafening slams of metal to metal around us with huge pallets and crates being loaded.

Distinctly stood napping in his box as if nothing was going on. He was unruffled by the commotions, took the flight from Johannesburg to Durban like a frequent traveller and stepped out on the other side as if he was walking from his stable and onto the track back home.

I'd never seen as many people on a racetrack as that Saturday, 5 July, 1975. There was an incredible atmosphere and the regular July fashion fanfare preceded the races in the build-up to the race. By the time the July field came on parade - mid-afternoon in a typically humid Durban - the air was thick with anticipation. The crowd buzzed, punters and paddock pundits sat on the stands around the parade ring and stood ten-deep behind that; others were gathered in colourful masses on every level of the grandstand overlooking the ring.

My raiding party included my wife Norma, fellow-owners Bennie Peznik, Dave Kopping, Harry Suckerman and Mordley Zimmerman. While we were tense and our palms were sweaty, we did have a quiet confidence among us and when Distinctly stepped into the ring he took our breaths away. His coat was shining and he was quiet and composed, as we'd come to know him.

Our rivals were the best around. There was trainer Fred Rickaby's freak athlete, Sledgehammer, a racing machine with 15 wins to his name before he turned five. His regular jockey Michael Roberts had been booked and they were the popular favourites at 2-1. Arion, the Cape Derby winner, was second favourite at 5-1 with the highly talented Gatecrasher at 6-1 and Distinctly at 7s with the grey, Jamaican Music. Queen Of All was at 10-1 and Yataghan, who'd won the race in 1973 and ran third to Riboville in 1974, was next on the boards at 16-1. He shared those odds with the Oppenheimer-owned Principal Boy, trained by John Breval.

I reckoned we had a good chance of winning the race if Distinctly could stay out of trouble. He may have been a bit lucky in the Dingaans when a passage opened for him at the right time, but in the company of these big guns no inches would be given. If he got stuck behind in a wall of runners, that would be tickets and tax for us.

Tobie van Booma and I discussed our tactics at length in the days leading to the race and on the morning of the event. We had a perfect draw at six and so, ideally, a position five or six lengths off the pace would have been best, and I wanted Distinctly to find his rhythm so he could relax during the early running. Tobie had to find the quickest way into the open when they turned for home and wind him up immediately in the short run-in.

We'd identified Gatecrasher as a potential problem. As brilliant as Herman Brown's runner was, he had a terrible habit of hanging out badly, sometimes across the track. I warned Tobie to steer clear of Gatecrasher. "Stay on his inside, stay away from him. He's going to hang out. Don't go to his outside, he will carry you out!" Gatecrasher was drawn at 14, eight berths away and perhaps unlikely to get close to us at the business end but, while Brown had declared his runner with a pair of blinkers, I still felt that Tobie had to watch him.

The few minutes before any Durban July, and the start of the race itself, is something to behold. There is a palpable tension, and then an almighty roar from the crowd when the gates open and the starter sends them on their way.

This time, two runners, My Hyacinth and Principal Boy, broke out prematurely and were reigned in, but it was smooth sailing at the second attempt and the field started perfectly, with Arion going out to set the clip with High Glow and Kentford handy, followed by Principal

Boy. Distinctly and Sledgehammer raced together in midfield and Gatecrasher was somewhere in the mix behind them.

Principal Boy, whose jockey Robbie Thomson had managed to place on the running rail from a wide draw, bounced off the false rail and set sail for home, in full cry. The other runners started spreading out across the track, like they often do in this great race, and everyone was screaming home their favourites over the spine-tingling last 400m.

I was watching Distinctly, who was just a few lengths off now and placed for a strong bid in the stretch. I expected Tobie van Booma to keep his position, to stay away from Gatecrasher as we'd discussed, and to step on the pedal at the 300m-mark.

Then, my heart jumped into my throat. Distinctly, running powerfully and about to hit the front, started drifting wide towards the outside under sudden pressure from a horse hanging out badly on his inside. It was Gatecrasher!

Gatecrasher was at his best, and worst, on this day. In a frantic finish, he carried Distinctly out across the width of the track and almost pushed him right over the standside rail with 120m to go. Van Booma was forced to ease our horse. He stood up in the irons and had to stop riding for a few vital seconds, allowing Gatecrasher to edge ahead.

Gatecrasher crossed the line a short head clear of Principal Boy, who had run perfectly straight, 40m across on the other side of the track. Distinctly got third, a neck behind Gatecrasher and still fighting for galloping room.

We awaited Distinctly in the third box, in a disjointed blur of bitter disappointment, and being almost numb I could hardly express my anger at what had happened. It struck me that jockey Garth Puller didn't use his whip in his left hand to prevent Gatecrasher from hanging so badly. But I had to vent at Van Booma, who was implicitly instructed to stay on Gatecrasher's inside and lost the race by going to his outside.

The Horse and Hound reported a week after the race: "The hooter sounded. The Greyville Stipes had objected and this virtually meant death to the winner. The long wait started, the tears flowed, suggestions raised, hopes dashed. How did Van Booma manage to stay in the saddle? After this, the meeting fell flat.

"Indeed, the strain was far too much for everyone and, when the result was finally announced – Principal Boy first, Distinctly second, Gatecrasher disqualified – more tears and heartaches were the order. There is no doubt that, had Distinctly made his run in the centre of the course, he would have won by four to six lengths."

Brown, Puller and the followers of Gatecrasher disagree to this day, believing their horse would have won regardless of what had happened, but there is no reason to argue. It is what it is, the popular experts' opinion is that we were most unlucky, indeed, not to have won, and to this day the 1975 Durban July remains the biggest disappointment of my career.

Van Booma said in an interview in Aidan Lithgow's Legend Of The Turf Series that I watched recently, that he shouted at Puller to get out the way; Puller told him he wasn't aware of them, yet in the same interview claims he didn't put his stick in his left hand because he would have hit Distinctly. There is a head-on photo taken close to the finish line that seems to show Puller leaning over in the saddle on Gatecrasher. No precautions there. Gatecrasher's jock was suspended for two months for that ride. I don't know. I just don't know.

There was chaos after the race, with supporters of both Distinctly and Gatecrasher demanding the 'right result'. We were unsettled, agitated. I remember our guest, Mordley Zimmerman, a prominent owner, promising after the race that he was so upset he was going to sell all his horses and stop betting altogether. In the weeks following the race, he delivered on his promise.

I had a temper in those days and I had to keep my words and emotions in check. It was hard. I suspect that, if not for the captain, crew and friends around me, I might have thrown Van Booma off the plane on the flight back to Johannesburg the next day. Then again, he was just an apprentice riding against some of the best jockeys this country has ever seen.

As they say in the classic terminology of this game: "That's Racing!"

CHAPTER 24

Early in 1975, the clouds unleashed everything they had over the Highveld and other parts of South Africa. Extreme rains turned the streets into rivers and homes in certain suburbs were flooded. In Johannesburg, individuals were reported missing and, in Durban, 12 people drowned in a flash flood on 22 March.

We weren't able to use Newmarket's grass training track more than once a week at most, and our work programmes were severely interrupted. It was a small wonder that race meetings were staged at all in this period but, having had a few of the stable's runners ticking over and approaching their best before the rains came, we were able to compete in the Graded features that were squeezed in on the odd sunny day.

The track difficulties that started with the rains at Newmarket got worse and I was not prepared to endure it for much longer. When the water table became saturated under the training tracks, the formerly good Newmarket surfaces turned into a morass of thick black clay. The clay stuck to horses' feet and they were slipping and falling, with high risks of injury. Working them became near impossible.

One day, I drove home thinking what we were going to do to get our horses fit. I'd paid off my loans on The Curragh, we were happy living on our smart property but I realised that, in due course, the worsening training tracks would take their toll. The track managers had no imminent solution as they hadn't been confronted by the effects of rain of this magnitude. We were in trouble.

The stabling facilities at the Vaal Racecourse near the town of Vereeniging were not as good as what we had at home, but their sand and grass tracks were first class. They drained well and there was no clay underneath the surface, so theirs was not a pressing concern over water levels like we had in Alberton.

I phoned Maurice Passmore, who was in charge of the Vaal, to find out if there were any stables available. Perhaps, I could train my runners approaching races on the Vaal tracks and bring the others over when I needed to, until the Newmarket tracks were safe again.

"Ormond, there's only a few trainers here, you can have as many stables as you want," Passmore said.

The call gave me some hope, but I was somewhat apprehensive in leaving our base at The Curragh where we'd put in money and so many hours of love and hard work.

I didn't ponder the matter too long. When I browsed through the racing programme for the next few months, I saw dozens of suitable races for my up-and-coming horses. If I couldn't get them ready, those races and stakes would be lost to the stable.

Right there and then, I arranged for two trucks to pick up my 30 horses at the Curragh and take them to the Vaal Triangle, destination Vaal Racecourse, in the shadow of the Sasol Petrol Company's massive chimneys.

THOROUGHLY!

This was a spur-of-the-moment decision which disrupted life at our smart and professional operation at Newmarket, but I had no choice. Within weeks of moving lock, stock and barrel to the Vaal, the floodgates opened and I never looked back.

Ralph Halket, Trevor Lange and Jean Barnard were the only trainers based at the Vaal at the time, so with not much horse traffic it was an absolute pleasure to train there, and my string settled in quickly and enjoyed their surroundings at the country course.

I commuted from Newmarket to the Vaal every day for a few weeks, a two-hour return trip every day, sometimes twice. Having to get up even earlier for a drive on the dark Vereeniging highway was not ideal, so we decided to put The Curragh in the market and look for a new house in the Vereeniging area.

This brings me to an interesting memory I'd like to share. After a week or two of searching for a suitable family home, we found an absolutely pristine, multi-levelled home on the Vaal River near the suburb of Three Rivers. The house was situated on a bend in the river and the owner had cleared away a grove of trees so there were uninterrupted views over a long stretch of it, with ducks paddling on the water and ample birdlife.

Can you guess who the owner of the house was? Well, none other than Frederik Willem 'F.W.' de Klerk, the Member of Parliament for Vereeniging, future Prime Minister of South Africa and joint Nobel Peace Prize winner in his later years.

I'd heard that 'Frikkie' was on his way to bigger things in political life and that he was moving his own family to Cape Town. I never got to meet him personally, but dealt with him through the estate agent – I remembered this detail when Mr De Klerk passed away of cancer in November 2021.

My boys, initially hesitant to move, loved their new home. Alan went to General Smuts High School, David enrolled at the then new Riverside High and Paul at Milton Primary. David has described this time as special in his life - he got involved in the tensely contested River Regattas and had his baptism of fire when he was pulled into an older team as coxswain one day and steered their boat into the river banks. He was much better after that and was a good rower in the school leagues.

Among the runners that started a winning roll from our new base at the Vaal were Barrack (Carnaervon Blues), Born Bold (Bold Lad), Miller (New South Wales), Red Neon (Royal Pardon) and Easy Glide (Galliot).

―――

The quiet feud between trainer Roy Unsworth and I continued. I was upset by this, because we were friends before the Van Booma/Turner incident and I'd helped him in difficult times at Turffontein and Newmarket. The only good thing that came from this was that Unsworth's jockey, the superb Michael Cavé, ended up in my yard. Tobie van Booma, in turn, started riding for Unsworth.

We were at the track one morning late in 1975, when Tommy van der Linde came running over and said that Cavé wanted to have a word with me. "Tell him to piss off," I said. "The last time I gave him a ride he got off because Unsworth told him to."

Tommy came back a while later. Cavé insisted on a quick meeting, so I hesitantly gave in and met him at the rail on the side of the training track.

"Mr Ferraris," Cavé said, "Mr Unsworth fired me, I won't ride for him again, it's over. Please sir can you spare a few rides? I will be here every day to ride work for you, too."

I may have been a man of poor temper at times, but I was no fool. If this was a jockey of lesser talent I would've turned him away, but Michael Cavé had already proven himself to be potentially in the league of Roberts, Rhodes, Schoeman and Turner, so this was a big opportunity to get regular access to his services.

"Okay, you can come ride a few, but I don't want more nonsense from you!" I told him, and he started riding work the next day.

This was one of the best decisions I'd made. Over the next few years, Michael and I developed a wonderful professional relationship with a spate of winners that was perhaps better, pound for pound, as any I'd enjoyed before or since. We never had an argument. If not for his personal problems and constant battle with weight and illness, ours would have been a combination that lasted much longer than it did.

Michael started riding Distinctly after the Durban July fiasco. Our stalwart kept his good high-level form going, but we just couldn't manage to win another feature with him. He finished second to Archangel in the 1975 Hawaii Stakes and third to Majestic Crown in December's Holiday Inn. He was the favourite to win on both occasions. He raced all the way through to 1977 and won a few more handicaps, but we retired him following a midfield finish in the 1977 renewal of the 'July'.

Distinctly was really a pony who ran his big heart out, but due to his size was never able to make the jump from top class racehorse to champion. Physically, he didn't have the improvement in him. Our time with him was memorable, however, and, to this day, I think about the gentle little horse often.

CHAPTER 25

The year 1976 started on a high note for South Africans because the SABC (South African Broadcasting Corporation) launched our first television service to great expectations on 5 January. Everyone who could afford the then black-and-white model television sets were glued to a news bulletin, a children's programme, a sports report and some basic documentaries between 6pm and 9pm to start.

Soon, we were able to buy custom-coloured plastic covers that fitted over the black-and-white screens so that the available shows could be watched in a semblance of colour. But that didn't last long. Within months there was a rush for the available new colour television sets and the country was literally TV-mad.

I am mentioning this because horseracing, already highly popular as the only legal gambling activity allowed, received chunks of airtime on National TV. The Saturday sporting show, 'Sport 76', which became Sport 77, 78 and so on, featured live crossings to racecourses for all the Jackpot races, every Saturday. The presenters included David Hall-Green, Martin Locke, Retief Uys and Jan Snyman. Remember them?

Racing was as much a part of the South African fabric as 'braaivleis', rugby, sunny skies *(and maybe Chevrolet?)*, betting pools flourished, totalisator technology was improved and racecourses were jam-packed, midweek and at the weekends. Racegoers queued for sometimes 20 minutes at the turnstiles, paid a fee to get in and wore badges for different enclosures. Yes, believe it.

The Durban July was arguably the biggest and most revered sporting event in the land, competing only with the occasional Springbok-All Black rugby test. Top horses and racing personalities were celebrated and some were household names. This was the start of what many refer to as South African racing's Golden Era, a period of phenomenal growth between the mid-1970s and the early 1990s.

While the political stage was volatile, the simmering racial tensions did not boil over to the racing industry. The racecourse was 'the great leveller' - a place where people of all races could enjoy a day of high-octane thoroughbred racing, compare notes from race cards and 'inside info', shout and jump for joy together and lament their losses afterwards.

There was a separate grandstand for 'Blacks and Indians' at all the venues, but if you were a racegoer in those days, you will remember that the racetrack was perhaps the only place where people of colour could pay a fee for a Day Member's Badge which allowed them access to the luxury enclosures in front of the main grandstand. Everyone at the track shared a love for the horses, and the sport. For six hours a time, twice a week, we were all equal and peaceful.

The racecourse was a place where camaraderie existed, week after week, away from increasing incidents of violence, protests and the growing dissent among parents for compulsory military service for their young sons. There was confusion in the air, mixed with anger, justified or misplaced, and some hot and bothered individuals in the mix.

THOROUGHLY!

While the country was experiencing a relatively low growth rate and a high rate of inflation, opportunistic businessmen were on the prowl, as they always are. There was a proposal for the takeover of Newmarket by leading racehorse owners, Reuben McCarthy, Lou and Izzy Schenker. They were property developers in the region and wanted to turn the racecourse into a major commercial site.

The management of the Owners and Trainers wouldn't stand for this. We were a strong unit, men with balls who'd just started the Benevolent Fund for our retired colleagues and stood together. We didn't even get to the 'consider the offer' stage. Selling Newmarket was a no-no.

McCarthy and the Schenkers, brothers as big as the mansions they were selling, called a meeting. When they came to the course to see us, we were ready and waiting. The moguls were intimidating, but OTA Management - Alf Peerman, Henry Eatwell, Pat Wright, George Azzie and I – were not about to start negotiating. We loaded our guns and placed them on the boardroom table, in clear view of our visitors. I kid you not. We'd set the stage for a shoot-out at the Alberton Corral and our scare tactics worked!

They were barely in the room when we shouted at them, "Bugger off, both of you, and don't come back!" When they saw the weapons, they turned a shade of red, retreated and left, never to be seen again. That was the end of our dispute. They took their development to the other side of Alberton, near today's town of Katlehong.

Thirty years later, the jewel of Highveld racing that was Newmarket Racecourse would be sold for way under its value to fund the bottom line of the gluttonous corporate, Phumelela Gaming & Leisure. Such a pity there were no men with guns around when that deal was concluded.

We entered Black Bishop (Prince Sao) and two others for the G1 SA Derby on 27 March 1976 and he was the second-most fancied runner in the market to JBK Cooper's The Maltster. We had a game plan and Raymond Rhodes made a sensible clip for us on Beacon Lad, who was drawn best of our trio at Number 5. Black Bishop (8) and Lead The Pack (14) were dropped out to come from the back and this suited their style of running.

Desert Sands, Simon Magus and The Maltster were the first to grab Beacon Lad, who'd done his job and was a spent force with 450m to run. Tobie van Booma had moved Lead The Pack into a challenging position from the rear. With the best horse in the race under him, Michael Cavé was biding his time on Black Bishop but at the 200m-mark they quickened up smartly, ran straight into contention and won going away from Lead The Pack and Double Haig.

Black Bishop raced for Barry Gebhardt and Tony Mansour and, like Distinctly, he won the G3 SA St Leger over 2850m, just a month later. He wasn't near as good, however, didn't shape with the best in the Natal Derby and the Holiday Inns later that year and we retired him after 14 runs. He was a decent soldier, winning six races.

Our 1976 Oaks contender Pretty Border, in turn, was a filly in a class all of her own, the type of horse that 'makes a trainer get up every morning' – to use that popular phrase. She was a smashing chestnut with a big white blaze, sired by Herbaceous from Deroneo, unfashionably bred at Gert Strydom's Rossmead Stud. She was bought cheaply at the National Sale by the Motortown Group of Distinctly fame's Dave Kopping, who registered her to race for his wife, Rachel.

Pretty Border was beaten in her first two starts at two, early in 1975, but she went on to win the T.R. Lewis Memorial over 1200m and the Transvaal Breeders over 1400m in a canter before being touched off by the good colt Bahadur in the G1 Allan Robertson Memorial, then contested over 1600m at Gosforth Park. She was good enough to race against colts again in the Benoni Guineas later that year, but she couldn't get into the hunt from a wide draw and finished in midfield.

We gave her a short break going into 1976 and she started a new campaign with three excellent wins on a trot, the first in the Coco Rico Jockeys International Invitation Stakes at Gosforth Park on Valentine's Day, when we were lucky to draw our own Michael Cavé for the ride.

Michael also rode her to a narrow win in the Autumn Fillies Stakes early in March and then she hacked up at the end of March in the Newmarket Fillies Plate, a 3.75-length success over Off The Hook. Each time, she came from well back in the field, preferring to be left alone so she could settle and do her own thing while her rivals were sizing each other up, elsewhere.

Pretty Border was on fire and I gave Michael a leg up for the G1 SA Oaks on 17 April. Racing editor, Robert Garner, described the race in The Star: "Pretty Border broke first from the pens but by the time 200m had been covered, she was in her customary position at the tail end of the field. There she remained until well into the straight when jockey Michael Cavé steered her to the middle of the track for her challenge.

"The chestnut filly took a little time to get into top gear but when she did, just inside the 400m-mark, she began to fly. Unwinding her breath-taking finishing burst, she swept past one rival after another. She struck the front approaching the 200m-mark and the race was over as far as she was concerned. Pretty Border has no equal among the Transvaal's three-year-olds and I know of no member of her own sex in the whole country I would back to beat her."

Commentator Peter Duffield called Pretty Border as being about 40 lengths off the pace at one stage. My patron, Boet Oosthuizen, the owner-breeder and big punter, turned to me after the race and said,

"Ormond, I was ready to catch you. You went white. I thought you were going to pass out!"

Pretty Border gave my stable a Derby-Oaks double, achieved only once before this when Henry Eatwell won with Home Guard and Mast High in 1968. This was my first SA Oaks, a race that was always dear to my heart and one I enjoyed winning a further six times in years to follow.

Like many top horses before and after her, Pretty Border didn't enjoy her first experience at Scottsville in Pietermaritzburg when we entered her for the G1 Natal Oaks a month later. She was odds-on at 6-10, but despite having every chance going into the last 250m, she didn't give her customary late kick and was beaten into second by the outsider, With Pleasure.

We trucked her to Durban next for June's G1 Rockgrip Guineas, the representative race for the best three-year-old colts and she gave a good account in fourth to Run Free, Bahadur and Tudor Blue.

In reading through a few newspaper clips from the 1980s and 1990s I see I was quoted as saying that Pretty Border was one of the best fillies, if not the best, I'd trained. Almost fifty years after she retired I'd stay with that statement. She was an absolute star who won 9 races from 22 runs, unlucky a few times and beaten on a few other occasions only by the best male runners in the land. I've never found one quite like her.

With mares like Pretty Border coming off the racetrack, I decided to invest in a farm to keep the best ones so I could breed with them, and Schalkie van der Walt found me a nice piece of land near Middelburg in the Karoo region, called Rooispruit. It had a typical farmhouse, paddocks, good water supply and limestone. I was never able to spend the time here that I wanted to, but I bred plenty of winners from the farm and it proved to be a sound investment.

I predicted a good career for Pretty Border at stud. She produced one promising early runner who was trained in the Cape by Peter Kannemeyer and won a few races but, sadly, Pretty Border got kicked on her head in a paddock early in her broodmare career and died, most untimely.

CHAPTER 26

Noon Flight, another son of New South Wales, was a high-quality colt who won a number of races for us from our base at the Vaal. He was a half-brother to the 1972 Durban July winner, In Full Flight, and one of 10 runners brought to me by owner J.P. 'Zwei' Herholdt, who farmed near Thabazimbi, North Western Transvaal. Noon Flight won five of his first 10 races.

I had an excellent spell of winners for Herholdt, who also raced the likes of Mellow Yellow (Oligarchy), Crafty Prince (Give A Hoot) and Sweet Victory (Filipepi). We had maybe 12 wins or more in the first half of 1976 and the same in the second half, including a few handicaps. The stable closed off the 1975/6 season with 48 winners and my first Transvaal Trainers' Championship in the bag. Michael Cavé was the top Highveld jockey for the season and Herholdt was the leading owner.

Herholdt was an intense, brooding individual who never once thanked or congratulated me, or his jockeys, when we won races for him. We were always one flare-up of bad temper away from a fall-out. Our relationship came to an abrupt end after a meeting at Gosforth Park during an International Jockeys Day. I'd won Race 6 on the card with Herholdt's runner Princemore and followed up in the next race with his Noon Flight winning the Invitation International Jockeys Stakes under Michael Roberts – a nice double landed!

The club gave silver plates as trophies to trainers for winning small features in this term and I received one for Noon Flight's win. It was twice the size of a saucer, if that big, but a nice gesture from the stewards. Only thing is, Herholdt came to grab it.

"This is mine," he said.

"Like hell it's yours," I replied and grabbed the plate back.

"It's my horse, my plate, give it to me," Herholdt said as his face turned red and blood started rushing up my own neck.

I held on to the plate, pushed him away and said, "Listen here, Herholdt, it was given to me as the trainer, not to you! Now get on a phone and call the truckers. Take your horses and go. Go. Go now. I want them out of my stable when I get back!"

Herholdt swung around, swore under his breath and walked away, and when I got back to my yard at the Vaal later, his horses were being loaded to leave. Some were going to Jean Barnard, others to Nick van Tonder.

My friend, Boet Oosthuizen told me to watch my step. He'd known Herholdt from farming and business circles out in the Western Transvaal and joked: "Ormond, don't mess with that guy. He doesn't take nonsense. Watch out, he'll shoot you!"

A week later, on my way to the Vaal, I was driving across the old steel bridge near the racecourse when a Mercedes Benz, some way ahead of me, came to a stop and a man got out of it, waving me down. I slowed down, stopped and discovered it was J.P. Herholdt, who was now approaching me on the bridge.

I thought for a few seconds that my final day on earth had arrived. Just a few months before this I'd heard on the radio of a guy called Jimmy Hoffa that went missing in the city of Detroit and was never found. 'Zwei' was going to put a bullet in my head and throw me over the bridge. But I faked bravery, got out of my own car to face him and he stopped a few metres away.

"Ormond, please take my horses back. Come on, let's forget what happened. Please man, can I send them back?" he asked, politely.

I simply said, "No, we are done. I told you. They're not coming back. Goodbye."

I got back behind my steering wheel and drove away, squeezing through a gap he had left with his car parked diagonally across the bridge.

That was it. We never spoke again.

Talk about volatile episodes, but on the political front things were far worse than an argument between two ill-tempered horse people. The situation in South Africa had reached its boiling point on 16 June 1976, when students from numerous schools in the township of Soweto, Johannesburg began to protest in the streets, in response to the introduction of Afrikaans as the medium of instruction in local schools. An estimated 176 or more people were killed by police who broke loose in uncontrolled fire. While the uprising began in Soweto, it spread across the country and carried us into 1977.

CHAPTER 27

It often happens that new patrons come along when old ones depart. Peter Dimakogiannis visited me at the Vaal just after J.P. Herholdt had left the stable, and sent me a few of his horses to train. I hadn't met him or known of this friendly Greek gentleman. He had been impressed with my results, liked the way my runners were turned out and approached me out of the blue, of his own accord.

Peter, an electrical engineer, was in the early years of his career and in the process of establishing an electrical firm in Ophirton, just around the corner from the Turffontein Racecourse in the Booysens district. He'd grow this to a major company over the next few decades, and he bought me at least one horse per year from 1979 to 2016. He was generous too. When I'd told him to have a bet and his horse won, he'd send an envelope filled with cash to my office the next morning. Peter enjoyed, 'carving the turkey'.

Peter was always a lucky owner. The first two colts I bought for him at the Rand Yearling Sale were the multiple winners Demon King (Welsh Harmony) and King Of Jazz (Fats Waller) and there were many good ones after that including Falconetti (Peaceable Kingdom), Simply Salmon (Western Winter), Natural Selection (Western Winter) and Santa (National Emblem).

Suitably I saddled my milestone 2500th career winner in March 2016 when Peter's gelding Romany Prince (Kahal) won the Drum Star Handicap under Muzi Yeni. Peter was popularly referred to as 'Mr Dimako' in racing circles when he became prominent as an owner and is still well liked today. He hasn't stopped investing in the sport after his recent retirement.

I'm getting well ahead of myself, but the introduction to Peter Dimakogiannis is appropriate here as it shows that long, good friendships between owners and trainers are possible when there is mutual respect. Peter was an absolute pleasure to deal with for more than three decades and we never had an argument. He left me to do my job.

Our front cover model (the nice one, next to me), is Wagga Wagga, one of the best colts I had the pleasure of training, and his story takes me back to Paddy Hinton, my good attorney-come-race-caller friend.

Remember those properties I told you about, the ones Paddy bought from the Boer War veterans? Well, at least one of those real estate investments paid off handsomely and made him a multi-millionaire. Paddy received a call one day from Bernhard Adelfang, a German entrepreneur in the business of manufacturing envelopes. He needed a property to build a factory and offices and he reckoned that one of Paddy's properties on the industrial side of Wynberg, Johannesburg-North, was the ideal spot.

Whilst negotiating, Paddy and Bernhard became friends and the German explained that the envelope business was booming and made

Paddy a partnership offer. A deal was struck on the property and Paddy received a share of Merpak Envelopes (Pty) Ltd, which grew from its inception in 1969 through the 1970s and into the 1990s to the biggest envelope business in Africa.

You'd have guessed by now that Paddy's personal wealth received an enormous boost from the mid-1970s onwards, so much so that he called a day to his career in law and also gave up his hobby of race calling to assist with the managing of his booming new business.

Paddy's coming into money was a blessing for my stable. He was keen on buying more horses, not shy of laying out extra if he was required to and now quite happy to race in his own silks. He registered a red body with black sash, emerald sleeves and cap.

We attended the Rand Sale in 1976 to buy Distinctly's half-brother, a colt by New South Wales from Instinctive, named Wagga Wagga. Paddy and I shared his purchase price of R42,000, the fourth-highest at that sale, but we didn't think twice when bidding. He was the one we wanted.

Wagga Wagga had Distinctly's handsome looks, but they were different in all other respects. Distinctly was a pony, Wagga Wagga was a big, imposing horse. Distinctly was calm, like a lamb, Wagga Wagga was a real handful. He had a bad nature and a vicious streak and proved troublesome to train, but boy, he could run!

We entered Wagga Wagga for a Maiden Juvenile Plate over 1000m on 27 November 1976 and while it was far too short for him, we expected him to win. Michael Cavé booted him home to a narrow success, but it was a classy show all the same. I knew that he'd improve a great deal and, with his first win under the belt, gave him a short break.

Wagga Wagga was a little ring-rusty when he reappeared in a Juvenile Plate on 5 February 1977, and Michael wasn't hard on him in a three-length defeat by Old Vic. That run was inspiring. He pulled up sound and full of beans and I decided to leave him in a strong race just a week later at Gosforth Park.

Wally Segal, the General Manager of Gosforth Park, was instrumental in a series of Invitational Jockeys Contests in the 1970s and 1980s. He was able to secure good sponsors and high-profile jockeys which made them popular among racegoers. These events received nationwide coverage and the stands were packed to the rafters.

Wagga Wagga was accepted for a Juvenile Plate over 1300m, the second of four test races between the South African team that included Michael Roberts, Michael Cavé, Gerald Turner, Raymond Rhodes and the team of overseas jockeys including Joe Mercer, Roy Higgins and Fernando Toro.

We drew French jockey Jean Claude DeSaint, someone I hadn't heard of before this meeting or thereafter, but he rode an excellent race on Wagga Wagga, who quickened away in style to beat Henry Eatwell's Welcome Boy (Roberts), a colt who'd become a formidable rival in months to come. Paddy and I were delighted.

Wagga Wagga ran three more times as a two-year-old, winning all three races at Gosforth Park.

He joined forces again with Cavé on 19 March in a Juvenile Plate over 1600m. We expected him to win easy, but he made it by a short head only, doing just what he had to do.

Then it was on to the G1 Allan Robertson Memorial over 1600m on 2 April, the race Pretty Border narrowly lost to Bahadur two years prior to this renewal. Again, this was a race we thought he'd win comfortably, but he didn't extend himself. Michael got Wagga Wagga up to win by a head from Soul Song, with good types Day Remember and Welcome Boy behind them.

THOROUGHLY!

The G1 SA Nursery Plate was raced over 1600m in those days and, on 16 April, Wagga Wagga made it four wins in a row with a decisive 1,75-win over Fashion Fling. Michael looked over his shoulder when they came to the winning post and Robert Garner reported in The Star: "Those who were brave enough to take 4-10 were not disappointed. Wagga Wagga won, hard-held."

We bypassed the two-year-old features during the 1977 Durban season and gave Wagga Wagga time off to mature and furnish into his big frame. We'd earmarked the prestigious G1 Benoni Guineas in December for him and brought him back to the track, at three, for his first of three prep runs on 19 October. Michael Cavé was suffering with a nervous condition and Raymond Rhodes was indisposed, so Ronald 'Tickey' Carr got a leg over our star in his first warm-up, a handicap over 1200m at the Vaal.

Tickey put Wagga Wagga adequately through his paces and they finished under five lengths off the winner, King's Ransom. He reported his mount giving him a very good feel, but being coltish. His spell away from the racetrack and more maturity hadn't quelled Wagga Wagga's foul temperament. He was as cocky as he'd always been, with his nasty streak surfacing at times. He tried to bite people around him on occasion, shook his head and snorted nonchalantly when he was approached.

Wagga Wagga started blossoming after this run. He improved several lengths every day and he appeared to get stronger and more muscular. He was growing from a teenager into man. We ran him a few weeks later in a handicap over 1200m at Newmarket and he turned in a most inspiring four-length win in the hands of Raymond Rhodes.

Next up, three weeks before his targeted race, we took Wagga Wagga to Pietermaritzburg for the G2 SA Invitation Stakes over 1600m at Scottsville. This was a popular provincial contest between top jockeys and featured Cavé, James Maree and Martin Schoeman riding for the Transvaal team; Garth Puller, Bert Abercrombie and Patrick McGivern for the Cape; and Michael Roberts, Bert Hayden and Basil Marcus representing Natal Province.

Wagga Wagga was close to his peak for this race and we'd drawn SA's champion jockey 'Muis' Roberts to ride him, but the Scottsville voodoo struck. Wagga Wagga, the favourite and well placed, just seemed to lose his way somewhat, first time at the undulating track. He was outgunned a length on the day by Camp Sailor, a rank outsider from Port Elizabeth, ridden by Schoeman. Welcome Boy, our old rival, also failed to run to his best, five lengths off at the line.

The result of the Invitation Stakes was like water off a duck's back, really. Wagga Wagga had to travel six hours from his home base, not ideal for a neurotic type like he was and, as noted before, Scottsville had been, and to this day continues to be, the undoing for many horses racing there for the first time.

A true setback came when the barrier draws for the Benoni Guineas were announced and Wagga Wagga was allotted a number in the 20s among 30 nominations. My heart sank because we'd pointed him at this career-defining race and he was going to be primed on the day. Traditionally, a wide draw from 1300m to 1600m at Gosforth Park was a ticket to nowhere.

I intended scratching Wagga Wagga from this race at the final acceptance stage and aiming him solely at the G1 Richelieu Guineas in the Cape, but when Raymond Rhodes took him for a final gallop at the Vaal a few days before acceptances, he returned to the paddock, all smiles. "This horse will win the Guineas. Don't worry about the draw. Leave him in!"

And so I did. And Wagga Wagga won. Raymond dropped him in from that wide draw, they had more than 15 lengths to find as the talented classic field straightened up. Street Fighter, Welcome Boy, Camp Sailor and Sun Tonic looked likely to contest the finish coming to the 400m-mark, but our jockey had set Wagga Wagga alight. The big bay flashed up on the outside of Altogether Now, who had hung under pressure, swept by all his rivals and won by 2,25-lengths, easing up from the second-placed Welcome Boy.

Raymond's smile didn't say, 'I told you so!' after the race, but more like, 'Hell, he proved me right, he's very good!' and it was a moment to behold with this great rider. I had to stay focused however, because the lunatic thoroughbred in the winner's box was trying to push me into a corner with his strength and presence. If he'd kicked out at a certain point like he enjoyed doing, I wouldn't have been here writing this today.

"Wagga Wagga is a true champion. Experts were floored by his brilliant victory," wrote Mike Hessenauer in The Citizen.

We wanted to have a crack at the G2 Dingaans over 1800m, scheduled for 17 December. Wagga Wagga had pulled up sound and well after the Guineas. On the manner he'd been winning over a mile, we didn't have any concerns about the extra 200m. We were proven wrong, however. Wagga Wagga was well placed in a small Dingaans field, had every chance to win, but became flat-footed over the last 200m. He was comfortably beaten by Welcome Boy and Queen's Rebel, finishing third.

Maybe it was an off day for him, or perhaps he was just below his best following his four previous races in a relatively short period. But whether Wagga Wagga would see out 1800m and further as an older horse we'd never know.

I had to ease off him after the Dingaans. He was a badly mannered bugger again, kicked his own hock while going ballistic in his stable and we had to nurse him back to health, missing some work ahead of his next mission, the G1 Richelieu Guineas in Cape Town.

We flew Wagga Wagga to the Cape on 3 February, 1978 – a day before the race - and the trip was arduous and tiresome. His half-brother, Distinctly, wasn't fazed by the noise at the airports and the loading process, but Wagga Wagga, of course, misbehaved as expected. Getting there was one thing, racing him was another. Unsettled and troubled, he didn't give himself a chance and finished a rather one-paced eighth, beaten just over five lengths by Welcome Boy, who was markedly inferior to him over 1600m on the Highveld.

Back home, Wagga Wagga signed his own, early pension application. Just a few days after returning from the Cape he started kicking out again, hurt the same hock and this time failed to make a full recovery. We did everything we could, but were unable to nurse him right again. This niggle, coupled with his increased coltishness, put an end to a career that spanned just over a year and yielded seven wins and three places from just 12 starts. Wagga Wagga was a terrific horse we fully appreciated and respected despite his nature. He was revered by the public and his retirement was met with disappointment by his many fans, the media and rival stables.

Paddy and I sent Wagga Wagga to Gary Player's Stud in Colesberg. He sired 14 crops to race from 1980 to 1993, with 144 foals, 120 runners and 56 winners. His stakes winners were Exodus, a decent top division handicapper who won the Java Handicap twice; Askari, winner of the Transvaal Bookmakers Handicap; Ready Wit, winner of the Maurice Nathan Memorial Handicap; Indian Wells, who won the

EP Guineas and Kamma Wagga, who won the Ladies Mile and Olympic Duel Stakes. Hydra Bay was his best daughter. She managed a third in the Cape Fillies Guineas. His winningmost son was My Advantage. He won 11 races in South Africa and Mauritius.

GALLERY
PART 1

My sister Ethne and I with my mother, Jose (left back) and my father Ernest. My mother's teacher friend, Jessie Stacey, at the back (right) – 1939.

Jockey Arthur Victor.

My school in Koch Street, Johannesburg.

George Weale's stables in Booysens.

Business tycoon Norbert Erleigh, early patron.

My first winner, Shenendoah on the old Benoni track 14 August 1954.

Hitch-Knot, winning at Benoni in April 1955.

Beaujolais, winning at Newmarket in March 1961.

Bennie Little (left), owner Alec Morris (right) and I on the beach at Margate, 1957.

Cucumber cool, Raymond Rhodes, stable jockey and friend.

Young Tobie van Booma as an apprentice at The Curragh.

David (left), Paul and Alan Ferraris (right), early 1970s.

Michael Cavé, ill-fated star jockey.

The amazing Pretty Border on the canterdown.

Pretty Border and I after the 1976 SA Oaks. (Photo: H.F. Kenny).

Norma and I with Distinctly, prior to the 1975 Durban July

Gatecrasher (left) and Distinctly (right), in the last 100m of the 1975 Durban July. Does it look like Garth Puller (left) is taking precautions to stay away from us?

Tobie van Booma on Distinctly in the paddock after the 1975 July. Was '13' our unlucky number, maybe?

Michael Roberts on Noon Flight, 12 February 1977

Wagga Wagga (Rhodes) on parade before the 1977 G1 Benoni Diamond Guineas. (H.F. Kenny)

Wagga Wagga storms to victory in the Guineas. (H.F. Kenny)

Here I am, caught smiling, probably after a big win! (H.F. Kenny).

CHAPTER 28

Wagga Wagga was our kingpin for the 1976/7 season, a horse whose exploits illustrate the aforementioned highs and awful lows of racing. If he'd been sound of mind and we were able to persist with him, I have no doubt he would have won his way through to the top as a three-year-old and as an older horse. His short, but remarkable career would have been even more impressive.

This was a fantastic season for the stable, overall. Wagga Wagga's success aside, I saddled a career best 83 winners, just six short of a record set by Howard Ginsberg in 1952. This secured back-to-back Transvaal Championships Titles for Michael Cavé (106 winners) and I, and we were looking forward to bettering that in the term that followed.

We also won our second, successive SA Oaks with Siberian Wonder (Persian Wonder), owned by my long-time patron, H.A. Mackenzie.

A few of my older horses had retired or moved on to other centres but I felt we had a string of runners capable of producing a third title.

Things didn't go all that well, however, and during the first half of the 1977/8 season we were suffering second place upon second place; third upon third, not near the success rate of the previous term.

Come January of 1978, I'd sent out only 20 winners for the season and I was flummoxed. There was nothing wrong in the stable, no injuries or illnesses, and no viruses I could blame for our below-standard results. My runners were placed in the right races, well-conditioned and ready, but they weren't winning as they used to.

In looking through the race results, I saw that we were getting beat most of the time by horses trained by Jean Barnard (later Heming), based then at a private facility near the Vaal. She had a growing and impressive band of patrons with good horses and was churning out winners as if they were coming off a conveyor belt. She was well on her way to her own first title with runners like Mr Universe, Flight Path and Hold Me Close winning multiple races.

I've never begrudged anybody for their success in racing, but I've always had a competitive nature and while I wasn't overly concerned about the title race, something else was bugging me. I am mentioning it here because it was one of the main reasons for my move away from the Vaal to Cape Town. I've been asked to touch on it as it serves the progression of my story and the stable's timeline. *I could not believe that Mrs Barnard's horses found so much extra when mine had cried enough in their races, and it was hard to fathom out why this was happening.*

If you can't beat them (or you're not willing to join them), how about moving away from them? I was not going to lose any further sleep on the matter and, as at most of the junctions in my career that called for action, I made an impromptu decision without contemplating matters for days at end: I decided to move my string of 26 horses, and my family, to the Milnerton Training Centre in Cape Town.

Alan, my eldest son, decided to stay in Vereeniging. He was in his Matric (Gr12) year, enjoying his school and friends and wanted to see out his scholastic career in the Vaal Triangle. This also gave him an opportunity to keep an eye on the handful of young horses I'd left behind, stabled at the Vaal.

David and Paul had no choice and, on our arrival in Cape Town, enrolled at Milnerton High School. My boys weren't near as happy as they'd been living on the banks of the Vaal River, though we all enjoyed our racing among new acquaintances, friendly fellow-trainers and passionate racing folk. My neighbour was Peter Kannemeyer and we got on very well. I also befriended Bill Prestage, a good mate until his passing in 2021, and several others including Lionel Witkowsky, Ralph Rixon and Terrance Millard, at the time based at his magnificent training centre in Bloubergstrand across the road from Blouberg beach.

I wasn't going to ask any of the high-profile jockeys on the Highveld to join me at Milnerton – Michael Cavé and Raymond Rhodes had established careers in Transvaal and were travelling to Durban to take good rides, so they didn't offer to come with me, either. I decided to give apprentice Jannie Gouws a chance. He was one of the most promising youngsters at the Germiston Academy, had ridden a few winners for me and was strong and capable. He was the type of hard-working lad I needed as a permanent stable rider in the Cape.

The Milnerton training tracks were well-maintained and from our first week at the new centre, early in May 1978, I saw my horses thriving. There is something about the Cape and horses. Most enjoy the fresh sea air, they work better at low altitude and they just love going to the beach for walks on the sand and in the water.

Our string included two-year-old Crown Pearl (Kingbenitch), a beautiful colt owned by Claude Gainer and Vaal hotellier Harry Rootenberg. He was the last winner I saddled on the Highveld before our departure, a top class run in the East Rand Juvenile Stakes over 1000m for cucumber cool Rhodes, who rode him from a seemingly hopeless position at the 400m-mark to win as he liked. We had high hopes for him as a three-year-old.

Other promising sorts were Brave Persian (Persian Wonder) a stayer starting his career, the filly Lone Waters (Loves Violin) and Havana Kid (Jamaico), three quality types who won a dozen or more races between them over the next few seasons.

We prepared four runners to race at our first meeting at Milnerton on 27 May and they all won, getting us off to a spectacular start and on the radar of the active Cape racing media, who enjoyed visiting the Milnerton training centre.

'Triangle Trainer Wows the Cape' read one newspaper headline after Ms Jenny, Mrs McCrim, Daisy Chain (Jamaico) and Flight Savon (Savonarola) won their respective races.

'Recondite' wrote in the Cape Times: "Ferraris is a great boost for Cape racing – in spite of what a few readers of this column and a few trainers might think. At the risk of inviting this sad coterie to hurl its next round of thunderbolts at me with powder-puff force, I would like to welcome Ormond Ferraris to the Cape and say keep up the good work!" *(Not sure what those words were based on, entertaining as they were!)*

We struck again the next midweek with Lone Waters, and then had two further wins the following Saturday. Tiny Girl (Garim), got off the mark and Flight Savon won again, this time with owners Mervyn and Liz Gribble on course, having made the flight from Johannesburg in support.

The winners kept flowing throughout the year and well into 1979, with Jannie Gouws quickly losing his apprentice's allowance and at one stage challenging Garth Puller for the lead at the top of the Cape Jockeys Table.

Lone Waters, owed by Rachel Kopping of Pretty Border fame, won three feature races that season – the Republic Handicap (1000m); the TBA Trophy and the G3 Fairmead Handicap over 1200m in which she beat Blazing Inferno, a top sprinter who'd go on to win 15 races, in a riveting finish at Milnerton. Lone Waters herself won nine races from just 23 starts, a super performer for the stable.

Havana Kid was our other feature winner. He defeated Gay Ray and a future J&B Met winner, Queen's Elect, in the Listed Midwinter Juvenile Handicap over 1200m in July 1979.

Prince Mehari (Commentary), who didn't seem to enjoy his previous stable, came to me from my old patron H.A. Mackenzie and we turned him around, winning five on the trot. Mackenzie, never shy to put down the cash, had an incredible all-to-come betting roll with this gelding. We shared the joy and adored the horse for being a money machine. Prince Mehari, as an older horse, went on to end his career with several places in Port Elizabeth.

The disappointment of the term was our losing of the promising Crown Pearl, whose owners decided that stakes in Cape Town were too low for their liking. They took him back to Johannesburg to be trained by Ricky Maingard.

I'd bought many yearlings by the underrated stallion Kingbenitch and Crown Pearl was one of them, acquired cheaply from Dawie Marais at Kalkfontein Stud. He was absolutely beautiful, a rich chestnut with a wonderful nature. He especially enjoyed going for walks on the beach, so much so that he wanted to go deeper into the surf every time and I had to ask his groom to bring him out.

Crown Pearl was beaten in his first two starts in Cape Town, favourite on both occasions but not wound up at the start of his preparation for the big summer features. I guess this also played a role in owners Gainer and Rootenberg's decision to relocate him. It was supremely disappointing as he was a horse I was truly fond of, with a bright career ahead of him.

To the credit of his new trainer, Crown Pearl won 11 races including the G2 Keith Hepburn Champion Stakes. I always kept an eye on Crown Pearl, perhaps the most striking individual that ever came through my yard. I can see him walking in the waves as I think back to those special days at the start of his career.

My stable was going great guns midway through 1979 and we ended the season with 38 winners from a limited number of runs and a fourth spot in the Cape Trainers' Table behind the big names Millard, Kannemeyer and Rixon.

Again, however, fate seem to play a role for the start of yet another period of personal turbulence. I developed a serious ear infection – boils in both ears and extreme pain - brought about by the damp climate, wind and sand at the Milnerton training tracks, and they just wouldn't heal. On the sheep farm in Kimberley, I looked like the Mummy Tutankhamun rising from Egypt's Valley Of The Kings. This time the trainers and grooms at Milnerton must have chuckled at what looked like a crazy old rake with cotton wool in his ears and a scarf around his neck. Our doctor advised a return to the Highveld.

I saddled a treble at Milnerton on 4 August 1979 – Havana Kid, Lone Waters and Jet Comb. After this, we wrapped up our operation and set out on the road back to Johannesburg on 27 August.

On top of my own battles with health my father, Ernest, who'd suffered a long bout of illness, passed away in the South Rand Hospital. We buried him in the West Park Cemetery in Johannesburg. Everyone deserves a father to be 110% behind you and my sister Ethne and I are so blessed to have had one in our lives. We were fortunate to enjoy his love, support and humour for many years as a grandfather, a mentor, a patron in the stable and a fellow racegoer. I am happy he got to see our stars of the time - Distinctly, Wagga Wagga and Pretty Border, and I was taken by his enthusiasm.

I have wondered at times whether I would have continued training in the Cape if it wasn't for my ear trouble and I don't really have an answer to that. Maybe yes, I loved it there. While we didn't stay on permanently, what came from our 14-month spell at Milnerton was the confidence to take a string of runners back there every winter in the years that followed. Those who wintered in Cape Town brought us some sensational results.

CHAPTER 29

During the 1980s, conservative politics and 'Reaganomics' held sway as the Berlin Wall crumbled, new computer technologies emerged and blockbuster movies and MTV reshaped pop culture.

In South Africa, in 1980, the African National Congress (ANC) intensified their campaign of terror aimed at the National Party Government with bombs planted at strategic targets and the constant threat of brutal attacks against civilians.

Racing retained its unifying culture throughout political upheaval and the racecourse was a place where peace and goodwill existed and the search for winners and big payouts was often a joint venture between people of all race groups.

The Ferraris family found itself back at Newmarket and we moved into a house just up the road from our old 'The Curragh' establishment, rented to us by my patron Peter Dimakogiannis. The Curragh had been bought in our absence by leading trainer Syd Laird, who had moved his operation from Durban to Alberton. I think we sold the property to Syd for R80,000 and made a small profit on what we'd invested back in 1970.

Our 'big blessing' of the early 1980s was that racing administrator Sandy Christie commissioned the building of a massive, modern stable centre on the Turffontein racecourse premises, following the increased unsuitability of the small stable complexes scattered around the suburbs in Johannesburg South. I'd requested, and was granted, three adjacent barns housing 60 horses, but it was business as usual training from Newmarket in the interim.

I was very lucky to come across Ermelo-born John Sibeko, one of those wonderful individuals who grew up on a farm working with horses. With all the moving around I had some trouble re-establishing a good group of grooms and I employed John after meeting him at the TBA stables in Germiston, where I had a few extra horses stabled away from Newmarket. Even though he was a youngster, John helped me to get a team of decent handlers together, formed a unit and soon became my 'Boss Boy' or Head Lad. He worked for me until 2019, aged 71.

I'd told jockey Jannie Gouws to stay in Cape Town, where he'd built up a good reputation and some relationships with trainers. I wasn't able to guarantee him any regular rides back in Transvaal, but his father insisted that he returned and, in the long run, Jannie didn't make it. He suffered weight problems and eventually faded from the scene.

Tobie van Booma, my prodigal son, returned in this period. He came begging for the job he'd lost after the Distinctly fiasco of 1975. With all of the top Highveld riders involved with other stables, I had no choice but to take Tobie back under my wing and, barring a few serious blow-ups and 'time off' after unavoidable arguments, we enjoyed a wonderful spate of winners over the next five seasons.

Tobie was more mature now, seasoned and experienced and he was at his peak as a rider. The Dutchman was strong as an ox, able to place his mounts well and not many could hold a candle to him in a close finish. His dark and unpredictable moods remained, however. There were times I just shook my head, gave him a leg up and looked the other way.

Two regular visitors to my yard were my son David and one of his school mates, Mike de Kock. David had his sights set on becoming my assistant and I could see that Mike had a lively interest as well. I was wondering at the time when (or whether) the pair of them actually went to school at all. They were among the regulars at most Highveld meetings and they were undoubtedly putting their heads and their pocket cash together to bet on horses they'd identified as winners from the stable. They were two typical 'victims' of thoroughbred racing from the moment they could pee straight, but as it turned out in later years, both became top horsemen too!

Despite our move back to Transvaal mid-term, we managed 46 winners in the 1979/80 season and, to that point our second-best season in 1980/81, when we sent out 70 winners from a stable of 30 horses. We eagerly awaited the completion of the new Turffontein stables.

Our original Cape contingent stood their ground – Prince Mehari, Brave Persian and Havana Kid kept earning, and new on the scene for us were several horses owned by prominent breeder Henry Devine, who joined the yard on recommendation from Paddy Hinton.

Devine had a reputation for being a difficult man and I told Paddy I was concerned about this. "Hard-headed people don't get on with me. I'm not in the mood for arguments and nonsense, please!" But Paddy insisted and after some debate I took Devine's horses as a favour, mainly because Paddy told me he was ill and in hospital after an operation and needed some good news, and because his son Richard had married Paddy's daughter Sue. I couldn't really say no.

Among the runners that came to me was the 1980 Derby winner Smugglers Den, a light-framed, but hard-as-nails horse by Sea Cottage formerly trained by David Bullock, a good sprinter named Red Cascade (Red Mask) and a number of decent bread-and-butter types that gave us a hot run of wins.

Other achievers in this period were T.L. Rudling's Livagen (St Cuthbert), Basil Starke's Spinning Coin (Contraband) and Peter Dimakogiannis-owned Goulburn (New South Wales). Goulburn was one of our best performing horses in 1980. He won five races including the Transvaal Handicap over 3200m under lightweight rider Cecil van As and the Sunday Times called him a horse of 'Solid Gould'.

Starke, who owned a massive road building operation, offered to put us up at his Bloubergstrand beach cottage whenever we needed it. Considering our success in Cape Town and the way our runners performed on the Highveld on their return - and with my ear infection having cleared up - I decided to take a small string down there again in April 1981. Something that stuck me with me was a few friendly chats with South Africa's famous soprano Mimi Coertze, who was our neighbour at the Blouberg Cottage and also a horse fan.

I had plans, especially, for Brave Persian, who I considered a better stayer than Goulburn. He'd beaten the classy Smugglers Den in a handicap over 2450m in October 1980 and went on to win a competitive Stayers Handicap over the same distance in February 1981.

I had two winter features earmarked for Brave Persian and he won both, starting with the Listed Lonsdale Stirrup Cup over 2400m at Milnerton on 13 June 1981, in which Tobie van Booma rode a good race; and the G2 Gold Cup over 3200m at Greyville on 1 August, 1981.

The Gold Cup was a more prestigious race then than it is today and we'd planned this carefully so that Brave Persian would travel from sea level in the Cape to sea level in Durban. He left from Milnerton on the Tuesday before the race, on 28 July, and went into the care of trainer Brian Cherry at Summerveld.

The rules at the time stipulated that the trainer of a visiting runner had to be physically present for a big race like this. Due to my commitments in Cape Town, I had no option but to register Brave Persian as being trained by B.A. Cherry. We booked Grant Kotzen for the ride, and Hinton's just-turned five-year-old defeated Garth Puller on Big Charles by a neck in a stirring finish. The runner-up had won the Durban July just a month prior to our encounter with him in the Gold Cup.

It's safe to say that my career record with stayers is better than most and I guess the Gold Cup was a race I should've won several times in 70-odd years of training. But I was always more focused on races for stayers on the Highveld. The single Gold Cup that was due to me, was recorded for posterity as having been won by Brian Cherry. Brian, of course, never took the credit for the win himself. He was a good man and a good friend. Bless his departed soul!

CHAPTER 30

Tobie van Booma rode like a man possessed in 1981. He was successful on several of our runners in the Cape, and his good form continued when we sent our small string back to Johannesburg from Cape Town midway through the year.

Spinning Coin was a little below her best in her first two Cape runs, but she finished a good third in the Boland Breeders to the Cape's rising champion Prince Florimund late in July and was a different horse back home in the weeks after that.

Like our Cape runners from 1980, she came into her own and blossomed in her Newmarket stable. She was a relative outsider in her first start back, the G3 Enterprise Handicap over 1400m at Gosforth Park in August, in which she beat the much-vaunted colts Captain Ekels and Champs Elysees out of sight.

The racing writers were dumfounded. They couldn't figure out how Champs Elysees, who ran Ricky Maingard's Wolf Power to half-a-length in a G1 at Greyville just a month prior to this, was no match on the day for our Spinning Coin. Frankly, neither could I, but we took the G3 honours and the cheque and went home. In December, Spinning Coin finished third to Breyani in the 1981 G1 Gosforth Park Fillies Guineas and that's about how good she was. She never won again. Champs Elysees became a top handicapper and the grey Wolf Power won 18 races and is still one of the most talked-about horses in South Africa's racing history.

I have good memories of two others that started their careers in 1981. King Of Jazz, a son of Fats Waller owned by Peter Dimakogiannis, was a cracking little sprinter who reeled off four quick wins as a juvenile and later won his way through the divisions. Royal Line, by Bosworth Farm's superb stallion Hobnob, was an all-class chestnut who started off in sprints, in fact was an understudy to King Of Jazz as a two-year-old, but developed into one of the better stayers I'd trained. He was owned by Joan Ruffel, the wife of then Jockey Club Chair Tony Ruffel, and Stephen Mulholland, an outstanding journalist and writer high up in the ranks of Times Media, publishers of The Sunday Times.

Among the more ordinary handicappers were The Nazarene, Sea Baby, Galactic Warrior and Record Review, but they added to our tally. Most of them were ridden, most of the time by Tobie van Booma, who was suffering some jealousy in the jockey's room for his consistent winning strike rate and his assault on the Transvaal title. The nastiness of his colleagues bugged him and contributed to his sombre states of mind.

I dislike rumours and bad-mouthing, but a few of the senior jockeys came complaining to me that Tobie was extremely moody and unpleasant. He was also hard on horses on the work track and at the start before races. "He can be cruel," said one. "He gets cross when they play up and he handles them too hard, he's going to get in trouble."

I was weary not to let the remarks about Tobie go to my head, I knew what he was all about and could live with most of it. But I started watching him more closely on the work tracks in the morning. He could be tough on his mounts at times. He'd try to enforce respect by screaming at the difficult ones or hitting them hard on their quarters with his whip. Some horses are troublesome by nature and need discipline at times, but after watching my jockey closely for a few weeks I felt that the complainers had a point – Tobie was reaching a point where his handling of certain horses became too severe.

Early on the morning of Monday, 7 September, 1981, I was watching Tobie through my binoculars when I spotted him actually mishandling a filly on the work track. She was playing up and he was tugging forcefully at her head, left and right, so much so that I could see her teeth through her skewed mouth. He was also giving her a hard and prolonged beating with his whip.

Blood rushed to my head and I tried to control myself when Tobie brought the filly back to the paddock, but I couldn't. I pulled him off the horse by his arm and when he landed, I came close to slapping him. "Get the hell out of my stable," I shouted. I dragged him along to his car. "Go. I never want to see you here again, and you're off my runners for tomorrow!"

In my office, a little later, I informed the stipes that I'd be taking Tobie van Booma off all his mounts for the Tuesday meeting at Newmarket. We'd entered eight runners, all with chances. With big fields on the day, all the top riders had been booked so I'd effectively snookered myself by firing my jockey. But I had a flash of inspiration. I took a chance, phoned up champion jockey Michael Roberts in Durban and asked him to deputise for Tobie on all eight rides. To my delight, 'Muis' agreed, and jetted in from his base the next day, proverbially boots 'n all!

To say we swept the boards would be an understatement. Roberts booted home five winners, a second and a third from his eight rides and aside from the personal joy and satisfaction it brought the stable, it was refreshing to work with a no-nonsense professional at the top of his game. This was my first of five career five-timers on a day.

We started off in Race 2 with Don Pedro, who ran on for second place to my old friend Boet Oosthuizen's runner Magic Bull, trained by Nick van Tonder and ridden by my former stable jockey Michael Cavé. But then, the floodgates opened and we took the next four races in a row. First, Ronnie Burg and Sid Bernstein's filly Imperial Plum (Plum Bold) won a handicap over 1200m, followed by Henry Devine's My Fair Lady (Elevation) breaking her Maiden over 1600m. Next up, my new Cape-based patron Syd Harris' colt On Guard (Harry Hotspur), skated home over 1300m and Sea Baby (Peaceable Kingdom), cracked it for Ronnie Bell in a Graduation Plate over 1300m.

Peter Duffield wrote in The Rand Daily Mail: "The applause that greeted Roberts when he returned to the winner's enclosure after Sea Baby's win was reminiscent of that accorded a winner of the Holiday Inns.

"Roberts' riding of the ninth-race winner Blue Bandit (Copper De Lux, Henry Devine) showed just what a difference he makes to a horse. He rode one of the most vigorous finishes I've ever seen on a horse to force Blue Bandit home by a head from Cosmic Prince."

The brigade of punters on course were suitably impressed and happy. They included David Ferraris and his friend Mike de Kock, who'd found themselves a lovely spot in an unused stipes tower to watch the day's races and ran down to the winner's box after every strike. Judged by their exuberance after the fifth winner, they must've collected enough dough to afford a month's burgers and shakes at The Casbah Roadhouse up the road from the racecourse in Voortrekker Street.

THOROUGHLY!

The year ended on a high note when Smugglers Den (Michael Coetzee up) won December's Johannesburg Summer Handicap from Danish Courage and Welsh Harp.

CHAPTER 31

In 1982, Michael Jackson released his record-breaking album 'Thriller' – the title track of which seemed to be played endlessly on radio. It was also a suitable description for my year, in more ways than one, and not always thrilling in the 'joyous' sense of the word.

It started with a move to a family house in Winchester Hills, in close proximity of the newly built stable complex at Turffontein, where the facilities installed by Sandy Christie were modern, spacious and simply wonderful. I had access to 60 stables for the first time in nearly 30 years of training and they were filled in a jiffy by old and new patrons, making us more competitive than ever before. The existing training tracks were good and there were plans afoot for the installation of an additional wood fibre work track that was said to be the talk of the town in the US and Australia for its all-weather suitability.

This was a juncture of some proportions for our family. Alan left to manage our Karoo Farm, Rooispruit, David was drafted into the South African Airforce for his compulsory military service, Paul was approaching the end of his school career, my mother Jose passed away and Norma and I decided to get a divorce – something I am noting for the purpose of our timeline but won't be elaborating upon.

My mother lived for three years after my father died. She was a small woman, but the strongest one in the family who made peace when we had rifts or disputes, always had warm advice, a hug and a cup of tea for those who needed comfort. She was especially close to Alan. Jose and George Weale's wife, Yola, remained the best of friends until her last days. They loved to come racing and celebrated the many good days with us. They enjoyed having a bet and were there in full support of the stable. We buried my mother next to my father at West Park. They were our pillars of support and stability for decades, and are still sorely missed today!

On the track, our higher number of runners meant more success, and in the 82/3 season I saddled 80 winners, the second-best of my career in the company of newcomers in the trainers' ranks, including Stanley Ferreira. Jean Barnard was still at the top of her game, with Spike Lerena, Nick van Tonder and J.F. Coetzee in the Top 10 on the log, young Michael Azzie at the start of his career and the formidable Syd Laird firing on all cylinders from The Curragh. I didn't really have their firepower at the time, but there was strength in numbers, as I expected, and my stable turned out more one, two and three-time winners than I can remember.

This was a time in which the brilliant young jockey, Bartie Leisher, literally had racing in Transvaal wrapped around his finger. I wasn't able to use Leisher as he was in big demand and wouldn't have signed with a single stable. Michael Cavé was still plagued by personal problems and only riding periodically. Raymond Rhodes, still very good, was freelancing and doing well as a first choice-jock for Laird. I was still giving my friend the occasional decent mount, but he was on the senior side now and I didn't feel like ordering him around the paddocks as a stable jock in the morning.

You'd guess who I was left with. Just a few months after I'd fired him in September 1981, Tobie van Booma started showing up again every morning, asking to put a few through their paces. I ignored him at first, chased him again, but he persisted. He came to annoy me every day and by May 1982 I gave in and, to his credit, Van Booma proved himself to be valuable with many powerful and well-judged rides. We really were a good team when things were going smoothly and it's a pity that his strange, dark demeanour came to spoil it almost every time.

In looking through an album with old newspaper clippings and photos I came across several articles written about Henry Devine's long-distance gelding Don Pedro (Selenio) and Anthony Joseph's filly Bright 'N Blue (Great Brother) a sprinter miler. Neither would feature in my Top 20 of horses trained, but they won eight and 10 races respectively and were two of the better ones that kept the tally ticking through 1982 and 1983.

Don Pedro was a punters' favourite due to four quick wins as a young stayer, but he wasn't as good as our up-and-coming ace Royal Line, who beat him in the Owners and Trainers Handicap over 2850m at Newmarket and a subsequent handicap at Turffontein. He trained on well though, and in the absence of Royal Line he won the Transvaal Handicap on New Year's Day in 1983 and the Len Harvey Memorial in January of 1984.

Bright 'N Blue raced alongside some top-class fillies from other stables, including Poetic, Liberty Silk, Breyani, Larne and Tecla Bluff – a few lengths inferior to the best in 1982 but good enough to win the 1983 G3 Summer Champion Stakes at and the G3 Helios Fillies Stakes, both wins at Turffontein in the hands of the in-form Van Booma.

The warrior, Smugglers Den, continued his winning ways. He captured the Racecourse Bookmakers Handicap in October 1982 and then posted a smart, follow-up win in the Transvaal Handicap in which he got the better of Lawn and North Island.

The Sunday Express reported: "Smugglers Den carried only 49kg when he won the race last year, but despite having a hefty 7,5kg extra on his back, he again showed his class. He has earned himself the title of the best of the sons of Sea Cottage."

Smugglers Den was the third leg of a stable treble that day, as we won the opener with Paddy Hinton's Sandfly (Sledgehammer), a five-length victor on his debut, and the speedster King Of Jazz outpaced his rivals in the fifth race.

Another memorable day came on 28 December, 1982, when Van Booma and I had four winners on a balmy Tuesday at Turffontein. Dave Mollett, who'd written several good articles about the stable since I tried to have him deported in 1974, reported in the Daily Mail: "Ormond Ferraris and Tobie van Booma began their New Year Celebrations 72 hours early with four winners. The Ferraris success was a significant pointer from the Turffontein trainer that Messrs Payne, Brown, Millard, Maingard and Mrs Barnard can expect strong competition for the SA Trainer's title in 1983."

I was in contention, yes, but would have to wait another several years for my first National Title. Early in 1983, I parted ways with Henry Devine following an incident at Turffontein, and the loss of his string was a setback as much as it was a relief!

I am not sure which horse had been the subject of our argument, maybe it was Devine's sprinter Red Cascade. One Saturday, at Turffontein, I'd put a little cotton wool and an Elastoplast over a small wound on the hock of this runner, who was in the habit of cutting himself in training and had suffered a minor scratch. In the saddling enclosure I was called to the stipes room to discuss an issue with the stewards, so I left David to saddle the horse for his race.

When the runners had left the parade ring on the way to the track, I came out of the stipes room onto the veranda when Devine approached me and said, "How's he doing? Can he win?"

I said: "He's fit and ready, yes."

He replied: "What's wrong, he has a bandage on his hock?"

I explained: "He cuts himself when he gallops. It's just a plaster over some cotton wool so the cut can heal."

Devine walked forward, came right up to me and stuck a finger in my face: "Now listen here," he said. "Don't you ever run a horse of mine in a bandage, you hear me?"

I'd had this feeling of blood rushing to my head before, perhaps when J.P. Herholdt threw his toys out of the cot a few years earlier. Again, I saw red and grabbed Devine by his jacket. My binoculars went flying. We were swearing at each other and ready to trade blows when trainer George Baleta stepped in between us. He pushed me away, shouting, "Ormond, stop! Leave it, they'll warn you off!"

I took a step back with George's arms around me and with Devine also retreating, I shouted at him: "Do me a favour, go fetch your horses, you're a horrible man. I want them out of my yard. Out!"

I can't recall if the horse won or not. The rest of that day was an emotional blur. But when I got to my stables later, Devine's runners were being loaded on a float and were on their way to a new trainer at the Vaal.

You win some, you lose some. Some, you don't mind losing.

CHAPTER 32

David Ferraris, who got called up to the South African Airforce, was fortunate to be transferred to Pretoria after his basic training in 1983. He was stationed at the Army's Transport and Supply Division in Voortrekkerhoogte, Pretoria. The seed was planted early. He was dead keen on becoming my official assistant trainer and, having pulled a few strings with his friendly commander, was allowed to leave his Pretoria base long before daybreak to join me on the training tracks at Turffontein, and to return to his post, mid-morning.

David was always going to be my natural successor and I appreciated the help with my now 60-strong stable of horses. I needed an extra eye. Good grooms weren't as easy to come by as they were in the 1960s and 70s, because the horsemen who traditionally came from the outlying farms were now starting new careers in the growing industries around Johannesburg that paid better salaries than we were able to afford in racing. Thankfully, the talented John Sibeko was in my stable to stay and he kept our assembled team of handlers in check and doing their duties.

First to announce himself in the early part of the year was a R42,000 yearling purchase Sandfly, a colt by Sledgehammer who raced for Paddy Hinton and I. He posted a commanding win in the G1 Allan Robertson Memorial Plate for two-year-olds over 1600m at Gosforth Park on 23 April.

Sandfly was a big, strong horse and from a wide draw Tobie van Booma had no option but to drop in behind his rivals, where they lagged quite some way behind with the speedier sorts galloping away. Van Booma took the easiest route home. He shook Sandfly up on the bend and sent him to the inside rail, where an opening appeared. He picked the leaders off one by one and ran on well to win by 2,25-lengths.

Sandfly caught the eye of most racing scribes despite setting a slow time, and they were in agreement that the manner in which he won, and not the time recorded, was the yardstick by which his performance had to be measured.

We entered Sandfly for the G1 Adminstrator's Champion Stakes over 1400m in July and he drew gate 12 of 14 at Greyville. The Durban track was not as tight then as it is today, but from an outside draw in top company he was up against it. He still ran into fourth, beaten just two lengths by Bold Speed.

Sandfly had a few starts as an early three-year-old and in November of 1983 he won a B Division Handicap over 1400m at Turffontein before we gave him a rest into 1984 ahead of his preparation for the G1 SA Derby.

We had several juvenile winners that year including Final Conclusion (Wagga Wagga) and Lord Lieutenant (Lords), but an older horse stole the show along with Sandfly. Four-year-old Royal Line was coming into his own as a stayer and won three successive handicaps in just six weeks approaching year-end. A pleasant memory from that time is of his co-owner, Stephen Mulholland, arriving at my office with an envelope full of bank notes for me every time he backed Royal Line to win. I had the 1984 Gold Cup in mind as this quality gelding's main mission and his preparation would start with a spell in Cape Town like we did with Brave Persian.

Another outstanding prospect was Lost Chord's daughter Winter Lass, owned by racing administrator Kim Latilla and his wife Carol, a striking redhead who was as firey as Kim was reserved. Winter Lass had an injury setback as an early two-year-old, but once we got her to the track, she reeled off a few quick wins to start her career and we knew she was well above average, though we couldn't win a feature with her in 1983. She was beaten into second in both the G3 Breeders Fillies Champion Stakes and the Listed Morris Lipschitz Memorial and then ran a cracking third in the G1 Gosforth Park Fillies Guineas behind Enchanting.

But Winter Lass improved considerably when she started maturing as a three-year-old. Her first start in 1984 was in February's Gosforth Park Fillies and Mares Stakes, in which she packed too many guns for two top rivals in Julia Goes and Novenna. In March, she finished second in the G2 Revlon's Charlie Fillies Handicap over 1600m, beaten almost 10 lengths by Herman Brown Sr.'s Eliza, but that was considered a freak result because this power-packed field included the Guineas winner Enchanting, the talented Cape raider Wild Hyacinth and Jean Barnard's top-class pair, Julia Goes and Spring Wonder.

I'd sent a small string to Cape Town, in David's care, and stayed on at Turffontein to oversee Winter Lass's preparation for her seasonal target, the G3 Helios Fillies Stakes at Gosforth Park. We put lightweight rider and Highveld log-leader Cecil van As on her in her final prep, a B Division handicap over 1300m in April and she skated home by four lengths.

We booked Van As again to ride her in the Helios Fillies on 26 May and this time the jock had to work harder for his share of the stake. She pinged the gates and immediately took up the running, but he kept her on a tight reign, just marginally clear of Spring Wonder and Lady Mollison. On the bend, however, Winter Lass' saddle slipped back and my heart sank. We were in trouble. Van As, with a loose saddle under him, had to let her off the bit and she raced several lengths clear coming into the last 400m.

Now, however, the pressure was on with Van As trying his level best to keep Winter Lass going, but the challengers were in hot pursuit and she appeared under big pressure to hold on. The Star's Robert Garner described the latter part of the race: "It was touch and go over the last 200m but Winter Lass clung to her precarious advantage as if her life depended on it. She had a head to spare over Lady Mollison at the line. It was a thoroughly game performance by one of the toughest and most consistent fillies you'll find anywhere."

To my dismay, this would be Winter Lass' last win for us. I was ready to send her off to Cape Town to join my string at Milnerton, but her owners were not keen. I tried to explain the benefits of wintering horses in the Cape and that they came back like cars with new engines. But Carol Latilla felt that Winter Lass would be better off staying at home and just refused to let her travel. They took this super filly away to Jean Barnard, for whom she won another four races and even had a tilt at the Durban July.

The departure of Winter Lass was a loss for the stable but by then I'd had more than enough experience of unhappy owners and I wasn't going to go on my knees to keep her in the yard. I let the filly go on her merry way. One can only do so much.

CHAPTER 33

I wanted something for the introduction of this chapter about the year 1984 and its significance at the hand of George Orwell's famous novel. There was much self-congratulatory coverage in the US that the dystopia of the novel and the 'Big Brother' scenario had not been realised at the time, but one can only wonder what those same critics would have said if they could see a decade into the future. And today, well…

If someone had Orwell's crystal ball, they would've told Sandy Christie and his decision-makers not to install a wood-fibre track to replace the sand training track at Turffontein, but of course there was no internet, instant messaging and e-mails. Some decisions were made without a broad, worldwide perspective and detailed information on issues, products or, in this case, synthetic tracks. I, for one, was sceptical about this track, but there was too much going on to worry about a new training track as 1984 would be another engaging calendar year that brought much joy and heartache to us.

With David home, at times, but also away in Cape Town, I employed another aspiring trainer who'd just completed his military service –

one Michael de Kock, as it happened another natural horseman who showed the right attributes, but needed some tutoring at 20 years of age. Alongside David, Mike didn't escape my watchful eye and, may I add, some of my temper. They comically recall incidents of being "barked and sworn at" as young assistants in my yard. I hope that their memories bring them joy for life!

Mike was born for landing with his arse in butter, it seems. He joined us at a time there were some stunning runners in the yard. Every horseman deserves a chance to train top thoroughbreds. For some, it comes only late in their careers. We had some proper stayers in this period, as mentioned, and Mike's allocated barn included Royal Line, a horse, I remember, he enjoyed working with.

Sandfly, meanwhile, put up two encouraging Derby runs when he reappeared in February 1984. He slammed a B Division field by seven lengths over 1800m at Turffontein and then ran a fair race in a talent-laden G1 Administrators Champion Stakes at Gosforth Park, midfield behind the likes of Bodrum, Turncoat and North Star. He wasn't course suited in this league, needed time to unwind and the Germiston track was too tight.

On 31 March, Sandfly took his place in the SA Derby. Paddy and I had been impressed by jockey Basil Marcus, who'd ridden a few winners for us on occasional raids to Durban. We'd booked Marcus for the ride on the big day, leaving Tobie van Booma on the bench, perhaps still sore on July Day memories from 1975. We put Van Booma on Chapter Two and Raymond Rhodes got the mount on Demon King, both instructed to ensure a good pace.

Basil acquitted himself well in a race described by Francois Wolfaardt as "the most exciting Derby in a decade". The Natal raider Brubaker started favourite at 2-1. He'd finished second to Charles Fortune in the Cape Derby and was ridden by the mercurial jockey Jeff Lloyd, who was booting home winners like they were going out of fashion.

Chapter Two and Demon King pulled the field up the hill in the back straight on a good clip, followed by Aberperth, On Gold and Raider with Sandfly on the rail, several lengths back. The leaders dropped back after the tough first three quarters of the race and it was Raider who shot into the lead with Sandfly looming up railside to take him on at the 400m-mark.

Sandfly drew level with 200m to run, but Raider kept fighting and edged marginally ahead at the 100m-mark. "It appeared as if Raider had broken Sandfly's heart", wrote Wolfaardt. But Marcus kept coaxing Sandfly, he came again and dropped his head down first as they hit the wire. Sandfly knocked half a second off the race record in going that had some give in it, a reflection of a true-run contest we were happy to have won. That Sandfly produced such a resolute finish was heart-warming. He disliked soft going and that he threw everything he had into the duel, showed his class.

There were suitable celebrations after the race, although Paddy Hinton said he was annoyed that, a little while after the race, Marcus reminded him that the cost of his flight had to be covered. They must've had an arrangement and Paddy paid up, but he asked me not to put Marcus on his horses again. I can only smile today as Basil probably flew around in his own jet after taking Hong Kong by storm just a few years later.

In April, Sandfly ran another good race in the Sun International over 1400m, taking third place to Rise and Rule, but that gruelling Derby battle took a lot out of him and he never quite reached his best level of form again. He placed a few times at high level and won again in October 1985, but we retired him after the G3 Allen Snjiman Stakes at the end of 1985. He'd won eight races in total, placed five times and was a workmanlike campaigner throughout his career. If we were ever to compile my roll of honour, Sandfly will make it to the list.

I sent David to Cape Town for our annual raid from the Milnerton Training Centre and his string included Royal Line, who was being aimed at the Gold Cup and was taking the same route we successfully employed with Brave Persian. Others were Demon King, Kunhild (Do Battle), Acacia (Fats Waller), Supreme Spirit (Lords) and Port Au Prince (Jamaican Music).

Supreme Spirit was a smart filly raced by Capetonians Syd and Sabine Harris, a couple I'd met during a previous visit and who became good friends and patrons. They had a store in the city that sold second-hand wares of all kinds, they loved animals and donated most of their proceeds to charities. We were pleased to win two Listed features with Supreme Spirit late that winter. She got up to win the Ladies Mile over 1400m at Milnerton on 30 June and a month later ran them ragged in the Champagne Stakes over 1200m. 'Rooies' Fourie was her pilot.

Royal Line was a better stayer than Brave Persian, but this time we failed to win the Gold Cup. He had two nice prep runs at Milnerton, placing both times, and David sent him to me in Durban a week before the race in the last week of July. He was fit, fine and tuned, but on the day found three too good in Terrance Millard's Durban July winner Devon Air, Hawkins and Luciennes.

We took it on the chin. The 1984 Gold Cup was contested by a strong field and it was not an easy race to win. With Millard in his prime, we were always going to compete for second. But I knew Royal Line's big day would come.

The OK Gold Bowl was scheduled for Saturday, 13 October, 1984, and I found the perfect race to keep Royal Line ticking over. We entered him for the Spring Stayers Handicap over 2450m at Turffontein on 22 September and he stayed on well for fourth behind David Bullock's top class 1982 Derby winner, Oakland Bay.

We were rounding off Royal Line's preparation five days before the Gold Bowl, on Monday 8 October, when a piece of shocking news spread around the training paddocks and left me near dizzy and weak in the knees. My erstwhile stable jockey, Michael Cavé, was reported to have died earlier that morning, on his 32nd birthday. I confirmed the news with a phone call from my office, where I sat thinking about him for hours.

Michael was a big talent but also a man with deep personal problems that plagued him throughout his career. I'd spoken to him not long before his death and he revealed some of what was going on in his life. To this day, I think about Michael, a professional with whom I never had a single fallout in our short and successful spell together. He was said to have choked to death in his sleep following an incident of acid reflux, but I've always wondered about that.

Michael's weight problems got worse as he got into his 30s. He ran in tracksuits with plastic bags underneath to sweat as much as he could. Every afternoon before the next day's races he would run around the track at Newmarket. On race days, he had to spend an hour or two in the sweatbox. He wiped streams of sweat off his body into cups to measure his weight loss. He ate very little, salads, perhaps a boiled egg a day with some brown bread.

The late Kelvin Haarhoff, Michael's friend and confidant, said in a profile of the jockey published in The Citizen: "He started using the appetite suppressor 'Obex' – the big yellow pill, for weight loss and energy. After a while he battled to sleep and suffered from anxiety and heart palpitations. He also suffered a serious bout of the nervous condition 'shingles', with unsightly sores and marks covering his head and body.

"Michael withdrew at that point. I found him crying a few nights with his head between his legs, his forehead, cheeks and hands covered in sores, he was often in discomfort and he went backwards. He had to receive morphine for the pain. He became briefly addicted to the drug and had to be strapped to a bed for two weeks to dry up and recover.

"His weight became a bigger problem than ever and at around 55kg he was battling to ride competitively. The sweating and dieting brought heart palpitations to the extent that Michael collapsed in the jockey room one day. And then, on the night of October 7, 1984, he took a prescribed sleeping tablet with a glass of whiskey before he went to bed. He was due to ride work at the Vaal on his birthday and wanted an early night. But as the autopsy showed, the strong sleeping tablet must have clashed with the whiskey and around midnight Michael suffered a reflux from his stomach and into his throat which choked him to death in his sleep."

This was a devastating end to the life of a good young man with a very promising career. Michael could have been one of the greats but the dreadful perils associated with being a jockey defeated him. Ironically, just four years after he died, in 1988, Mrs Bridget Oppenheimer commissioned an investigation into jockeys' eating habits and lifestyles and shortly thereafter the bottom weight was raised from 45 kg to 50kg and the top weight to 57kg. Along with it came much more nutritional information, exercise routines and other health pointers from which Michael would have benefited greatly.

———

The G2 OK Gold Bowl had a long and famous history, having first been run as the Woolavington Stayers' Cup in 1925. The race was run as the Black & White Gold Bowl from 1977 and became the **OK Gold Bowl** from 1984. The stake that year was R200,000, South Africa's richest race for stayers.

The OK Bazaars Group was headed by a fine gentleman named Gordon Hood, whose aim it was to make this not only the best race for stayers, but the most popular race in the country. They came pretty close to achieving that in their first few years of marketing the race. Hood and his team produced hundreds of thousands of 'scratch cards', hugely popular in the day. They marked them with specific numbers linked to prizes and gave the cards away to everyone who shopped at the OK stores. The prizes were fantastic – from electronic sound systems to television sets, furniture and even cars, and they advertised the promotion in community newspapers, the national daily papers and on TV.

OK Bazaars improved the footfall through their stores tremendously and with all the fanfare Turffontein was packed to capacity on race day. To claim the prizes, scratch card holders had to be present on course and they arrived in thousands. Hood, dressed in what became his familiar cherry red jacket, announced numbers after each race and the racegoers scratched feverishly to see if their cards matched the winning numbers. They were still queueing at the gates before the running of the main race, because the prized cars would be given away after the running of the OK Gold Bowl.

As luck, or fate, would have it, we enjoyed some good rains during the week of the Gold Bowl and that suited Royal Line who, being by Hobnob, had big, flat feet and enjoyed soft conditions. He could take as much work as we could give him. There was more rain on the morning of the race and we knew he'd be hard to beat. Tobie van Booma went through the motions, they bowled along handy for most of the long journey, galloped clear and won by 3,5-lengths from Big Bentley, incidentally another useful son of Hobnob.

The 1984 OK Gold Bowl was a good plan that came together for all.

CHAPTER 34

The Southern Hemisphere's racing seasons stretch from August to August, so all Southern Hemisphere-breds have their birthdays on 1 August. That's also a time when the National Statistics are published in South Africa and places likes Australia, and racing's champions are announced.

The closest I'd come to winning the National Title was in the 1976/77 season when I was pipped by Syd Laird. I enjoyed Top 3, Top 5 and Top 10 finishes since, including Top 5 finishes in 1984/5, 1985/6, 1986/7 and 1987/8 when Terrance Millard and Jean Heming alternatively won the titles between them. I wasn't overly concerned about National honours. I competed well with the stock I had, and at the back of my mind I believed I'd make it to the top of the log at some point. I didn't have any real stars in my string, so I set this hope aside to focus on maximising the potential of the horses in my care.

There were a few milestones I achieved on the way, including winning the annual Turffontein Trainers' Competition every year between 1983 and 1986, passing the 1000-winner mark and building the Trainers Benevolent Fund. Even in those good years for racing, there were trainers retiring without a brass penny to their names, and they needed help to stay alive.

In looking back through the respective racing calendars, I also noticed that we often had winners on New Year's Day. Whether that was just a co-incidence or whether by entering horses for those meetings I wanted to ensure that my assistants and jockeys went to bed early on New Year's Eve, I can't remember. But, in the Ferraris family, New Year's Day was often celebrated with a winner or two.

We kicked off 1985 with a victory by Northern March, a four-year-old gelding sent to me by owner Andre MacDonald, the founder of Lido, the electronics supplies giant in Boksburg. Northern March was previously trained by Neville Pearce in Durban. There wasn't much wrong with him, he was one of those horses that didn't enjoy coastal conditions but thrived on the Highveld and seemed to have more ability than his form showed.

I'd given the ride to Raymond Rhodes, who'd come to ride a few gallopers in the morning as Tobie van Booma and I were having another spell apart. With Raymond up, my runners never started at odds good enough to win more than a handful of lowly coins, but at least I knew what to expect from this seasoned master jockey. Northern March won going away over 2000m and Raymond promised there were more wins to come.

There was a lower division handicap over 1400m at the Vaal on 24 January and Northern March got in with 54kg. Punters climbed in and took the opening odds of 5-2. He started the race at 9-10 and won without much fuss.

Northern March was sound and well after the race, but there were no suitable races for him in February. We placed him in a handicap over 1800m at Gosforth Park on 2 March. This was a competitive middle division race with a few hard knockers against him, but Northern

March was again handily weighted at 54,5kg. Raymond only had to go through the motions again as they beat Tallyman and Rockbuster going away.

Andre Macdonald was happy with three-on-the-trot, I'm not sure if he had bets on his horse every time, but he looked chuffed with himself in the winner's box and asked about Northern March's next run. I was thinking of a few minor features in Durban, though not sure what to expect at the coast considering his race record at sea level.

On 15 March, we entered the gelding for another middle division handicap, more or less the equivalent of a MR95 race today, and this was his first try at 1900m. Bartie Leisher on Totally Bold made this a keenly contested finish and went head-to-head with Northern March for the last 250m, but Raymond kept his cool and his mount prevailed, by a head.

On the strength of this courageous win, we decided to try our luck in the G3 In Full Flight Stakes over 1600m at Scottsville. I gave Northern March a short break into April and prepared him for this 15 May event. With 52kg to shoulder, we had to engage a lightweight rider and Patrick Wynne was our choice, though jockeyship didn't come into play. Northern March failed in a strong renewal of this race and trailed in 16 lengths behind Petrava, Up The Creek and Grey Sun.

The mentioned fillies happened to be three of the best females to race in that era, so we accepted that Northern March was out of his depth, though I did expect him to finish closer to the winner than he did. We decided on what looked to be an easier Durban feature next – the Republic Day Handicap over 1900m at Greyville. He was as fit as I could have him, but was again found wanting to the tune of 16 lengths in a race won by Ralph Rixon's Grey Sun.

Northern March was a solid handicapper, and it was clear after the pair of disappointing runs that he was not from the top drawer and simply hated the coast. Back home, he showed the same sparkle as we'd previously seen and I decided to leave him in the Nomads Handicap, just a week later at Turffontein, over his favourite 1800m.

We booked the up-and-coming lightweight Lawrence Riley at 51,5kg and he rode a super race. Northern March dominated the finish and won by two lengths from All The Rage. With five good wins from seven runs between January and June, and some easy pickings available in the winter of 1985, I was confident that we could win several more races with Northern March. But that was not to be.

Owner Macdonald brought his bookmaker friend Nic Claassen to the stables the day after the Nomads to show him the horse. I smelt a rat and told my assistant, Mike de Kock, that something was brewing. I must have had a sixth sense. Macdonald appeared in my office again one morning, a week after his first visit, and said he wanted to have a chat.

"Ormond," said Macdonald. "You know, Nic (Claassen) has started training now at the Vaal and my other horses are with him, about 10 of them. I was just wondering, man. I think it's better if I have all my eggs in one basket. It will be more convenient for me. I think I should move Northern March over to Nic's stable so I can visit them all at the same time."

I considered what Macdonald had just said and then spoke my mind. "You know Andre, I agree. I don't want you to wait. If you wait, you're going to risk injury. You may just end up in a clinic. So, please, arrange a float. The quicker, the better. And then, get out!"

Mike happened to be there that morning, too. When he stepped into the office with an unrelated query of his own, I told him to fetch Mr Macdonald's set of purple and red silks as this patron would immediately be on his merry way.

THOROUGHLY!

Mike handed over the silks. And that was it. Andre Macdonald marched out.

———

The new wood fibre track was finally laid over our best sand track at Turffontein at a cost of R650,000. All the trainers decided to give it go, make it work, but within the first few weeks the majority of us realised that the officials had made a mistake. The track proved wholly unsuitable. Horses were slipping and breaking down and, within a few months of installation in July 1985 we were only using it for slow work or when the other tracks were waterlogged.

The fibre track was a white elephant for officials, an embarrassment really and only one trainer, Alan Forbes, had praise for it. The part-time businessman told Turffontein's Sandy Christie that this was the best track he'd ever worked on. Excellent track work didn't reflect in Forbes' results, and most of us suffered a slump in success too. When I came to Turffontein, I saddled 83 winners in the 1982/3 season, but that figure fell to 57 (1986/7) and 59 (1987/8), something I attributed directly to the loss of the old sand track and the poor, new fibre track.

Forbes refused to discuss the matter with anyone, insisting that the fibre track was the best thing to happen to racing. He was a strange fellow – a big, tall man who stabled horses for his wife as owner-trainer and ran what I think was an engineering business in Booysens. Sometimes he was accompanied by his son, Arnold, also a tall man with a large, protruding Adam's Apple. They'd drive from the stables to the track and back, four times a day, something we found quite peculiar.

Forbes had his own, specific methods of training – nothing wrong with that, but he had an unsettling habit of cantering his horses on the back stretch at Turffontein for only 300 – 400m. They would stop, turn and run back against the flow of horses from other stables, getting dangerously in the way. I, and a few others, had shouting matches with the big guy until he stopped doing this. But he'd start again, doing what he wanted, and didn't win any popularity contests among his fellow-trainers.

In August 1986, Ronnie Napier released his 'Napier Report' which called for the establishment of the Highveld Racing Authority (HRA), a united, corporate type, top management structure to manage matters of common interest in the Transvaal.

"As conceived, the HRA has the makings of a dictatorship that will grow to control every facet of Highveld Racing including perhaps even the functions of the Jockey Club," wrote Robert Garner in The Star.

Following recommendations, The HRA was officially formed in 1988 to encompass the two race clubs operating at every centre. Vaal/Vereeniging Turf Club became Vaal; Benoni Turf Club/Gosforth Park became Gosforth Park, Rand Turf Club/Newmarket became Newmarket and Johannesburg Turf Club/Turffontein became Turffontein. The HRA also branched into HRATS (the broadcasting unit) and Racing Services, which rationalised nominations, scratchings and final acceptances.

The Owners and Trainers Association (OTA) was replaced by GOA (The Gauteng Owners' Association) and TTA (Transvaal Trainers Association) to serve owners and trainers separately.

We prepared Royal Line again for the 1985 running of the OK Gold Bowl. We brought him into the race via the Gold Cup (unplaced) and the Spring Stayers (4th), runs that were not on a par with his 1984 warm-ups. He gave a good account in the Bowl, however, finishing second to Petit Prince, beaten only by a length.

Tobie van Booma came back to the stable, like he always did after our fallouts. He rode a few winners for me again, but one day I received a call from my friend, Brigadier Des Tee, at Booysens Police. He said one of his squad members had been driving along the highway late the previous night when a man came speeding by in a car. His arm was out of his window and he was shooting wildly into the sky with his gun. The officer took down and traced the number plate and discovered that the car belonged to one Tobie van Booma.

A few days later, when I got to the stables at 4:30 am, Tobie was already there. He was booming music from his stereo system and rocking to the beat in his car seat. The sound reverberated through the stable complex and he only saw me when I hammered on his window and asked him to turn down the music. "For God's sake, Tobie, what the hell are you doing? You are disturbing the horses!"

I fired Tobie van Booma again and this time he didn't return. He started taking rides for other trainers, travelled around the country for a while and we actually booked him for a few winning mounts when he based himself in Durban. The man was a very good jockey, after all.

CHAPTER 35

I've been giving you notes on important people and events I have lived to see, and there was no shortage of explosive happenings in the period between 1986 – 1989 in South Africa and the world. I can deliver a history lesson that will take a while – suffice to say this was a period of intense political upheaval as the ANC escalated their campaign of terror against civilians and the National Party's armed forces made attempts to counter them. Bombs were detonated, or diffused, almost every day at strategic targets. Newspaper headlines were written in blood.

Elsewhere in this period, a nuclear reactor at Chernobyl exploded, causing the release of radioactive material across much of Europe; the space shuttle Challenger disintegrated 73 seconds after launching, killing all seven astronauts on board; Mad Cow Disease broke out; the US Stock Market crashed spectacularly; a Libyan terrorist bomb exploded on a Pan Am jet over Lockerbie in Scotland; 96 people were killed in the football fanatic disaster at Hillsborough; and the Berlin Wall came crashing down after 30 years of the Cold War between East and West.

The racetrack remained a place where hordes of peaceful people gathered twice, sometimes three times a week to enjoy the great racecourse buzz. Away from the tension in the streets they could have a snack, a drink and a bet and shout their fancies home alongside a few thousand like-minded others.

The racetrack always smelt good. There was a little hamburger shop next to the bookmakers' ring at Gosforth Park, the Curry Den at Turffontein, a restaurant under the main pavilion at the Vaal and a Schwarma Stand at Newmarket where a chap called Rafael prepared this tasty walkaway dish for punters on the move. There were bars on the ground floor and on every level of the grandstand where groups of punters took a few shots, combined their skills and their cash to take joint bets.

On our tracks, senior jockey Michael Roberts was winning title after South African title and setting his sights on riding in the UK. Bartie Leisher, Basil Marcus and Felix Coetzee had similar ambitions. The crown prince was the unstoppable Jeff Lloyd, a rare and unconventional talent. In the Transvaal, Gavin van Zyl, Rhys van Wyk, Robbie Sham and Cecil van As were chasing Bartie for provincial honours. Robbie Fradd, Anthony Delpech and M.J. Odendaal were the emerging stars in Natal. Garth Puller and Karl Neisius ruled the roost in Cape Town and, in the league of young apprentices Piere Strydom, Douglas Whyte and Weichong Marwing announced themselves as big names of the future.

In 1986, my youngest son Paul completed his compulsory military training – he was stationed near the war zones in South West Africa, but received a logistics posting and was one of the lucky ones. Many other young men of his age died in battles on the Angolan border.

Also in this year, I married Maureen Summerly, whom I'd actually known in racing circles before I met my first wife Norma in the 1950s. I vividly recall going to a wedding in or around 1949 when I was asked to be the best man to a friend named Edgar De Gouveia. Maureen was a close friend of his bride, Veda, and it so happened we danced a few times that night. That was a special evening. Maureen came back into my life at a time I needed support and encouragement and she provided that not only as a devout horse and racing fan, but as a loving partner.

David, meanwhile, was taking on more responsibilities in the stable, travelling with our raiding horses and liaising with established and new clients. Mike de Kock left to join Robbie Sage at Randjesfontein. He felt that, as first assistant to Sage, he'd have a better chance at realising his own ambitions and his departure carried my blessing.

With all of Royal Line, Sandfly, Bright N Blue, Don Pedro and Chapter Two reaching the end of their careers I was a little worried that a lean spell without decent runners may set us back but, as always, a new battalion of young horses started coming through the ranks. A number of graduates from my Middelburg farm, Rooispruit, also started coming into the yard, many of them progeny of our stallion Bel Byou (IRE), and to my delight there were among them a few that could run!

Bright N Blue's full-brother Never Blue (Great Brother) was almost as good as his sister. He won as a two-year-old in 1985 beating the top class subsequent Computaform Sprint winner Military Song over 1000m at Gosforth Park and then won his way through the divisions for owner Anthony Joseph. He was versatile, won up to 1700m and we had a go at a couple of big races. He wasn't quite up to scratch in the majors, but won seven career starts and placed nine times.

Rhys van Wyk, one of the strongest jockeys around, rode a few for me at the time, including bookmaker Bill Ferguson's filly, Kamadeva (Kama). Bill was perhaps the best known figure in the old bookmakers' ring, a legendary turf accountant who could lay you a bet to win a million and ask immediately, "Would you like some more?" Perhaps that's why Bill liked to have Rhys on his runners - a jock known for keeping his cool on well-backed runners and bringing them home for the cash!

Kamadeva, also versatile with a few wins down the straight, posted her first notable success in the TBA Newmarket Fillies Plate over 2000m in which Van Wyk rode her to victory. She was placed in the G1 Lancome Fillies and the Rand Turf Club Stakes over 1600m and then perhaps a bit unlucky not to get more black type, finishing fifth in the 1986 Garden Province Stakes on July Day.

We booked Jeff Lloyd on Kamadeva in the G1 Natalia Stakes a month later and she won it narrowly under a peach of a ride, not only a memorable success but the race which started a fruitful association with Lloyd, who agreed to travel from his Durban base to ride for us on the Highveld as often as possible. Our association yielded a spate of winners over the next few years as Lloyd was chasing the National Title and wanted to better Michael Roberts' number of wins in a season, which at the time stood at 203. Kamadeva won us eight of 16, another classy filly that brought us many thrills in her short career.

When Lloyd had other engagements, I spread my rides between Van Wyk, Robbie Sham, Christie Blom and Tobie van Booma's younger brother Charles, an apprentice that had the good riding qualities of his brother and used every chance I gave him to the best of his ability. Mark Nel got among our winners, the relocated 'Rooies' Fourie and Natal's ace, Kevin Shea, also picked up a few good mounts.

The main arrows in our quiver in 1987 were Bookbinder (Meadowville), My Advantage (Wagga Wagga), Copper Tan and Lines Of Power (Instrument Landing).

I trained Copper Tan for Pretoria-based owner Henry Breitenbach, a likeable, ginger-haired man who bred horses from an imported stallion called Bold Voyager (His Majesty), with which he enjoyed a notable amount of success for a small breeder. Henry also trained for several months at a time when he felt like it. Copper Tan came to us during one of Henry's 'off' spells and we won three races with her, including the G2 TAB Fillies Futurity, in which Kevin Shea rode a big race winning despite suffering interference from M.J. Odendaal on Jean Heming's Love Of London.

Bookbinder was one of those big plodders that could just run all day, the further the better. There were plenty of races beyond 2400m in this era and he earned stake after stake over 2400m, 2700m and 3200m, winning four races and placing nine times.

One winter's day, in a 2700m race at Gosforth Park, he ran on late to win under Mark Nel at 48,5kg, a race he wouldn't have won with a bigger weight. He was just a moderate one-paced gelding in the right race with a light weight, and reached the post first. One newspaper called Bookbinder 'The Saviour' the next day, because he'd gotten up to beat two rank outsiders and kept punters 'alive' in their Jackpots. One remembers the average horses too, especially when they gave their best in a race.

Mark also got on well with another stayer Lines Of Power, who won two races in 1986 en route to plenty more in 1987. Particularly memorable was his B Division win in July 1987, when we changed tactics. I asked Mark to send him to the front in an 1800m event at Turffontein. Having finished downfield in his two previous races, Lines Of Power enjoyed only minor support in the betting market, starting at 10-1. But he was well ridden and held on to win by a head. The racing media was crafty again. Robert Garner titled his review of the race 'Lines of Power's win shocked!' and Graeme Hawkins came up with 'Lines Of Power short-circuits punters!'

Gary Player owned My Advantage in partnership with Des Bolton. This was the smartest colt ever produced by our Wagga Wagga and Player came to the course on occasion to see his home-bred in action.

My Advantage notched four quick wins in a row between August and December 1987. Gary actually attended the Vaal meeting for his November win over 1700m, when a strong head wind blew and Jeff Lloyd had to keep his mount covered for most of the race. Gary was very pleased that day, the man who always remarked that the exhilaration of leading in a winner was on a par with winning a big golf tournament. Especially when you've bred them, too!

A highlight for Lloyd, the stable and his legion of fans came on 29 July 1987 when the jock equalled Michael Roberts' record of 203 wins in a season aboard Miss Quickstep (Fordham) and then setting the new benchmark of 204 on the same day with my own filly Island Paradise (Elliodor) in the Maurice Passmore Handicap over 1800m. My good friend Mr Passmore came to the track and led Island Paradise into the winner's enclosure at my side.

Talk about unforgettable days. Lloyd's record hunt was big news in the papers that week and there was a bumper crowd at the grand old Alberton track. The big parking lot was packed to capacity and racegoers were still streaming in from allocated parking strips at surrounding shopping centres as late as the fifth race to cheer Lloyd on. I know there will be any number of readers who will remember that sunny winter's day. If you were a racing fan in the 1980s, and you were based in Johannesburg and surrounds, you would have been there that afternoon. Memories are made of those.

CHAPTER 36

This book will be historically incomplete without the story of Have A Deal and Kiev – two runners involved in the 'Ringer' scandal of 1987. I am covering it because of my own (second-hand) experience with a 'ringer' as relayed in Chapter 11. It also fits into our timeline and is as interesting and entertaining as it was outrageous.

In researching the case, we spoke to a number of individuals and, as with other controversial matters, details are sketchy and tails have been added (or taken away) over the years. There were prominent press reports, but they contained lots of mumbo jumbo. The base of our research was the article on display in the TBA's Museum at Gosforth Park, but that written piece just scraped the surface and I'll give you an account below of more or less what happened in the weeks before 29 September 1987 at the Vaal Racecourse, on the day itself and in the weeks thereafter.

Among our trainers on the Highveld in this period was W.F. 'Barney' Barnard, who owned a farm and a sand track near Putfontein on the outskirts of Benoni. Some 15km away trained his acquaintance C.J.

'Neels' van Baalen, the headmaster at Jan van Riebeeck Primary School in a village called Sundra.

Early in 1987, Barney went to a dispersal sale at the old showgrounds in KwaZulu-Natal and purchased a good horse, a seven-time winning Top Division gelding named 'Kiev', formerly trained by David Payne. He took Kiev to Putfontein and started putting him through his paces. Kiev showed that he was indeed a good and speedy sort, beating every other horse he was tested against in gallops.

Up the country road in Sundra, schoolmaster Neels trained a moderate one-time winner called Have A Deal, who'd fluked a Maiden win in Bloemfontein and was battling to place just one division up in the ranks. But here's the thing: Have A Deal looked remarkably like Barney's horse, Kiev! They were both dark bay geldings of the same height, exactly alike apart from the white marks (blazes) on their foreheads. While in the same position between their pairs of eyes, Have A Deal had an uneven circle, Kiev's was more in the shape of a star of the same size. At a glance, untrained eyes could not tell them apart.

Whether Barney approached Neels or Neels went to Barney first is unknown, but between the pair they hatched a plan. Neels was to enter his moderate Have A Deal in the weakest race he could find, and then take Barney's powerful Kiev to run in his place. It follows that the carded 'Have A Deal', with his poor form, would start at long odds and a big betting coup could be landed with Kiev at the track to do the actual racing!

In those days, horses weren't micro-chipped like they are now. Today, we have detailed passports and individual barcodes to ensure that the right horses run in the right races. No confusion can arise and no cheating can be attempted. But Neels and Barney, 35 years ago, had what looked to be a failsafe way of fooling the stipes and the punters, and bagging some serious loot for their ingenuity.

Neels entered Have A Deal in a Novice Plate over 1000m scheduled for Tuesday, 29 September, at the Vaal and while the field was weak, Have A Deal's form seemed even weaker than average. He was a good, traditional, rank outsider. Of course, Have A Deal spent the day in his Sundra stable while Kiev was prepared for the race and trucked to the course. Jockey Gordon Sterley was booked for the ride.

As their initial good fortune would have it, there was plenty of rain in the days leading up to the race, so the punting public expected upset results. Have A Deal had won a race, but hadn't finished closer than 11,75-lengths behind the winner in four subsequent starts.

All went according to plan. Kiev was saddled and paraded before the race as Have A Deal. In the betting market, the odds disseminator at the Vaal reported to Tattersalls around the country that some support had come for Have A Deal, who'd been backed from 25-1 to 20-1. Nothing to frown at really, perhaps someone thought that the Neels van Baalen runner would do well on the soft track, as he'd been reported suffering from sore front legs after a few previous races.

But then, after the canterdown, Have a Deal's odds shortened dramatically from 20s into 14-1, then 10-1 and 6-1, and bookmakers started 'taking back' odds with other bookmakers to cover their potential losses. Shortly before the off, more bets were struck and Have A Deal went off at 4-1, now among the favourites to win.

There was a bit of argy-bargy between runners at the start, but 'Have A Deal', represented by the top galloper Kiev, jumped well for Sterley, led for most of the way and won easing down. Gamble landed.

Outsiders win races, especially at the Vaal and often following rain, so this was perhaps just one of those days for punters. Another roughie had won, this one must have been fancied. Good luck to the boys who backed him! But then the objection hooter sounded and, curiously, the photo of the lead-in shows Neels with a concerned expression on his face, an 'anxious look'. He promptly got nauseous, ran to an on-course lavatory and didn't come out until 15 minutes later, when it was announced that the result stood. The stipes had noted some interference at the start of the race, but it did not concern the winner, Have A Deal.

As it were, Have A Deal was reported to have left the track to return home via a truck. Neels stayed on to have a celebratory drink. Barney wasn't seen on course.

The Jockey Club's Investigsting Officer, Captain Dirk Blignaut, set about investigating the matter and gathering evidence. A Jockey Club Inquiry began on 19 October 1987, with legal representation for Van Baalen and Barnard, who were called in jointly to face Advocates Clive Cohen and Altus Joubert, representing the Jockey Club.

The bulk of evidence for the prosecution centred on video footage of the race and on photographs taken by the on-course photographer, H.F. Kenny, also on photos taken by Blignaut at the stables of both Van Baalen and Barnard during the week after the race.

The defence argued that the whole 'Ringer' case was nothing more than a conspiracy by the conservative Afrikaans community who disapproved of Headmaster Van Baalen's involvement in horseracing and gambling. They also felt that the photos presented an 'optical illusion' due to the poor lighting on the rainy day and the angles at which they were taken.

The Jockey Club were, however, satisfied that the evidence brought against the pair of trainers was good enough to warrant a guilty verdict. They were convinced that Kiev had run the race as Have A Deal, and imposed a 'warning off' (permanent banning from racing) on both Barnard and Van Baalen.

Barnard accepted his fate; Van Baalen took his warning off on Appeal to the Jockey Club's Inquiry Board but was unsuccessful. Both were also found guilty of fraud in the Johannesburg Magistrate's Court in May 1988, for which fines were paid.

It's all conjecture, but there were stories 'around and behind the story', worth mentioning:

-Barney and Neels had been in trouble for a previous 'Ringer' incident in which Barney's top horse First Base ran in a race on behalf of That's A Deal, another struggler trained by Van Baalen. This was referred to in the case heard before the Magistrate's Court.

-In another case in Bloemfontein, a grey filly trained by Van Baalen won a race and was removed from the course so quickly nobody could get to her for dope testing or identification.

-Barney actually went to the Durban sale specifically to buy a lookalike for Have A Deal, and found Kiev.

-To overcome the problem of the slight difference between the white markings between their eyes, Barney and Neels concocted something they found within the inner layers of an old radio battery, mixed with water for a dark, sticky paste. Kiev's mark was touched up so it could look more like the mark on Have A Deal. Some of it came off during the race.

-Somebody sitting at a Vaal bar later in the day (which may have been Van Baalen), bragged about Kiev having won the race, not Have A Deal. This was overheard by trainer Andre Kotze, who alerted the Stipes. Interestingly, however, one report claimed that, 'the same informant later gave evidence that he regretted that he only had R60 on him at the time, which was to pay for petrol to get the horse home as he had only taken odds of 4-1 and not 20-1.'

This suggests that the informant, allegedly Kotze, was told of the scam beforehand, missed the coup, split on his colleagues because of that and drove Kiev home with his last few bucks. But Kotze was also a trainer so he was probably referring to one of his own horses. We were told that the truck was driven by one Hilton Wright, and not Kotze. There were grey areas here, and poor reporting.

-Neels van Baalen, perhaps overcome with emotion, was seen in the muddy stable area at the Vaal some time after the race. He'd put on a pair of gumboots to walk in the mud, but they were the wrong way around and he battled to get them off.

-H.F. Kenny joked with Barney Barnard a few weeks after the race: "Hey Barney, you should have put blinkers on Kiev!" Barney chuckled and walked away.

- The 29 September race was a trial run, just an experiment for a bigger coup later, and neither Neels nor Barney struck bets on Have A Deal. They were left penniless.

-Barnard and Van Baalen won hundreds of thousands with bookmakers around the country.

Here is an interesting, and somewhat bizarre, true story from veteran racing enthusiast David Safi, the founder of Formgrids:

"The Ringer scandal took place at the time when I started SARA, the South African Racegoers Association, with the specific view of bringing dishonesty in racing to the attention of the public and the stipes.

"Barney Barnard approached me, as a racing expert, to testify for him. I hadn't seen the race, only heard the rough details. Barney said, 'If that winner was really Kiev, how do you think he would have won?'

"I replied: 'Well, Kiev's a good horse. He would have jumped three lengths clear and won by three or more!' Barney said: 'Nevermind' and walked off.

"Later, Neels van Baalen asked me to testify at his hearing in front of a Tribunal assembled by the Department of Education. They wanted to strip him of his duties as a schoolmaster and take away his benefits. This was a huge scandal in the Afrikaans community.

"I went to the hearing and testified as I was asked to do. I said that skulduggery was not uncommon in racing. Indeed, I'd started my organisation SARA to protect punters from dishonesty on the part of trainers and jockeys. I told them about doping, jockeys pulling horses up, tricks they employed at the start and during a race. The argument was that inventive methods to gain an edge was a part of the fabric of horseracing and that the Ringer case was nothing out of the ordinary.

"The impression they wanted to create was that Messrs Van Baalen and Barnard were simply one step ahead in a dishonest game and my testimony came in handy. Van Baalen was found not guilty and was allowed to resume his duties with full benefits.

"I want to add that racing, and punters, were going through a turbulent time with some unbelievable results at the order of the day, so I'd stick by what I said at the time. After this case, the Jockey Club started cleaning things up with sophisticated dope testing and introduced micro-chipping and more detailed horse passports. Technology was also vastly improved so that horses and jockeys can be watched within a race.

"Oh, and this is funny. During the hearing they showed the replay of the race to the Tribunal and all the others present. This was the first time I could see the race. Kiev jumped like a rocket, three lengths clear, strode along easily and won by three lengths!"

I was friendly with Barney Barnard. He was a good horseman who fed his runners well and looked after them properly. His son, Clive, is one of my best friends today. Clive bought my Karoo farm, Rooispruit, in 2016. I still visit there from time to time.

Barney never revealed to me, or to his family, what really happened that day. Clive told me that Barney said he didn't have a cent on Have A Deal. He was as poor as he'd ever been after he was warned off, there was no cash lying around and he eventually went to the United States to get involved in the lucrative (and legal) cockfighting industry.

Neels van Baalen resumed duties at Jan van Riebeeck Primary School and according to the school's website was replaced by a new headmaster in 1991. His whereabouts since are unknown.

CHAPTER 37

The dissatisfaction with the fibre track at Turffontein peaked in the early part of 1988. In the two previous winters of its existence, the track was unusable because it froze over to the extent that salt and anti-freeze were added to the irrigation system, but not even that could break it down.

Turffontein's retiring boss, Sandy Christie, called a few meetings with trainers and track staff and it was agreed that we should investigate similar tracks and call for help and advice. After some discussions, I was designated to fly to Australia alongside track manager Don Borchers to visit some of the venues at which wood fibre was being used, and to come back with viable suggestions.

While it was exciting to get an all-expenses-paid first visit to Australia, Don and I had no time for sightseeing. We weren't sure what to expect, but this journey put the matter beyond doubt: The wood fibre track was a disaster. We jetted to Sydney and Melbourne, visiting a number of racetracks and we also went round to Adelaide, where Hall-Of-Fame trainer Colin Hayes (father of trainer David Hayes) advised us and showed us around his 800-acre establishment, Lindsay Park.

In a nutshell, what we established was that nobody in Australia was completely happy with wood fibre, most were in fact not satisfied all. Their wood fibre tracks needed constant moisture and even in the coastal centres, where it rained a lot and there was moisture in the air, the tracks did not retain the levels required for competitive training and racing.

In cases where the wood pieces were too large, they did not settle and became lodged in hooves; if the pieces were too small and lightweight, they got loose and blew around in the wind. At times, horses slipped on the surface like they did back home. If the drainage conditions weren't good, the surfaces become waterlogged. Wood fibre wasn't as durable as made out to be and freezing was a problem too, like we had to endure in South Africa.

We returned to Johannesburg with our findings in a report and, following a few meetings with the administrators, trainers, jockeys and track officials, our advice was heeded. Turffontein's new General Manager, John Alexander, announced that the fibre track would be lifted and replaced with a fast sand track. The majority of Turffontein trainers were happy with the decision and supported us all the way.

The new track comprised washed plaster sand, which was selected from several sands recommended by track consultant Arthur Reid after being subjected to laboratory analysis. The cost of replacing the fibre track was about R200,000, far less than the R650,000 initially spent on installing it, and R50,000 was recovered selling some of the redundant fibre.

The new sand track was excellent and most Turffontein trainers saw markedly improved results. My winners in the 1988/89 season had dwindled to 58 from a high of 80 in 1983/4, but in 1989/90 and 1990/91 I would set two career-best tallies.

THOROUGHLY!

Of all the horrible things to have happened in racing's history, the Hennenman air disaster of Tuesday 12 April, 1988, must rank near the top.

Our horseracing community lost 13 jockeys, along with two trainers and racetrack officials in an aeroplane crash that occurred near the farming town of Hennenman when the group was on their way back to Johannesburg having performed their duties at a Bloemfontein race meeting that afternoon.

Mike Moon wrote in The Citizen on the eve of the 2022 memorial of the tragedy: "The official inquiry into the Hennenman air disaster appears to have been at best half-hearted and at worst botched. No-one was ever named as responsible for the Dakota catching fire and crashing into a Free State mielie field, killing the 24 people on board.

"From the eyewitness account of a local farmer who saw the horror unfold in the early autumn night sky, it seems fuel leaked from the starboard engine, caught alight and eventually consumed the craft in a ball of flame.

"A logbook revealed the aged twin-engined plane had not been properly and regularly serviced. There were also allegations that its airworthiness certificate had been falsified. These lines of inquiry seem not to have been vigorously pursued by government investigators.

"By the time of the probe, operator United Airlines had gone bust and no-one in officialdom seemed inclined to cause its owners any more grief."

Of those lost, the individual most readily remembered is Johannes 'Rooies' Fourie, who was destined for greatness as a jockey on the South African turf – at least the match of the later great generation of Strydom, Whyte, Marcus, Lloyd and co., according to old-timers.

Many of the riders were under the age of 22, some of them married with young children. Rooies, and many other jockeys on that flight, rode for me regularly, in work or in races. Keith Basel, Lawrence Riley, Warren Bailie, Bennie de Wet, Greg Holme, Douglas Roper, Danny Lombard, John McMurtry, Mark Nel, Michael Coetzee, Simon Rahilly and Gordon Sterley all had a turn in my paddock at different times. Teenage jockeys Riley and Bailie, not long out of their apprenticeships, had shown that they were top riders of the future, and all the other guys were good at what they did.

I was fond, especially, of Mark Nel, a regular at my paddock most mornings, and a worker as hard as I'd seen. Mark loved me like a father. His wife Sharon told us after the tragedy that Mark told her in casual conversation a few months before the crash that, when he died, he wanted to be buried wearing my black-and-red silks. I was emotionally taken and duly obliged.

Race caller Clyde Basel, who lost his brother Keith, told the Sporting Post: "When getting to the bottom of what caused the crash, it seemed to be due to negligence. Despite a judge ruling that this was an act of God, none of the families could accept this. It was rather obvious that this plane should never have been allowed to fly."

It was discovered that the right fuel pump had withered away, which resulted in a fuel leakage that may have instigated the crash. The log book also showed that the aircraft was well overdue a service (it wasn't serviced for thousands of flying hours), and it also became apparent that the company, United Airlines, who owned the aircraft was insolvent. This was the same plane that was used in the movie 'The Wild Geese' in 1941!

I am sure that many of you remember when news of the plane crash broke in the media that Wednesday, 14 April, 1988. This was a dark day by any stretch of the imagination – memorable for tears and disbelief - and the industry reeled in shock.

The Highveld racing authorities stage an annual race day in memory of the Hennenman disaster and invite the families of those lost, one of their few commitments to preserving the history of the sport, but a gesture nonetheless.

CHAPTER 38

We entered Lines Of Power for the Politician Handicap over 2000m at Greyville on 12 March 1988 and David accompanied him for our Durban raid. We got lucky as it were, because rain had severely interrupted training programmes for the Natal trainers. Having prepared him at our Turffontein base, Lines Of Power was the fittest horse in the race. He won it quite easily in the hands of our old friend Tobie van Booma, the temporary Natalian, who was in good form again.

Lines Of Power, at six years of age, had served us well and was coming to a stage of his career where he'd done most of what he was able to do, so we sold him on to a Mauritian owner after eight wins and 11 places in South Africa. Amazingly, this warrior won another nine races on the island and became one their most popular runners.

Jeff Lloyd continued his midweek visits from Durban to the Rand and rode most of my winners, including Paddy Hinton's up-and-coming stayer Almanac (Bold Voyager), who posted three wins during the course of the year; another Hinton-owned stayer Budget (Elliodor) and the O'Connor family's sprinter Pi Are Squared, by Piaffer.

We also had some early success for my new patron, Dr Hilda Podlas. Racing administrator, Chris Botha, introduced me to Hilda and her husband, Emmanuel Cambouris. Hilda was an authority in the field of radiology, Emmanuel was an erudite businessman who spoke seven languages. They were wealthy and it showed – always immaculately dressed and they resided in a mansion in Hyde Park, Johannesburg where the interior reminded me of a smart antique store.

Hilda was the boss, Emmanuel took a back seat in most of our dealings and acted as an advisor. She was (I hear, still is) a successful businesswoman, good at what she does and as a couple they were getting involved in horseracing at a high level. Their desire was to win the major races and they had the funds to make their dream a reality. I recall going to the launch of Hilda's tastefully designed Radiology Centre in Johannesburg, the best of its kind in a building constructed with state-of-the-art glass blocks. They meant business and I was comfortable to train for them.

Hilda and Emmanuel had gone horse-hunting, here and abroad, and were keen on getting the best overseas blood they could find into the South African market to improve our stud book. In the UK, they secured four horses with stallion potential in Emerald Point (Mill Reef), Icelander (Kris), Lord Balmerino (The Minstrel) and Vigliotto (Blushing Groom).

Shopping around in South Africa, they were offered a grey filly by Foveros, named Miss Averof, courtesy of Colin Palm, the brother of Bobby Palm who rode my first G1 winner in 1956 and who later became a friend. Colin had trained for a while himself and when he retired, handed over to young gun Paddy Kruyer at Milnerton. He remained involved with Paddy as a consultant.

Paddy had won a Maiden Juvenile Plate with Miss Averof in December 1987. She followed that with an easy Juvenile Progress success in February 1988 and - a month after that - a third in the Ascot

Nursery in the company of future stars Epoque, Wainui and Fanciful. The trainer described her as 'explosive' and her regular jockey Karl Neisius shared the praise.

Colin insisted that I should see Miss Averof in the flesh to approve her for Hilda and Emmanuel, who partnered with Sid Gervis for the purchase of the filly. I travelled to Cape Town, was suitably impressed by her conformation (though she needed some time to furnish) and her temperament. The deal was done. We trucked her to Johannesburg and gave her a chance to mature into her three-year-old career.

Among the first runners in their soon familiar pink-and-black silks was two-year-old Picture Search (Northern Guest), who won a Maiden Juvenile Plate over 1200m at Newmarket on 4 May, ridden by Charles van Booma.

Next was General Blake (Commodore Blake), a little black gelding with courage. He had good pace, but failed in the Nursery over 1200m in April. He showed his calibre, however, when winning the Transvaal Breeders' Plate over 1600m in July from Kadarko, a good stayer who'd go on to win the Derby in 1989.

Another early winner for my new patrons was the imported filly Angel Light (Electric), who was decent, and won her Novice Plate debut under Lloyd in good style, on 24 May. She wasn't the soundest of fillies, so we raced her sparingly and hand-picked races for her.

I had Angel Light beautifully lined up for a Graduation Plate on 14 July but Hilda was worried that the filly was not well enough to win. This left me surprised and a little annoyed. Hilda had heard about blood pictures taken by a handful of other trainers. She was told that they were a fool-proof indication of a horse's health and well-being, so she wanted me to take a sample from Angel Light to have it tested before the race.

I'd never used blood tests in all my years of training and wasn't about to start. It's a load of bull. Any trainer worth his salt should be able to know by his eye and experience alone when his horse is healthy, fit and ready to win. When they've trained well and eaten well, and if you know their levels of energy, habits and peculiarities it is not hard to see when they reach the peak of their condition.

I recalled that my old mate J.B.K. Cooper had experimented with blood samples in the late 1970s and early 1980s when our fellow-trainer Bert Sage. He had enjoyed a fantastic spell of winners and gave his taking of blood tests from his runners much of the credit for his success. But Cooper just couldn't get it right and it drove him mad. After a while he was so confused, he wanted to give up his career altogether!

Hilda insisted on having a sample taken. I said, "Angel Light is flying, she is very well, she will win," but she kept nagging so I called a veterinarian to draw blood and perform the required tests. I don't remember what it showed and I didn't really care, but my patron was told that Angel Light's blood was definitely 'not right' and following this information she wanted me to scratch the filly from her Newmarket race.

I remained calm (can you believe it?) and repeated to her that Angel Light was as well as she could be and that she would win the race 'on her coconut'. I guess that, at this early stage of our relationship, Hilda was also intent on remaining amicable and avoiding arguments. She carried on, insisting that I respect the blood results, but let it go on the eve of the race saying that she was concerned that we'd be running a sick filly. I can't remember whether they came to the course to watch her run the next day, but Angel Light won with her head in her chest. No contest. Hilda's awkward request had me a little worried, however. When owners show a desire to be trainers, well, tears invariably lurk on the horizon.

Mill Reef's son Emerald Point was a tall and quite athletic horse, but no more than an ordinary stayer and we knew early that he wasn't going to Hollywood. But we had him race fit - he finished not far off in his debut for the yard over 2450m, so we decided to have a crack at the 1988 Gold Cup. He was likely to come into the race with a low weight, maybe 48kg, which would give us an outside chance on his natural staying ability.

To my surprise, Emerald Point was allocated 58kg, joint top weight with G1 winning stayers Aquanaut and Pedometer. Emerald Point had only won two low class races in England, one over 1700m at Lingfield in 1986 and one over 3200m at Bath in 1987. Handicapper Colin Buckham told me that, because Emerald Point had only run once in South Africa, he was in at weight for age.

With no flexibility forthcoming, I withdrew Emerald Point's entry and decided to boycott the Gold Cup meeting on principle. I pulled all of our other entries from the meeting. It was laughable that the handicapper didn't have the authority to make the correct call.

Emerald Point won two B Division races on the Highveld, one over 1900m and another over 2000m, both in small fields in which he carried 48,5kg and 49kg respectively. That was the extent of his ability. He was retired to stud where he achieved moderate success.

Vigliotto, on the other hand, turned out to be a really smart stayer. He was a small, flashy chestnut horse with a big heart and he liked to race. Lord Balmerino also showed quality, but he was not in Vigliotto's league. Both would perform with distinction for us in 1989.

Jeff and I hit the board three times at Newmarket on 2 August, 1988, to start the 1988/9 season with a bang. Hiltonian (Hobnob), Almanac and Pi Are Squared won three of the four Jackpot legs. They were all punters' favourites, and the Jackpot returned just R42 that day.

The Pick 6 reflected in my newspaper clipping from the meeting shows the pool for this bet reaching almost R4,1-million. Today, if we reach a Pick 6 turnover of R600,000 at a midweek meeting, we consider ourselves lucky. Again, I am overwhelmed by a sense of nostalgia for those wildly successful years when our sport was revered, widely supported and managed by individuals who had its best interests at heart.

Picture Search went from strength to strength. She won a Graduation Plate over 1600m late in October, and on 11 November Jeff Lloyd rode her to a good win over Kyle and Margot in the Executive Fashion Stakes, a Listed race over 1600m.

The race was sponsored by the Abrosie Brothers, who opened their Executive Fashion store in Bedfordview in 1970 and are amazingly still in business in their original shop. As racehorse owners, the Abrosies were also big in the 1980s and 1990s with horses like Brainteaser, Golden Loom. But they were lost as investors, disillusioned like so many others, by what became racing's plundering bureaucracy of the 2000s.

CHAPTER 39

Among the many astounding events of 1989 was the invention of the World Wide Web (www), by Tim Berners-Lee, a British scientist. I can tell you, if the internet had been invented in the 1930s, this book would've taken perhaps six months to complete instead of the best part of two years.

We had to dig into library archives and old racing calendars to confirm facts and racing results and, if you want to start a search for quality racing photos from the early and middle part of the 20th century in South Africa, good luck to you!

We couldn't find, for example, a single photo of my mentor George Weale, oft-mentioned in the first few chapters, to include in our picture sections. He was a highly accomplished trainer, had won many G1 races but unless we're lucky to unearth a surprise photo from a reader for a revised edition, nobody will ever know what George looked like.

I was quite diligent at keeping my own scrapbooks updated – my single photo of George disappeared after a robbery at my office, but despite that we were often left scratching our heads at the lack of racing information and images at hand. Charles Faull and his crew at aro.co.za have done what they can to recycle some wonderful old stuff, but one can only do so much with limited resources. Chunks of history from South African racing are lost to posterity.

Information and photos were more readily accessible as our research headed into the late 1980s and 1990s when I was in the prime of my career and the stable was consistently in the Top 3. This era came just before the takeover of the world by cell phones, digital images and social media, but we found suitable images to go with some riveting memories.

Our association with a talented new stable apprentice probably had much to do with the yard's momentum. An 18-year-old lad named Weichong Marwing came along from the Academy to knock on my door. He'd shown true ability riding winners for Michael Azzie, Scott Kenny and others, but had been going through a lean spell and, as a young man with big ambitions, wanted high-profile winners. Already.

I saw immediately that what we had here was a champion jockey of the future. Weichong was 'pocket dynamite' – strong as they come with balance and good hands, a fine judge of pace, a hard worker and not scared to ride with any of his peers.

We decided to take Weichong with us as stable jockey for our 1989 winter raid to Cape Town, the sojourn that brought us much success in the past. There were a number of runners in my 30-strong string that weren't suited to the hard winter tracks on the Highveld, and all would benefit from the weaker opposition.

Centre Bill (The Eliminator) and Budget got us off to a good start with wins at Kenilworth, and then, on 24 June, Weichong and I won our first feature race together with Miss Averof, who ran on well to win the Champagne Stakes over 1200m at Milnerton from Dainty Di.

I'd given Miss Averof runs in three features on the Highveld leading to the Champagne Stakes. These included the G1 Lancome Fillies at Gosforth Park in May, where she was beaten by Alistair Gordon's Saintly Lady and the star fillies Mill Hill and Roland's Song.

She finished within four lengths off the call that day and I guess most trainers would have been happy with this run at G1 level, but Miss Averof gave me the impression that she was just holding back a little, that she was better than this.

Of all my raiding runners in the Cape that season, Miss Averof benefited the most from the coastal air. Before and after the Champagne Stakes I saw that she was putting herself into her work and improving tremendously. She was turning into a prospect of note.

The Cape's racing media loved Miss Averof and they were all over Weichong too. Graham Potter of The Argus spotted him early. He wrote: "Marwing is no ordinary apprentice and putting that designation in front of his name could be misleading to those armchair punters who have never seen the youngster in action. His first attribute is his strength; he's also shown himself to be a 'thinking' jockey, seldom being conned into compromising his mounts' chances by accepting a false situation."

There were more press accolades for Weichong when he booted Vigliotto home to win the Lonsdale Stirrup Cup over 2400m at Milnerton on 1 July. Vigliotto wasn't wound up when we stepped him out for a B Division pipe-opener over 2000m at Turffontein in April, but won it anyway and then blossomed in the Cape. The gutsy little chestnut, patiently ridden early in the Lonsdale, ran down the free-striding Bold Messenger in the stretch and kept him at bay for a 0.75-length win. We were starting to get excited about Vigliotto, and we pencilled in October's OK Gold Bowl as his main mission.

Jeff Lloyd, on a midweek visit to Cape Town, rode our well-travelled filly Wot-A-Hussy (Peaceable Kingdom) to win the Valmary Stakes at Durbanville on 4 July, with Weichong missing out. I sensed he was not 100% content sitting on the bench for this one. Even before he came out of his apprenticeship, the confident youngster wasn't happy to stand back for any senior rider. Not even for Lloyd, the accomplished South African champion.

Weichong and I chalked up a double again on 8 July when Fair Dancer (Fair Season) won a Maiden Juvenile Plate over 1600m by 7,75-lengths and Miss Averof followed her Champagne Stakes victory with another smart feature win in the Ladies Mile where she accounted for up-and-coming filly Kissagram. This was my apprentice's 120th career win and I was pleased to see his commitment and continued improvement. Likewise, Miss Averof was improving still and I couldn't wait to get her back to the Highveld for the Summer features.

The other notable winner in this term was owner Lawrence Potgieter's High Function, by unfashionable sire Dukedom. Lawrence bought him as a yearling for R200, nobody wanted him but I was glad he found his way into my stable because he was improving nicely at the age of five. High Function won a minor feature, the City Handicap over 1800m at Kenilworth, on 9 August, just before we wrapped up and prepared for a return to the Rand.

One newspaper called our winter spell in the Cape in 1989, 'Ferraris' Winter Of Content' and reported that we'd sent out 124 runners over 22 meetings, yielding 24 wins and a further 50 stake cheques. I commented on the racing experience in the Western Cape, saying, "I am amazed that the Cape Clubs can offer the stakes they do because there are so few people here and the pools are so small compared to Johannesburg. I have nothing but admiration for the committees of the race clubs who so valiantly try to keep the stakes gap between themselves and upcountry to a minimum. I honestly don't know how they managed to come up with their last stakes increases. I enjoy being here, Cape Town is a cheap place to race, from transport to bedding to vet bills to feed. Everything is half the price."

At this very moment, 33 years later, I'm looking at a headline from the Sporting Post website, which reads, 'Cape Racing Puzzle – Conflicts, Capture?' in which racing in the region is reported to be on its last legs, with infighting and politics at the order of the day and no solution in sight. *(Note: There have subsequently been several positive developments for Cape Racing).*

Once again, I feel privileged to have lived my career in the glorious days of South African horseracing.

CHAPTER 40

Our Cape sojourn in the winter of 1989 was like a fertile garden and, when we transplanted our seedlings in Highveld soil, they sprouted bright and green that summer.

Runners I'd considered to be average, like Fair Dancer (Fair Season), Prime Factor (Royal Prerogative), American Affair (Volcanic), Legal Cargo (Over The Air) and Fearless Spirit (Foveros) all ran out of their skins over the next several months. Vigliotto, Miss Averof, Budget, High Function and Almanac came to the racetrack for several Listed and Graded races and slammed their opposition.

I didn't have much doubt that Vigliotto would see out the demanding 3200m of the Gold Bowl – his Lonsdale win at Milnerton taught me a lot about him and Weichong Marwing reported there was plenty more to come when he ran past the line. The Turffontein circuit with its uphill before the final bend would be a different kettle of fish, however, so the OK Trial over 2450m was the perfect prep into the Bowl.

All went according to plan. There was an easy pace throughout, Vigliotto entered the straight behind pacemaker Kharg Island and raced up in Weichong's hands to take command at the 400m-mark. He stretched away to a 3,25-length win over Sky Safari and, again, the apprentice reported that this US-bred had still had much fuel in his tank. We were pleased and confident for the Bowl, just three weeks away.

There was a good deal of media attention on this race. OK Bazaars had once again thrown their weight behind it with colossal promotions within their stores, backed by radio and television campaigns in which the company MD, Gordon Hood, spared no cent.

The race itself attracted what I reckon was one of the best fields ever assembled for a South African stayers contest. Mark Watters' star stayer, Aquanaut, was coming to defend the Gold Bowl title he'd won in 1987 and 1988. He'd taken the The Gold Cup and the Chairman's Handicap in between and his '89 prep had come via the G2 Computaform Champion Stakes, in which he ran champion filly Roland's Song to 1,8-lengths over a distance short of his best.

Mike de Kock had entered Evening Mist, the brilliant filly who took her rookie trainer to immediate prominence with a G1 Administrators win in 1988. Terrance Millard fielded Castle Walk, winner of the G2 Republic Day Handicap and, for a while, the ante-post favourite for the 1989 Durban July. He'd backed up with Cipayito, a multiple winner of stayer's features. Ralph Rixon raided with the Durban July runner-up Tropicante, who'd gone on to win the Gold Cup three months prior to the Bowl.

That wasn't all. Jean Heming's St Leger winner Chattaronga stood his ground, alongside Scott Kenny's SA Oaks winning filly Rootin' Tootin and Spike Lerena's Graded-performed pair of hard-knocking stayers, Cincinatti and Home Style. Vigliotto had 19 top runners to beat.

David Mollett was the only tipster who recommended Vigliotto as the winner of the race. The other scribes were in Aquanaut's camp - even

THOROUGHLY!

Charl Pretorius, then a junior reporter at Beeld who was friendly with my son, David. He was sniffing around the training yards at Turffontein on the eve of the race when he bumped into David, who invited him for a drink and told him to 'empty out' on Vigliotto. A good example of 'looking a gift horse in the mouth'?

A crowd of 32 083 was recorded at the city track on 14 October, with the entire infield cordoned off and turned into a makeshift car park. The stands were packed, even the area where the inside track is today was buzzing with racegoers. It was a beautiful day for racing, one of those rare occasions when everything just fell perfectly into place and things seemed to flash by in an animated daze of colour.

Despite her impressive march of feature wins into the Listed OK Fillies and Mares Stakes over 1400m, which started the day for Weichong and I, Miss Averof was easy to back at 5-1 in the wake of support for Roy Magner's smart galloper Not Now Darling and Backapound, an ace filly from Tobie Spies' yard. But Miss Averof was not aware of her odds, or who her rivals were. The explosiveness her first trainer spoke about was well witnessed here as she burst away from a talented pack with 250m to run and creamed them by 2,50-lengths.

Following Miss Averof's win, which preceded the big event, there was a stampede of racing fans to the available seats around the parade ring. Those who didn't make it stood five-deep trying to get an eye on Aquanaut, Vigliotto, Castle Walk, Evening Mist and company as the trainers and their assistants went out to saddle their contenders and a host of fashionably-dressed owners awaited them with bated breath. We were calm and focused despite the thrills the grey filly had given us a half an hour earlier. Weichong mounted the small, muscular Vigliotto - flashy, fit and on his toes for the biggest race of his life, and he had a short canter to the 3200m starting gates, positioned in front of the grandstand around the 200m-mark.

Weichong and I had discussed Vigliotto's style of racing in the week leading to the race and we agreed that he didn't enjoy being whipped on his behind. We decided that he'd ride the horse hands-and-heels, with taps on the shoulder and only a backside reminder if absolutely necessary. There was a lot at stake for all of us in this R600,000 race. For a young apprentice, especially, it would be tempting to call for the stick at the business end of the race when 19 other jockeys started cracking their own and shouting to spur their mounts on.

But Weichong showed his big-match temperament again. When the gates crashed open, there was a roar from the crowd who could see the first few hundred metres unfold. Thirty-two-thousand pairs of eyes at the track searched for their favourites as the runners jostled for position and perhaps a few million watched the race on SABC TV.

Vigliotto was handy early as nobody seemed keen to set the pace. Our runner led the 20-horse field past the post for the first time as they started their long roundabout. Soon, however, Robbie Sham, riding the outsider Lord Fonteroy, decided to hurry things up. He let his mount stride freely in front at a steady clip. In the back straight they went six lengths clear of Allied Party with Vigliotto settling nicely into third and just striding along ahead of Castle Walk, Power Of Jamaica and the rest of the field.

Lord Fonteroy found a rhythm that suited him well because he reached the hill before the home bend full of running and still comfortably clear of Allied Party and Vigliotto. When they turned into the straight he extended again, galloping strongly. With several others in the pack already off the bit, I started to get worried as one would do when your runner has the best part of 10 lengths to find. Weichong hadn't yet made his move. He was waiting, patiently, for Lord Fonteroy to come back to the field. Was he waiting too long?

As they hit the 400m-mark and patches of sweat under my shirt reminded me that this contest had reached the critical end, Lord

Fonteroy finally started to shorten his stride and for the next 100m I tried to gauge whether Vigliotto, still five lengths adrift, would have enough time to rope him in. Then, the heart-stopping bit where things go to slo-mo and every part of one's body seems to be moving without actually moving. Vigliotto clawed back his deficit, ranged up to Lord Fonteroy and into the lead with 200m to go. The stylish Piere Strydom's recognisable late run caught my eye. He was coming hard at us on Cincinatti, with Aquanaut suddenly in the hunt as well.

The consummate professional, Weichong did what we'd discussed. Instead of laying into his mount, he just waved his whip and tapped Vigliotto on his shoulder. Our runner found extra, strengthened again over the last 50m and won by 1,75-lengths from Cincinatti, Lord Fonteroy and Aquanaut.

As with all other major winners, the walk from the grandstand to the winner's enclosure seemed to happen without happening. Other trainers have reported this sensation too. Perhaps because your mind is still coming to grips with a dream come true. There are hugs and cheers and a flurry of arms and commotion. And then you're there, awaiting the return of your equine star, an almost maddening mix of emotions playing out inside your head and around you.

Hilda and Emmanuel led Vigliotto into the winner's enclosure, I think their son Shaun and a few representatives from his modelling agency were there too. Hilda was presented with the beautiful Gold Bowl Trophy by Gordon Hood.

This was a truly phenomenal day for all of us – the biggest win of my career - and it ended the way it had started. The little black soldier, General Blake, won a handicap over 1400m to give the stable three legs of the Jackpot and the Pick 6, which had reached a R5-milion plus pool and returned more than R70,000, with Hilda and company said to be among the winners.

Speaking to the media in the aftermath, Hilda announced that Vigliotto would be retired immediately to stud. As a Graded-winning son of Blushing Groom the six-year-old had a good chance of getting support from breeders. He would stand at their Swynford Paddocks Stud near Mooirivier.

Weichong, David, Paul and I didn't stay too long for the celebratory functions in the Steward's Quarters and private suites. We decided on dinner at the popular Lord Prawn in Braamfontein, Johannesburg. We skipped the Queen Prawns that night and enjoyed Kings with our champagne instead. A few dozen of them, I'd say!

CHAPTER 41

Once in a while, there is a charming racing story about horses and their lucky owners. Laurence and Sue Potgieter came briefly through our stable with a remarkable horse named High Function, a big-blazed chestnut bought for just R200 at the National Two-Year-Old Sale where he reminded Sue of a dressage pony she used to own.

Three days after the Gold Bowl, it was back to business at Newmarket and High Function picked up where General Blake had left off on Saturday afternoon. On a hat-trick of wins, he was priced up favourite for the Anniversary Cup Handicap over 1600m, for which 15 runners were entered, and had no trouble whatsoever in putting them to bed. This was Weichong's 30th winner for the new season and, with two months of his apprenticeship left, he was leading the Transvaal Jockeys log, side-by-side with senior jockey Gavin van Zyl.

My scrapbook shows a comment from Weichong to interviewer Gary John Knowles after the race: "I'd like to buy a house some day!" All these years later, I'm sure our erstwhile champion apprentice has owned a few of them.

High Function's sire, Dukedom (Connaught), stood at Winterhoek Stud in Graaff-Reinet and had only a handful of mostly unsuccessful offspring who contested thoroughbred racing. He was the odd one out, one of those tough little freaks who gave everything he had in a race and came to fitness quickly after a break.

High Function surprised us with a close fourth to super filly Northern Princess in the G1 Germiston November Handicap over 1600m and, on the strength of this we picked December's G2 Allen Snijman Stakes over 2000m at the same track as his next target. To our surprise, he improved even further after his November run and posted what was considered a shock win over Jean Heming's champion filly Roland's Song, the 7-10 favourite.

We gave High Function time off after this and raced him a few times in 1990, but he never reached the same level of form. Perhaps, one could argue, his pedigree caught up with him, but seeing that history delivers many unlikely stars bred from unfashionable pedigrees, this is an assessment that won't hold much water. This special horse just came to the end of his career, he'd had enough and we retired him with seven wins and six places from just 15 starts.

Miss Averof, too, remained in top form after the Gold Bowl weekend. She was just terrific, getting better with maturity and disposing of everything we brought to challenge her in morning gallops. We aimed her at the G1 First National Bank 1600, a helluva contest against several top-level winners including Roland's Song, Coolstar, Yardmaster, Sloop, Von Spee and others.

Roland's Song topped the bookmakers' boards at 2-1 with Miss Averof at 5-1, which seemed to be her favourite odds. She handled her first big step into major company with some comfort. She joined Roland's Song for a duel at the 400m-mark and, in the cosy way she was travelling, pressed Heming's filly to come fully off the bit first. Miss Averof, in a strong visual display, powered away from her rival in the last 100m and won by a length.

The strength of this line of form was incredible. Roland's Song went on to win another three G1s (14 career wins in all) and was described by Heming as the best she'd trained. Miss Averof herself won another three features as an older mare, but as it turned out the FNB 1600 was the last success she'd have for us.

Paddy Hinton's runners weren't left out in the cold. We'd bought consistently well throughout the 80s, Paddy and I, and our small yearling investments kept delivering, including Budget and Almanac, who came into their own when they reached four years of age and older.

Budget ended the year on a high note when he landed the G3 Caradoc Gold Cup over 3200m at Turffontein on Christmas Eve. He was a decent stayer, but we kept him out of the Gold Bowl – Vigliotto was the only runner needed that day – and he came into the Caradoc fresh and fit with a number of perhaps not so sprightly Bowl runners as rivals.

Weichong produced another fine ride. He kept Budget out of trouble when there was argy-bargy going on as the 12-horse field swung into the straight to head for the judge. Budget got away by a couple of lengths while Kadarko, Cincinatti and Born A Ruler were bumping and boring each other for position. Budget won, unchallenged.

In January 1990, on the halfway mark of the 1989/90 season, the stable was approaching 50 winners. We had six or seven runners competing at top level and a number of promising younger ones starting to emerge. Paddy and I were really enjoying our success and starting to toy with the idea of buying some stock overseas.

Hinton's six-year-old Almanac had reached the peak of his powers and struck early in the year when Weichong rode him to a good win in the Listed Turffontein Bookmakers Handicap over 2000m, defeating Jean Heming's Chattaronga.

The press corps found it quite amazing (and I guess so did I) when, next up, Almanac caught Roland's Song flatfooted in the G3 Newmarket Stakes and a runner from my yard beat the star mare for the third time running. "I found this a decidedly sad occasion," wrote David Mollett, describing the atmosphere on course and punters' faces. I don't take any delight in losses incurred by punters – I enjoy a winning bet too much myself – but this was a sweet victory in other ways.

Almanac's win, I recall, came at a time of sweeping changes in South Africa. State President F.W. de Klerk announced plans to end the system of Apartheid and the ANC's long-jailed leader, Nelson Mandela, was released from prison on 11 February, 1990. De Klerk also set in motion a series of steps that would lead to the formation of South Africa's first democratic government in 1994.

On his level of improvement we felt that Almamac would be good enough to point at the Durban July, and we'd identified the Podlas/Cambouris owned five-year-old, Lord Balmerino, as our other July hopeful. He proved to be a versatile horse who'd won two middle division handicaps over 1800m and 2000m early in 1990 and was also well on the upgrade.

Lord Balmerino's test, and his only way into Durban's flagship race was the G3 Woolavington Cup over 2400m at Clairwood Park on the last weekend in May. He shouldered only 50kg which gave us a big chance. Rainy conditions had cleared, but the track was on the sloppy side. In a slow-run race, Lord Balmerino rallied with good energy from midfield and Weichong pulled him away from the pack towards the stand-side rail. Nothing else ran on through the 300m-mark, no challenges were forthcoming and Lord Balmerino won easing down from Terrance Millard's Violero.

Hilda and Emmanuel were highly excited about Lord Balmerino, who'd now secured his spot in the Durban July and would come into the race with just 52kg. They got too excited actually, believing that their first July runner would be a winner. They started planning a trip for the July racing weekend for themselves and their acquaintances, and booked Weichong into the plush Beverley Hills Hotel in Umhlanga.

An improving horse with a low, galloping weight always has a chance in a handicap, but I wasn't sure Lord Balmerino had the makings of a July winner. He wasn't remotely in the class of a horse like Distinctly and would be facing several top horses including Terrance Millard's SA Guineas and Natal Deby winner Illustrador, and his Paddock Stakes and Fillies Guineas winner, Olympic Duel.

I didn't want to put a damper on the owners' enthusiasm. I'd seen too many horses improve almost beyond belief. We had a decent type of horse coming to his peak, and a chance of earning a July stake on his fitness and well-being alone.

We took Lord Balmerino and Almanac to the Clairwood Park training facility just outside of Durban, a few weeks ahead of the July to keep them ticking over and streamline their preparations. Everything went perfectly according to plan until about 10 days before the race, when Lord Balmerino turned in a below-par piece of work one morning. His coat was perfect, he was striding out well, eating up and had no temperature.

The next morning his work was average, again, most certainly below what he'd shown in the two weeks after winning the Woolavington. After another poor piece of work, we had Lord Balmerino fully examined by a veterinarian, from scoping his throat and lungs to checking his heart. We did everything possible to establish why he wasn't putting himself into his work. Absolutely nothing showed up and the strange thing was that the horse looked bright, happy and full of pep before and after every bad exercise gallop.

I reported Lord Balmerino's disappointing track work to Hilda and Emmanuel, who were not bumped off their cloud. They kept the belief that he was going to win the July and we agreed to push on, quietly hoping that he was just quirky and that he would wake up and produce a good run around several other horses and a racetrack full of July fans. Physically, he was a picture of health and fitness.

Here's the invariable twist. A week before the race, Weichong, his then girlfriend Annelie and two friends decided on a Friday night on the town and ended in a nightclub in Durban's city centre. During the course of the evening there were words between one of the men in Weichong's party of friends, and an intoxicated fellow-clubber from another group. This ended in a fight outside of the club. Things got physical, the drunk man fell and hit his head on the sidewalk curb. He died on the scene.

In the subsequent frenzy of police lights and media cameras, Weichong was eventually asked to fetch his car and drive his friends to the police station where their statements were taken. He wasn't even close to the scene when it happened - in essence, he drove his friends to and from the club. The media, however, latched onto the presence of our celebrity jockey. Early radio 'breaking news' and the first editions of newspapers reported that 'Durban July jockey Marwing' was being questioned in connection with a murder.

He didn't put a foot wrong, was just in the wrong place at the wrong time, and as a result Weichong was unfairly overrun with queries from worried family members, colleagues and reporters. He explained that he was completely innocent, but rumour about this kind of incident spread like wildfire and Hilda Podlas, for one, was highly upset that her horse's jockey was mentioned in connection with such a shocking occurrence.

Come July Day, with all the pomp and sparkle, the atmosphere in our group of connections, in the parade ring, is not exactly remembered for party streamers and balloons. There were sullen faces and Weichong got a few awkward stares.

Lord Balmerino, in turn, was a horse full of smiles. He looked as good as any of his seasoned rivals on the day and with his light weight, the hype around him and the apparent open nature of the race, went off as a firm 6-1 third favourite. Illustrador topped the boards at 33-10. On his looks, there was every reason to put our runner's weak work leading to the race at the back of our minds.

The 20-horse field jumped to the customary roar of the large Greyville crowd and Lord Balmerino survived the early scrum from his good inside draw. But he soon lost his position, came under pressure before the home run and flattened out badly. He stopped to nothing and finished last, beaten a distance by Illustrador, whose stable mates Olympic Duel and Jungle Warrior gave Terrance Millard a 1-2-3 in the race.

I can't recall if I saw Hilda or spoke to her again after that dismal Durban July. Weichong did. He was asked to leave his hotel as soon as possible and later heard that his 'involvement in a murder' was considered to have brought bad luck to Lord Balmerino.

The horse itself was found to have a sore back in the week after the race, and we had him treated by a veterinarian to start recovery. He hadn't shown any sign of a spine problem before the race, and to this day we don't know whether he was harbouring the injury or whether he hurt his back during the running of the July.

Back home, a week or so later, I received a call after the Gosforth Park meeting on 14 July – incidentally the meeting at which young riding sensation Piere Strydom rode all the winners of the Pick 6. It was Alison McKenzie, then editor of the SA Racehorse, who said she'd heard at the racetrack that Hilda and Emmanuel were moving their horses out of my stable.

"That's news to me," I said. "But thank you, thanks for that."

Early on Monday morning, 16 July, I asked David to gather Hilda and Emmanuel's horse blankets and their sets of silks from our colours room. Those were all neatly packed when Emmanuel arrived with his cheque book, mid-morning. Floats for their runners came later that day and their horses were taken to Randjesfontein, where jockey Garth Puller was placed in charge of them under trainer Peter Kannemeyer's banner.

As for the night club incident in Durban: The alleged murder was deemed to have been a case of self-defence and no charges were pressed against Weichong's friend.

The stable completed the 1989/90 season with 87 winners, a career best for me. I was about R75,000 clear of Terrance Millard on the stakes log going into the last meeting of the season at Clairwood on 30 July. But the Cape trainer's Olympic Duel won the G1 Mainstay on that day to give Terrance another National Title. I was pipped in the very last stride, as we'd say in racing. But we had some firepower coming through the ranks. A good season lay ahead…

CHAPTER 42

I want to take a brief step back to 1988 to tell you about St Just, a filly leased from Dr Neil and Lyth Orford of Bosworth Farm Stud in Klerksdorp, in the region then known as the Western Transvaal.

I'd trained a few offspring of the Bosworth stallion Hobnob (Gyr), including Royal Line. They were tough, sound horses that stayed all day. I often visited Neil and Lyth, who at times had unsold colts and fillies running around in their paddocks and gave me options to lease the ones I wanted.

One day, around September or October of that year, a diminutive chestnut filly caught my eye among much bigger fillies and colts in the Bosworth paddocks. She was just 'an inch and a ticky' high, would have been classified a 'pony' in the old days but she had good legs, everything in the right places and carried herself with a sense of pride. I liked that.

Neil Orford stood St Just's dam Cornish Rhapsody, a six-time winner he'd acquired in a lease deal of his own from a breeding farm in

Zimbabwe, where her owners revealed that she came from the most interesting of female lines. The story goes that, in the 1920s, three broodmares were on their way from England to Australia when the ship wrecked somewhere on the South African coast. One of the mares managed to survive the ordeal by swimming ashore courageously. She was the seventh dam of St Just and an educated guess can be made as to which of the mares she was, but that wasn't good enough for the Jockey Club.

A horse that carries less than eight crosses of thoroughbred blood, with 'thoroughbred' defined as 'a horse qualifying for the stud book of any recognised racing country', cannot be registered as such. St Just was a thoroughbred all right, but her registration was refused, and she couldn't go to a sale.

St Just's mystery seventh dam left a wonderful legacy through her third dam, Cornish, who bred no fewer than 14 winners including 14-time winner Corpora. Cornish's daughter, Cornette, as it were, found her way to breeder George Rowles in Mooirivier, and she visited Rowles' successful stallion Caerdeon, the nick that produced Cornish Rhapsody.

Registered all the way back or not, we can say with some certainty that gritty courage was passed through six generations to our powerful little chestnut who became a race filly of note, and one that will probably make my Top 10.

Leased on my behalf to Mervyn and Liz Gribble, St Just won her 1200m debut at Turffontein by 4,50-lengths and then placed in a couple of sprints on the Highveld early in 1989. But she was another who enjoyed her spell in Cape Town in the winter of that year, and she came back blossoming. She won over 1400m in August and, in October, was unlucky to go down a bob of noses to Alec Laird's smart colt, Warning Sign, in a C Division contest over 1600m at Turffontein.

THOROUGHLY!

St Just let loose after this, winning December's Gerald Rosenberg Stakes over 2000m at Newmarket, always a pointer to good staying fillies, followed by the John Lindbergh Memorial over 2000m at Gosforth Park in January 1990. This was a month before the release from prison of Nelson Mandela, one of the biggest events in the history of South Africa.

I hadn't won the SA Oaks since 1976, when Siberian Wonder took the honours, but I was certain that St Just would break our Oaks drought. I hadn't had this much faith in an Oaks contender since 1975, when Pretty Border won the memorable race described in an earlier chapter. On a hat-trick and in top form, I expected St Just to make light work of the 1990 Oaks over 2450m on 14 April, and we backed her to even-money favourite.

It was in St Just's nature to get involved in lengthy, nerve-wracking brawls. She loved to fight. This was a race that tested her mettle again, and had our hearts beating, double-time. Her rival this time was Proud To Be, a strong staying filly by Jamaico from Jean Heming's yard, and significantly bigger in frame than ours. They came together with 300m to run, with Frikkie Vermaak on Proud To Be throwing all but the kitchen sink at Weichong Marwing, riding St Just. They raced to the line virtually as one.

The pair of fillies and their riders were exhausted after the race, and so were all the shouting connections, because not the naked eye nor the race replay could separate them at the line. Frustratingly, the judge took his time too. This had been another tussle between two big stables and I'm sure Mrs Heming was holding her breath as much as I did. The photo showed that St Just had prevailed by the pearls of sweat on her nose! It could've gone the other way, I guess, but I was quietly starting to wonder whether St Just was one of those fillies who did just enough to win, even if she could do so with ease.

St Just recovered quick and showed no signs of fatigue in the week after the race so we kept her on target for the then G1 SA Fillies Guineas at Scottsville on 19 June, in which she would get to meet Terrance Millard's boom filly Olympic Duel for the first time. All went well, she took her place and ran a decent race, beaten into third behind Millard's runner, but looking just a little flat.

Perhaps her stiff outing in the Oaks did draw a little too much energy from St Just's reserves, but after the Guineas she sharpened again and we had her in tip-top shape for the G1 SA 2000 (today's Daily News) at Greyville, for which Olympic Duel was odds-on favourite and already the ante-post favourite for the Durban July.

With a few superb classic colts thrown into the SA 2000, including a future J&B Met winner in Divine Master and a future Durban July winner in Spanish Galliard, St Just came freely to punters in the 6-1 range, but she ran like she was the real deal in the race. And she was!

With her excellent record and weight advantage, Olympic Duel thrilled her supporters when she moved up from four lengths behind the leaders turning for home to join issue. She hit the front with 150m to run, but St Just, the little package of dynamite, raced right up to her for a memorable challenge. Olympic Duel gave her all under a typical, strong ride from Felix Coetzee, but St Just responded to her every move, took her challenger bravely to the line in a driving finish, and got up to win it under Marwing.

With seven wins from 13 starts, St Just was now recognised as champion three-year-old filly of South Africa and we were amazed at how this game little horse perked herself up and was ready for more after every race.

St Just's next big challenge was a showdown with Heming's Roland's Song, the champion older mare, in September's G2 Computaform Champion Stakes over 1800m at Turffontein. She was outpaced over the last 250m by the four-year-old, who was at her brilliant best on the day and beat us by 1,25-lengths.

St Just's encounters with Horse Of The Year, Roland's Song, captivated racing fans over the next six months. They met for the second time in December's Allen Snijman Stakes over 2000m at Gosforth Park in which St Just (Marwing), in receipt of 1,5kg, shot away from Roland's Song (Piere Strydom) in the short run-in and won by 2,25-lengths.

Both fillies were just short of peak fitness in March 1991, when they were beaten into second (Roland's Song) and third (St Just) respectively in Turffontein's Administrator's Champion Stakes by Gary Alexander's Naval Guest, ridden by Douglas Whyte.

I'd been 'oversubscribed', I guess, with the best jockeys riding in South Africa at the time. Whyte, Jeff Lloyd, Piere Strydom and of course Tobie van Booma were phoning for rides, and a newcomer from Peru had proven himself to be a jockey of note and was riding work regularly. His name was Guillermo Herrera-Figueroa, popularly known as 'Willy'. He couldn't speak a word of English, but communicated through an interpreter. His riding style was unconventional, but effective.

There are times in even the best of trainer-jockey relationships when one, or both, need a break from each other. While Weichong had proven that he was in the top bracket, SA champion Lloyd had made himself available to me as permanent stable jockey. Weichong wasn't happy to compete for my rides and decided he'd be best served as number one in another leading stable. He was instantly offered a job with my arch-rival Jean Heming, and left my yard.

I booked Strydom on St Just for her next encounter with Roland's Song, who now in the awkward change of allegiances had Weichong holding her reins in the G3 Newmarket Stakes over 2000m on 26

March. St Just received a kilo from the older filly at weight-for-age and she turned the tables smartly on the day, outpacing Roland's Song in the closing stages. There aren't many glances between former partners on days like these, it's a funny old game.

Personal splits and reversed rivalries are a part of the fabric of racing and it's something either party takes on the chin. Or hands back in a punch. I guess Weichong got his own back a month later, on 27 April, in the G1 Administrator's Champion Stakes, when it was Roland's Song's turn to beat us. I'd given Lloyd the ride on St Just, he didn't do much wrong but I suppose our filly simply got on better with Weichong, who would have enjoyed his victory on her biggest adversary.

The long and the short of it: Weichong was back in my stable after a few months in the employ of Heming, though St Just was never the same again. With the score unsettled on 2-2, she didn't cross swords with Roland's Song ever again, but also didn't win another race. She ran below her best in the Johannesburg Winter Handicap and the Jubilee Handicap. Not even re-uniting with her favourite jockey could recover her zest for racing – they finished downfield in the 1991 Durban July. She signalled that she'd come to the end of her time on the track. We retired her with 10 wins and 8 places from 23 starts.

St Just was the kind of filly every bloodstock investor wants to own, just once in a lifetime. Weichong described her as a filly with "a mighty will to win and a big heart".

She was all proud bravery, the little chestnut, a joy to train and we'll have the fondest memories of her, forever.

CHAPTER 43

Alan Forbes, fellow-trainer at Turffontein, was in the news in 1991. On the morning of 21 March, Forbes was sitting on the northern side of the racecourse watching his horses work, when he was attacked by a man wearing a balaclava. The assailant jumped over the fence and Forbes was hit over the head with a lead pipe.

The Star reported Forbes as saying: "Somebody gave me a helluva smack. I blacked out. I half came round and this bloke was spraying tear gas in my face. I thought this was the end. I kept getting hits to the head."

Police investigating the incident believed the intention was to kill Forbes, but the intervention of a passing jockey saved his life. The trainer suffered serious head injuries and was said to have spent several weeks in recovery.

The attack happened at a time when Forbes was fighting 'dope' charges pressed against him by the Jockey Club and fines imposed; and shortly after he and 16 other individuals instigated a Jockey Club investigation into alleged irregularities by stewards and officials in horseracing circles.

While this was going on, a series of other incidents occurred. There was a death threat against Wally Segal, the CEO of Gosforth Park, for whom, according to The Star, a Mafia-style hit was allegedly arranged at a fee of R100,000. Ronnie Napier, at the time Jockey Club Chairman, and Executive members Guy Hoffmann and Jules Horowitz, were threatened and had their properties damaged, while Hoffmann and Colin Dunn had shots fired at their homes and nasty slurs were said to have been spray-painted on their walls.

The matter was investigated by the Jockey Club's Investigating Officer, Captain Dirk Blignaut, as well as the South African Police, then a fully functional and competent unit. They interviewed a number of individuals, including myself, because there were some fingers pointed at me due to the fall-outs I'd had with Alan Forbes on the training track. Also, there was disunity at the time between the Transvaal Trainers' Association (TTT), who had Forbes at the helm, and the Owners and Trainers Association (OTA), of which I was Chairman.

I've been asked many times about the attack on Alan Forbes, even recently, and my answer is the same: *No, I had nothing to do with it.* There were dozens of people who had disagreements with Forbes over the years. He was not the most popular personality in racing circles. I was in the business of training horses and enjoying a wonderful season when he was attacked. I was not friendly with Forbes, but I didn't have the time, or the inclination, to be involved in an act of brutality against another person.

During his illness, Forbes was replaced at the TTT by Jackie Mills, who received a number of death threats too. It was reported that Wally Segal was opening a docket for defamation against Ian Jayes, a member of our OTA. Rumours and allegations persisted for some time. A reward of R100,000 was offered for information leading to the arrest of the perpetrators and anonymous tip-offs were encouraged by the Jockey Club, but to this day nothing's ever come to light.

Between 1990 and 1993, we had a terrific bunch of two-year-olds in the stable, and a dozen or so turned out be wonderful stayers. With the workload increasing and David making plans to take out his own trainers' licence, I employed Michael Clements as an additional assistant – a good move as he proved to be a horseman of calibre. We were a powerful team, saddling what I believe is still a record, 40 two-year-old wins in 1990/1 and 23 in 1991/2.

I'd bred a number of them at my Karoo Farm, Rooispruit, which made the wins even sweeter. They included Middelburg (End Of The Line), who won the G2 Gosforth Park Juvenile Stakes, and Colesberg. Other notables like Chasing Gold (Dancing Champ), Tight Drums (Hard Up), Peregrine Falcon (Fair Season), Piastar (Piaffer) and Sparkling Tandy (Crystal De Roche), won their fair share of races.

The stable's abundance of super staying types came to the fore as they matured, and lay at the heart of the two best seasons of my career, measured in winners and, at the time, in gross stake earnings. I didn't plan an assault on races for stayers when I bought them as yearlings. Things just came together when the members of this staying generation all happened to be well above average, and all were housed in my three barns at Turffontein. We racked up winner after winner.

The ones I will single out are Fast Break, Eaton Lad, Fluent Stride, Launching Pad and Fine Regent.

Fast Break (Foveros) showed her exceptional ability early for owners Syd and Sabine Harris. She reeled off a hat-trick of wins between May and August 1990, winning with consummate ease, stepping up from 1400m to 1900m and improving every time. She revealed herself as a definite SA Oaks contender.

Jeff Lloyd had to pull out all the stops to get Fast Break's head down in the SA Oaks Futurity Trial over 1800m at Newmarket on 5 March 1991, where Charles van Booma almost stuck us out with his mount, Cool Success.

Fast Break came to her peak after this run and was cherry ripe for the Oaks itself on 30 March, in which a surprise challenge came from our own LA Law, who was well inferior to Fast Break. Being by Hobnob, she kept grinding away at the favourite as they raced side-by-side over the last 200m. We had Piere Strydom on Fast Break that day and, he, too, earned his fee in a close finish in which LA Law was beaten a neck and we completed a 1-3-4 with So Sparkling running into the minor placing. Fast Break was my fourth Oaks winner.

Eaton Lad (Hobnob) was slow off the mark in 1990, but his staying ability was never in doubt and he got out of the Maidens over 1800m in October, at his sixth attempt. Weichong Marwing reported Eaton Lad giving him the feel of a decent marathon athlete that day – like most of the Hobnob progeny that came through my hands, this one just had endless reserves the further he raced.

I bought Fluent Stride for owner Chris von Solms at the 1990 National Yearling Sale, paying R85,000. He was a smart chestnut by the Alydar stallion, Steady Beat, who wasn't the most fashionable on the block, but the colt's looks and conformation had won me over.

We entered Fluent Stride for a Maiden Juvenile Plate on New Year's Day, 1991, and gave the young apprentice Andre Hoffmann a leg up. We quietly fancied him and the money came, but he found one too good on the day in Strydom's mount, Golden Galleon. Fine Regent (Del Sarto), bred for a mile-and-half, made his debut in the same race and that he managed to get within seven lengths of the winner was encouraging.

Fluent Stride won two Juvenile Plates over 1100m and 1200m in quick succession, one two weeks after his debut and another in February, both wins by three lengths in the hands of Jeff Lloyd. We fancied him to win April's G1 SA Nursery but, as fate would have it, we came up against Tony Millard's Empress Club, the so-called 'galloping gold-mine' – a seriously good filly who gave us a hiding on the day.

But I was impressed with Fluent Stride. We had a quality sort to work with here and I knew he'd furnish and improve over a bit further. In June 1991, still at two, he won a Graduation Plate against a good field of older horses by more than three lengths. Alec Hogg wrote in Racing Digest that this was the best performance he'd seen from a two-year-old in a decade. There were some expert retorts to this, I recall, but Alec was later vindicated in his opinion of our colt.

Fine Regent was all class. He had pace and stamina and won early over the specialist 1400m straight course at the Vaal, slamming Sir Como by over seven lengths in April 1991. As expected, he was also one to get better with maturity and he posted his second win as a late three-year-old in July 1991, winning a mixed Novice Plate over 1600m. He was shaping as a strong Derby prospect for 1992.

The career of Launching Pad (Great Brother) took a similar early trajectory as we saw with Eaton Lad. He, too, couldn't get out of his own way in races down the straight, but, stepped up in distance, he came to his powers quickly. He won his Maiden over 2000m and following that with a win in the Derby Trial to stake a Derby claim of his own.

Our 1991 Derby prospect, Eaton Lad, enjoyed a good preparation for his biggest engagement when he finished second to the useful Homero in a C Division Handicap over 2000m at Turffontein. But, like Fluent

Stride in the Nursery, he found one better on the day in Alec Laird's well-bred Sacred Jungle, who mastered him late in the race. Jockey Donovan Habib noted, like Marwing had done a few months earlier, that Eaton Lad had a ton in hand at the line, just failed to match the winner's finishing pace.

Eaton Lad had two ideal races to follow that year and he won both easily. He stretched home nearly two lengths clear in the St Leger over 2850m, beating a strong field, and then absolutely romped home in the 1991 OK Gold Bowl, giving us a third success in the stayers' showpiece. "Eaton Lad strung out the cream of South Africa's stayers like ducks on a pond," wrote Jeff Zerbst of the gelding's 6,25-length win in a race record 3:27,1s.

Eaton Lad was bred at Rooispruit from Syd Harris' mare Arniston, who was warned off after just one run because she was, as we say, a bit 'dilly'. She was assessed to be a danger to herself and others. But I advised Syd to breed with her and she had three foals before she died. We got lucky with Eaton Lad who ended his career a seven-time winner, and did us proud with a surprise sixth place to Spanish Galliard and a R35,000 cheque in the 1992 Durban July, drawn 18/19.

Fluent Stride started his three-year-old career winning a B Division Handicap over a mile by a whisker from Howitzer, showing his versatility. I wasn't sure that he'd be an out-and-out classic miler because my jockeys felt he'd see out 2000m and even further. We tried him in the G2 John Skeaping Trophy over 1800m, a race that always reflected quality. He was beaten into second, but it was another excellent run for a three-year-old.

With all the 'heavy artillery' in the stable, I was truly spoilt for choice when picking races for them in this memorable period. I had two, sometimes three or four decent horses to enter for races across the programme, across the country for that matter, and sometimes we had no choice – they had to race against each other.

Fluent Stride, Launching Pad, Fine Regent and two others named Valete (Take Your Place) and Copper Lustre (Beldale Lustre) were all good enough to contest the SA Derby. I nominated them for a race we expected to win for a fourth time, though they were at different stages of development and maturity and it was hard to pick between them.

They all had chances, perhaps I had a quiet fancy for Fine Regent, but Lloyd's mount Valete found most support on the day to start second favourite. Paddy Hinton's Launching Pad was at 5s, Fine Regent at 7s, Fluent Stride at 8s and Copper Lustre at 14s.

Mike Clements saddled our Derby quintet at Turffontein that day because Paddy and I had decided to fly to Australia for the Inglis Easter Sale (more about that in the next chapter) and David had started his solo training career with a small string in Cape Town. We were in our Sydney hotel, late on Saturday, 18 April, 1992, when Michael phoned to tell us that Paddy's Launching Pad had won the race by 3,25-lengths for jockey Willy Figueroa. Fluent Stride (Tobie van Booma) was second ahead of Fine Regent (Brett Smith) in third.

Launching Pad had turned out to be the most suited to the slow pace of the Derby and, whilst obviously overjoyed, we were surprised that he'd done it so easily. He won only one more race after this, the 1993 Len Harvey Memorial Handicap, and didn't train on the way we expected. Still, his name made the Derby Honour Roll, another feat for the Hinton-Ferraris partnership for which the best was still to come.

Fine Regent, who also raced in Paddy's Silks, turned into an awesome stayer. He was never beaten again. He and Lloyd settled the score with Launching Pad a month after the SA Derby in the Transvaal Tattersalls Bookmakers Stakes over 2000m, the first leg of the Newmarket Stayers Triple Crown.

On 2 June, in the second leg, the Computaform Derby over 2400m, he got the better of Launching Pad again, this time in Felix Coetzee's hands. Lloyd was back on him for a triumphant Triple Crown win in the St Leger over 2850m on 2 July. In between, Fine Regent also travelled to Durban to bag the Topsport Bloodline Derby over 2400m at Clairwood in which he rattled the cage of Space Walk, a horse who'd go on to win the 1994 Durban July.

Fine Regent won eight of 16 races before his retirement in 1993. A beautiful big, framed photograph of him winning the Triple Crown adorned the foyer of the Newmarket Members Facility for about 15 years before the course was closed in 2007. I wonder if that photo is gathering dust somewhere or if it was thrown out with the rubble when the grand old track was demolished.

Fluent Stride achieved his moment of historic glory at more or less the same time as Fine Regent. After the SA Derby, we prepared him for a try at the standard-setting G1 Daily News in which we were to face Empress Club, the filly who had captured the imagination of the racing public and had soundly beaten him in a sprint when they were juveniles.

The Racing Record reported a few years after the June 6, 1992, contest: "With every Gr1 race Empress Club won, the accolades got greater. Opinions in the popular press varied from 'the best horse in the country', to 'the best ever to race in South Africa'. She's the only horse in recent times to have had an official fan club. The first to have won R2 million. And if there was a Hall Of Fame she surely would be in it.

"After all this, the Gr1 Daily News 2000 looked in the bag. Bookmakers had the Empress at 1-10 with 10-1 bar, and rightly so as none of the nine colts in the line-up had any pretensions of being in her league. After breaking smartly (the way she usually does), jockey Coetzee dropped Empress Club quickly to the back-end of the field, in a position she had never held before. It looked to us like a dress rehearsal for the Rothmans July, where she was likely to carry a big weight and might not want to race handy.

"But in this race the tactics didn't work. The early pace was diabolical and Empress Club used her turn of foot as usual coming off the bend, but instead of carrying her comfortably into the lead she only just made the front and in a sandwich between Fluent Stride and Anarch at that. The filly fought back gamely (she certainly wasn't intimidated as some sources suggested), but simply had shot her bolt too early and through circumstances beyond her control. She was beaten a short head by Fluent Stride, with Gaelic Find running on well to be a close third. Empress Club ran some 15 pounds below her usual form. She wasn't seen out again after that."

It is probably true that we caught Empress Club on her off day, but it was most significant for us all the same. Fluent Stride, ridden by Anthony Delpech, helped me to secure a tight National Title race over Empress Club's trainer Tony Millard. Only R200,000 in gross stakes separated us at the end of the season on 31 July. The stats reflected my 116 winners (20%) and 298 places for R5,1-million in gross stable earnings. My first National Title came after 38 years of training, and it was a proud moment for my family and I.

CHAPTER 44

Now to the stories of two of my stable's most famous runners: Rakeen (1987 – Northern Dancer - Glorious Song), a noble and super horse who left a great legacy and Tracy's Element (1990 – Last Tycoon – Princess Tracy), an extraordinary race filly and a prolific dam of stars.

Larry Nestadt, the accomplished business tycoon and a patron in my yard from the 1980s until my final retirement, has been interested in pedigrees as long as I've known him. He was forever reading every available thoroughbred directory and the best local and overseas magazines. Late in October 1990, he stumbled across a horse for sale in the United Kingdom.

Not only was Rakeen the last racing son of the world's great foundation stallion Northern Dancer, but he was out of Canada's Horse Of The Year, the superstar broodmare Glorious Song (Halo), the 17-time winner and already the dam of the Riverman stallion Rivotious and an up-and-coming track star called Rahy. (She also sired Singspiel in 1992).

Rakeen had won his Maiden at three and had been entered for the Listed Cenotaph Stakes when Larry and partners Tawny Syndicate and Guy Landon made some inquiries with the office of his owner, Sheikh Mohammed bin Rashid Al Maktoum. After negotiating with Sheikh Mohammed, they put in an offer to purchase and their offer was accepted.

It appeared that Rakeen had issues with his joints – not the type of problem the world's major owners wished to deal with – and whilst he was a racing prospect still, he was considered best sold off rather than persisted with on the powerful UK racing circuit.

There was a sales agreement in principle and to his credit Sheikh Mohammed stuck to his word, even when Rakeen, trained by John Gosden and ridden by Walter Swinburn, won his second start, the Listed Cenotaph Handicap, on 10 November 1990. He was suddenly rated a high 99 by British form analysts, Timeform, who described him as an "attractive colt; useful and progressive."

Rakeen arrived at my yard early in 1991 and while he was an obviously impressive horse with a touch of class, his joints gave him trouble from day one, as we expected. I had to nurse him along carefully and patiently from race to race, taking the utmost care not only because of his stud value, but the actual ability he'd shown on the mornings we had him striding freely and running hard. He was a horse with the potential to win at the highest level, but his soundness was always a worry. He was unlucky, with his preparations frequently interrupted by days off.

The Citizen's Geoff Sinclair, a scribe known for his love of English racing, announced Rakeen's first start with fanfare under the headline "Big Horse Goes On Trial" and wrote on the morning of 23 April 1991: "If you hadn't heard the name yet, you will get a chance to see him at Newmarket this afternoon when the son of Northern Dancer makes his debut a Graduation Plate over 1800m. That Rakeen is actually racing in this country is possibly the coup of the decade for his owners."

One can't always blame the media for hype. Rakeen was worth it and while we felt some pressure, he raced to a never-in-doubt and decisive win under Jeff Lloyd, 4,50-lengths to the good in front of a crowd that included several old pedigree gurus dragged out of hiding for a visit to the Alberton track.

This eye-catching win made Rakeen a 'buzz' horse overnight and of course the media put us under pressure to get him into the 1991 Durban July. That was always the plan, but his joints were doing the dictating. I did not want to reveal too much to the press circus for obvious reasons, but we could only fit in two more qualifying runs of which he won a B Division Handicap over 2000m without fuss.

To our relief, Rakeen's Listed win in England and his two excellent local wins were considered good enough by the Durban July panel. He was allotted 51,5kg near the bottom of the handicap and while he was due to race in a truly powerful field (and having to be mollycoddled between prep gallops), he'd shown me enough progress in the six weeks leading to the July to get all of us excited. We confirmed Lloyd for the ride. Rakeen was better than his rating, ahead of the handicapper and, hence, in with more than an average shout.

Here's a few of what we had to beat on the big day: Al Mufti, Olympic Duel, Spanish Galliard, Flaming Rock, Bluffing, Sacred Jungle, Sand, Roland's Song, Naval Guest and our own St Just. The betting boards changed late as Flaming Rock was backed into favourite at 4-1 from Olympic Duel and Al Mufti at 5-1, Spanish Galliard at 6-1 and Rakeen at 7s.

Everything was in our favour except a 15-draw and one telling factor: the track condition at Greyville, which was rock hard on the day. It was the strangest thing, we had almost no rain in Durban that season and Rakeen felt his joints in the race. He ran his heart out, put himself powerfully in the drive to the line and challenged for victory, but was run out of it in the last two strides by a low-flying Flaming Rock, and Al Mufti. Just half-a-length covered the first three and I believe Rakeen would've won it if the sting was out of the ground.

We managed to get five more runs from Rakeen in the next eight months. He won the 1991 G3 OK Trial over 1400m and the G2 Allen Snijman Stakes over 2000m, retired at five with only one Grade 2 win to his name – not enough for stud glory on paper, but this is where things get interesting.

Larry and company stood Rakeen at Aldora Stud near Mooirivier in Kwazulu-Natal, where they were battling to get support from breeders. He covered two small crops and when his progeny got to the track in 1994, they all proved to be late maturers, sound enough and good-looking but slow off the mark. This was a death knell for future seasons as there was no confidence from breeders for the needed support.

A decision was made to sell Rakeen to Hill N Dale, the renowned Kentucky Breeders, where he stood for the next two seasons, but it was as if his departure lit a fire among his offspring in South Africa. Suddenly, as late three and early four-year-olds, runners sired by Rakeen in 1993 and 1994 were taking the tracks by storm from 1996 onwards. I trained a few of them, too.

First off the mark was Keeneland Gold (G3 OK Trial), followed by Jacob's Creek (G3 Vaal Stayers and G3 Worker's Day Handicap), Harvest Rose (G2 Gold Vase and G2 St Leger) and Keen Observer (G3). Then, as some pedigrees destined for greatness just seem to happen, Rakeen's mating with the ordinary two-time winner Jet Lightning (Rollins) produced Jet Master, the mighty racehorse, stallion and later sire of sires.

Given his obvious, but not immediately revealed talent as a stallion, Bernard Kantor and Mala Mala owner Mike Rattray decided to buy Rakeen back from Hill N Dale and bring him back to South Africa to stand at Lammerskraal Stud. He produced a host of further track stars in the 1990s including North By Northwest (G2 Premiers Handicap), Maiwand (G2 Premiers Handicap), Angelina (G1 Paddock Stakes), Young Rake (G1 Champion Stakes, G2 Colorado King Stakes, G2 St Leger), Rubirosa (G3 Spook Express Handicap) and well into the 2000s with Dream Idol (G3 Racing Association Handicap), Malteme (G1 Summer Cup) Likeithot (G2 November Handicap) and Red Rake (G2 Midmar Trophy).

Back to Jet Master. He had an astounding racing career despite being plagued by breathing problems. He posted 17 wins - eight of those being Grade 1 races, including winning the Queen's Plate twice, and was Horse Of The Year twice.

Jet Master's offspring won the G1 J&B Met five years running, from 2007 to 2011, left behind more than 70 stakes winners and over 130 stakes horses. He sired 22 G1 winners, who were produced by daughters of 16 different stallions. The champion left behind 48 G1 performers, and his offspring won the majority of South Africa's top races, including the Vodacom Durban July twice with Pocket Power and Pomodoro.

Jet Master was a R15,000 yearling bought and owned throughout his career by my erstwhile patron and sparring partner, Henry Devine. In his prime, Jet Master stood for R200,000 a pop!

I mentioned in a recent chapter that Paddy Hinton and I were away in Australia when his colt Launching Pad won the SA Derby in 1992, but this was the most inspiring and worthwhile trip of my life.

Due to the bloodstock import protocols we weren't able to buy in Australia when we may have wanted to, but the red tape had been cut and the Australians were keen to do business with us. The Inglis Sales Company made attractive buyers' packages available and a group of us, including Herman Brown Sr. and Len Salzman, left for Sydney in the second week of April to attend the Inglis Easter Sale.

I was excited about this auction because in my pedigree research I'd always been attracted to the offspring of Last Tycoon (Try My Best), a top racehorse in his own right who'd won a sprint and a Group Mile and was making a name for himself at stud, initially in Ireland. There were a number of his yearlings on sale and I hoped that we could get a blow in and perhaps buy one of them.

It was a long flight and when we eventually got through customs and booked into our hotel, Paddy suggested we rest a bit and start our search for a good buy the next day. But I told him I wasn't accustomed to sleeping during the day, so I unpacked and left for the sales complex alone, keen to see what was on offer.

I was only at the sales site for a short period of time when a string of yearlings from Segenhoe Stud came walking by and the leader of the group took my breath away. It was Tracy's Element, who happened to be a filly by Last Tycoon. Her female line also looked good because her dam, Princess Tracy, had won two Group sprints in Ireland.

Everything about Tracy's Element was perfect. She was physically outstanding from top to toe, with great legs, and I could hardly contain my excitement when I met with Paddy at the hotel a few hours later.

I said, "Paddy, I've found a Last Tycoon filly for us, she is perfect, we don't need to look any further!"

He replied, "You're joking, how many did you see? What about the rest of the catalogue?"

We discussed her pedigree and Paddy was sceptical, at first. He didn't think we'd be able to afford her. "I agree, this is a good pedigree but I'm not sure we have enough money to buy her!"

"But let's try anyway, I think she's special," I said, and eventually he agreed and we went to the sale the next day armed with a limited cheque book and a whole lot of hope.

Surprisingly, and to our eternal delight, we secured Tracy's Element for $AUS 100,000 in hardly a bidding war and that was it. We walked around with our chests out and believed we had bought the bargain of the 1992 Inglis Sale. She was shipped to South Africa for her proud new owners.

We've all heard hundreds of similar stories, and there are guaranteed thousands more of buyers through the ages who believed they outwitted their rival buyers only to be gravely disappointed when their runners got to the track. We, of course, were incredibly fortunate to be proven right by a rare specimen of superior thoroughbred horseflesh that became a track sensation.

There are many silent prayers that go up when one sends an expensive or highly regarded colt or filly through its paces for the first time. On the first day, Willy Figueroa, the Peruvian who was doing most of my work riding, reported something in broken English that sounded like lavish praise. 'Figgy' got more excited with every gallop and when she was ready for her first run, I gave him the ride.

Tracy's Element stepped out against winners in a Juvenile Plate at Newmarket on 17 December, 1992, racing in the dark blue and white silks of Maura Hinton. Our jock was never hard on his mounts and he tried to keep the filly in check for as long as he could, but sheer class and her natural galloping power saw her to a win of 10,25-lengths over Sister Shirley.

She won two more on the trot for Figueroa, including the Listed Morris Lipschitz, before we switched jockeys to Jeff Lloyd and then to Weichong Marwing. Wins in the G1 Smirnoff Plate and G2 JB Mcintosh Fillies Classic ensured that Tracy's Element ended her first campaign with acknowledgement as the best of her year. She was duly named the ARCSA Champion Two-Year-Old Filly of 1992.

That, unlike many other juvenile stars, would not be the final award of the filly's brilliant career. Tracy's Element went on to win a further six races, another ARCSA award (Champion Older Female Sprinter in 1994), and build a reputation for herself as one of the finest sprinting fillies to race in South Africa.

Her victories included a win in the 1994 G1 Star Sprint (where her beaten rivals included paternal half-sister, Super Sheila, and outstanding producer, Secret Pact), and gallant scores in both the G1 Computaform Sprint and SA Fillies Sprint in 1995 – two pinnacles for sprinters in South Africa.

Tracy's Element's career record showed 11 wins and 3 places from 19 starts and just under R1-million in stake earnings when she lined up for the G1 Golden Spur at Scottsville on 25 June 1995. She had an off day, ran unplaced and the Hintons decided to retire her. At this juncture, however, things went pear-shaped between Paddy and I. I clearly remember the Springboks beating the All Blacks in the Rugby World Cup Final the previous day. We were all overjoyed for them, but the filly's below-par run put a dampener on things. I wanted Tracy's Element to stay on for breeding in South Africa, in fact I reckoned she had another win in her, but Paddy believed she was too valuable for our breeding paddocks.

In the weeks following her retirement, I was aware that a deal was being brokered in which Tracy's Element would be sold back to Australia, but Paddy had suddenly gone quiet. My wife, Maureen, phoned me at the stables to say, "Ormond, surely you're entitled to your percentage of the sale? Look at what this filly has achieved, they're leaving you in the cold!"

Paddy and Maura arrived at the stable one morning, unannounced, and said they were coming to say goodbye to their special filly. I felt uncomfortable while they patted and hugged Tracy's Element. They still hadn't officially announced the sale, but it had clearly been completed.

When the Hintons left that day, without an official word of the sale, an era came to an end. I phoned him and said, "Paddy, this is not right. I am hurt, I feel like turning up training. Presents and commissions are a part of sales all over the world, and you owe me!"

That was the last time we ever spoke, and I never saw Paddy or Maura again. To this day, I do not know the amount they received for her, and I never saw a cent of the proceeds. And so ended a friendship of some 32 years that started in the 1960s. Paddy and I were almost unbeatable through the days of Wagga Wagga, Brave Persian, Sandfly, Fine Regent, Almanac and many others, and he made plenty of cash betting on them too. We were close, inseparable for many years, but our friendship ended abruptly.

Tracy's Element became a top broodmare in Australia, producing among her first progeny the unraced but later successful broodmare Traceable, also winning geldings Hanover and Baltic Cove.

Her first foal of real note was born in 2001, to the cover of top sire Red Ransom. This was the filly Kylikwong, who was placed in a number of group races, and ran a good second in the G1 South Australian Oaks of 2005. Kylikwong herself has made her mark at stud.

Kylikwong was then followed by her winning full sister, Element of Danger, and a Red Ransom colt named Red Element. A high-class racehorse, Red Element won a pair of stakes races and ran third in the G2 Sir Byrne Hart Stakes to G1 winner Swiss Ace.

Tracy's Element's finest hour came in the form of her 2005 foal – a full sister to Kylikwong and Red Element. This was the magnificent Typhoon Tracy, who won no fewer than six Australian Group One races, and was named Horse Of The Year in 2009-2010. In 2010, Tracy's Element herself was named the TBQA's Broodmare Of The Year.

Aggrieved and disappointed with Paddy Hinton and probably upset with the entire racing industry too, I decided to follow through on my final words to my former friend. At the end of the 1994/5 season, I turned up my stable and my horses were transferred to my son, David.

CHAPTER 45

I need to tie up a few loose ends between 1991 and 1995 for the sake of keeping this writing comprehensive and before I go on to 1996, a dark year for our family.

With the stable still growing after our first National Title in 1991/2, and with David settled on his own with a small string in Cape Town, I employed Weiho Marwing and John Buckler as assistant trainers alongside Mike Clements. Judy van der Merwe came on board as my personal assistant to take care of my growing administrative duties needed in the stable and the Trainers Benevolent Fund.

In 1992/3 we had fewer winners, down to 82 from 116 but there was still enough firepower in the yard to finish second to Tony Millard on the National Log. The best performers alongside Rakeen and our group of classic colts were Daddy's Darling (Elevation), who won the SA Oaks in 1992 and Lambarina (Dancing Champ), who gave us a fourth successive Oaks winner in 1993 and our sixth in total.

Daddy's Darling was leased from the Birch Brothers and she raced for Tony Pereira, who owned a butchery in Lambton, Germiston. Tony had only a brief career in racing but was quite lucky, though we battled to get a win from this little chestnut as a two-year-old. We tried her over 1200m-1600m between January and July 1991 and used Piere Strydom every time, but not even 'Striker' could get her into the winner's box.

In her first start at three, in August, Daddy's Darling turned the corner and won her Maiden at her sixth attempt for Weichong Marwing. She ran on well on the tricky straight mile at the Vaal and then won again over 1600m at Turffontein, in October. She made more progress into 1992 with a 1900m win in February.

We had some musical chairs going on with Marwing going freelance, Strydom in demand all over and Lloyd travelling between provinces, so I gave the ever-reliable Figueroa a leg up on Daddy's Darling. They won the Oaks Trial on 20 March 1992, following this just a month later with her Oaks win over Sparkling Tandy, Lazuli and Dancing By, a 1-2-3-4 for the stable.

On hardworking jockeys, let me throw in a quick tribute to Michael 'Muis' Roberts, who in 1992 rode winners for no fewer than 57 trainers in his quest to boot home over 200 winners in a UK season. He ended that British flat season with 206 winners and the UK title, a feat equal to winning a golf major but never really recognised as one of the greatest achievements by a sportsman in South African history.

It was Lloyd's turn to shine for us again in 1993, when Advocate Altus Joubert's filly Lambarina (Dancing Champ), also completed the Oaks Trial/SA Oaks double, for which she won Champion Highveld three-year-old filly in 1993.

Summer Line, another filly by the stunning sire Hobnob, was a chestnut in the St Just mode, not as good, but possessing her fair share of courage and a good deal of stamina. She was owned by Professor Willie Herbst and we thought of her as a potential seventh Oaks winner in 1994, but she failed by a long neck at that hurdle, going down to outsider, Victoria Bay.

The Scott Brothers were one of the Millard empire's major patrons and I only ever trained two or three runners for them, including a brief time with Sizzling Sun, a gelding by Father Rooney who'd won four races for Joe Joseph in Natal. He was on the upgrade when Des Scott sent him to me to campaign for the big prizes on the Rand late in 1993.

Sizzling Sun won the G3 Administrator's Handicap at Newmarket under Tobie van Booma, finished second in the G2 Allen Snijman and then, in March 1994, got up to win the R1,25-million Administrator's Cup over 2000m for Marwing. Des was very happy, he was there to lead the horse into the winner's enclosure that day.

Sizzling Sun was sold to a Mauritian buyer after his big win. He was a lovely horse that I really enjoyed training, but sadly died of colic before he could race on the island.

The stable's fifth and sixth SA Derby winners came courtesy of The Monk (1994) and Travel North (1995). Both had the attribute of class. They could sprint; compete over middle distances and stay over ground, like only the good ones do. I am sometimes baffled by some of today's younger generation of trainers who find it hard to map out careers of top horses using different yardsticks on the distance spectrum. When you find a good horse, they'll give you what you ask of them.

The Monk was bred as well as they come, by then champion stallion Foveros out of the excellent stakes-winning mare Winter Lass who, as I explained earlier, was taken away from me to a rival trainer because I wanted to send her to the Cape as a member of my customary winter contingent in 1984. Ironically, a decade later, The Monk found its way to me courtesy of his breeder and part-owner Gernot Eckert who raced him in partnership with, you guessed it, Kim and Carol Latilla, Winter Lass' original owners. Bygones.

The Monk went from his 1300m Maiden win to a Graduation win over 1800m and his G1 Derby win over 2450m under Marwing. He won the Listed Newmarket Stakes over 2000m for Figueroa as a late three-year-old and then, at four, won us another Gold Bowl over 3200m. This renewal was sponsored by IGN and was run a few days after the scheduled date following heavy rain. Lightweight, Stephen Jupp, was booked on The Monk, he rode a great race in a strong field to hold off the Tony Millard powerhouse, Surfing Home. Our own runners, Travel North and Pinehurst, took third and fourth, respectively.

I associate The Monk with John Noble (CBE), who worked for the British Trade Commission at the time and is today still involved with the British Chamber of Commerce. John was introduced to me by Tony Ruffel and, when he came to visit the stable, he took a liking to our stayer. A keen amateur rider, he actually started riding The Monk around the training paddocks and his visits became more frequent until he departed back to London.

John was (I am sure still is) a pleasant and likeable man I enjoyed spending time with and who has sent me postcards and messages ever since. Just last Christmas (2021), I received another note from him in the mail. There are still true gentlemen in this world.

The Latillas also partnered to race Travel North, a stoutly bred horse by Northern Guest out of Travel Along, by St Cuthbert. I bought him as a yearling for Chris von Solms of Fluent Stride fame and he was all quality and even better than The Monk.

Travel North won two races over 1000m, before a gutsy win in the Natal Breeders Challenge over 1800m, when he showed he was a serious thoroughbred. He was as game as they come again in the G2

Dingaans over 1600m when, partnered by Figueroa, he defeated the likes of future star racer and stallion, National Emblem.

By the time the Derby came on 22 April, 1995, Travel North had furnished into a big, strong and beautiful horse. He made his rivals look average in a three-length success under Figueroa. In December of that year, Travel North was one of my last winners before I called it a day. He was wonderfully brave again in fighting off Mike de Kock's filly Drum Taps in the Caradoc Gold Cup over 3200m. Travel North won several races for David, too, and ended his career with 10 wins and 14 places to his name.

I'd asked David to wrap up his Cape operation so he could take over, back at Turffontein. I was still upset and hurt by what had happened with the sale of Tracy's Element. Having been involved as my assistant for a long time, David knew and got on well with all my patrons, including the Hintons, Larry Nestadt, Greg Blank, Peter O'Connor and others. He had proven himself a good trainer in his own right.

As for me, the old man, I went out on a great high and a gloomy low. I'd won my second National Trainers' Championship, almost R1-million clear of David Payne, Patrick Shaw and Tony Millard, saddling 78 winners in the 1993/94 season, and a further 73 in 1994/95. But I was troubled and unhappy and my wife, Maureen, forever an inspiration, had to keep me standing and fighting to regain my composure.

CHAPTER 46

The leap year 1996 was perhaps a good year to retire, but after some consideration, I didn't. I took out an owners/trainers' licence to stay involved without the aggravation of patrons, and to keep my mind occupied. At 63, I'd probably fooled myself into thinking that it was time to buy a walking stick and hobble off into the sunset.

I was watching upsetting things unfolding around the world, a time of depression and fear and a popular belief that the end was nigh. I didn't want to sit in a rocking chair all day to wait for the outcomes. There were wars happening in the Middle East and on the borders of Russia. Suicide bombers, those craziest of the crazy, were taking their own and many other innocent lives in droves. A madman walked into a school in Dunblane, Scotland, and opened fire, killing 16 children.

Free-for-all violence ruled in Burundi, where the Hutu tribe wiped out over 800,000 Tutsis; just south of that a terrible dictator was re-elected as President of Zimbabwe; there were massacres in Lebanon, Egypt and Port Owen; hurricanes, tornadoes and heavy rains in the United

States; an assassination in Liberia and the election of Bill Clinton as US President. Locally, former State President of South Africa, F.W. de Klerk, made an official apology for crimes committed under Apartheid to the Truth and Reconciliation Commission in Cape Town.

The good that came of my handing over to David was that my son finally got his chance to be the master of a yard with many top runners, a spell that would lead to him winning his own National titles and later building a successful career in Hong Kong.

I moved to a small barn at Turffontein while David was running my old yard with great success, assisted by John Buckler. They were winning race after race and gaining popularity and new patrons. He had several feature contenders in the stable, including Divine Force, Storm Champ, Vogue, Kushka, Super Quality, Daphne Donnelly and North By Northwest.

David was doing well, getting everything right and the last thing I wanted to do was make a nuisance of myself or interfere. While I was missing my big string of runners, I could proudly watch as David announced himself to the industry as a horseman to be reckoned with.

Things took an unexpected turn at 4 am on the morning of 28 August, 1996, when I woke up to prepare for the day ahead. I'd just gotten up when I heard, 'Bam! Bam! Bam!' in the distance. Suddenly, I was wide awake.

"Did you hear that?" I asked my wife, Maureen. She did, and I said: "Those were gun shots, somebody's shooting down in the valley."

David and his wife Pam lived in a house in Glenanda, about eight blocks away from my own house, which was just up the hill in adjacent Glenvista, hence my concern.

THOROUGHLY!

To my shock, the phone rang right then and Pam, understandably in a state of distress, cried out: "David's been shot, he's been shot, come quick, please come!"

I will be correct in saying that one can only know what a message like this feels like when you receive one, and there will be readers who have gone through similar ordeals in our troubled land. It's a feeling of great concern mixed with desperation and anger and constant thoughts of what you'll find on the other side of the call.

The real ordeal, of course, was suffered by David, Pam and stable apprentice Derryl Daniels, who was staying with them at their residence for a part of his apprenticeship, and what had transpired was horrible.

I rushed to my car and drove down to David's house, where I found him lying in a pool of blood, with Pam and Derryl sitting by him, and an ambulance said to be on the way.

Derryl relayed what had happened: David and Pam got into their old, canopied Isuzu truck (bakkie), with Derryl and their two dogs on the back – from the inclined driveway of their house on their way to the stables – a routine they followed every morning.

When the driveway gate opened, David rolled the truck down in 'neutral' and moved forward slowly and out, waiting for it close. Just then, a man emerged from the darkness behind a tree, outside and close to the gate. He started firing at the car. Derryl said he saw two orange flashes as the first two shots went off and he ducked for cover. The gunman was a tall individual in a blue jacket with brown trousers. A balaclava covered his face.

Behind the wheel, David was hit in the neck by one bullet, miraculously missing four others. His saving grace was that the truck kept rolling, out of gear, so the gunman wasn't able to take precise aim. It ended up across the road, coming to a standstill against the sidewalk curb. Pam threw her door open, got out and escaped the bullets herself.

My courageous son, bleeding and in pain, retrieved his own firearm, fell out of the bakkie, got up and started chasing the gunman, who had emptied his magazine. He was running away as screams went up and other household lights went on.

But David didn't get very far when he felt, and saw, the extent of his injuries. He stumbled back to Pam and Derryl and collapsed.

There wasn't much we could do but wait, try to stop the bleeding and keep David as calm as possible for an agonising several minutes before the ambulance arrived. He was conscious, but battling when they picked him up for the nearby Mulbarton Hospital, where he was referred to Alberton's Union Clinic and emergency surgery was carried out.

I said to Derryl, "Let's take a drive and see what we can find", so we drove up and down the street and into the adjacent areas and got as far as the suburbs close to Turffontein Racecourse. Derryl kept saying that the gunman was unusually tall and this struck a nerve I couldn't put my finger on.

In Forest Hill, we actually found a scooter lying on its side, at the side of the road, and there were some people gathered around it. I asked, "What happened here? Did you see something?"

They told us that a man had abandoned the scooter and ran off to the next block, where there was a taxi rank. He was said to have gotten into one and had left the scene.

"He was tall, and he had a big Adam's Apple," said one bystander whilst gesturing with his hand on his own throat.

Then it struck me. The only unusually tall guy with a prominent Adam's Apple I was familiar with, was Arnold Forbes, son of Alan

Forbes, the former Turffontein trainer who had passed away several months prior to this incident. I felt weak and dizzy and had to sit motionless in the car for a while, pondering over this piece of information. What had just happened here?

David was in surgery for hours with a bullet having to be removed from his neck. He was lucky to be alive. Many friends and acquaintances came to Union Hospital, and there were gatherings in the waiting room as we discussed the matter, speculated and waited for news.

David pulled through. He was tough as nails. A typical Ferraris, all he wanted to do was get back to his horses. The bullet that had struck him in the throat caused extensive damage to his vocal cords. He battled for weeks to speak and during the course of time was left with a gruff-sounding voice that took many years to recover sufficiently and still sounds hoarse.

Detectives came to investigate the matter soon after the shooting and we were questioned. I told them I believed that Arnold Forbes was the gunman and I warned that he would try to skip the country. But they missed an opportunity to catch him and a few days later we were informed that Forbes had left South Africa on a one-way ticket to the Indian Ocean Island of Reunion. That may have been (a very unlikely) coincidence, but Forbes was later also identified by the shop where he had bought the scooter. It was him, all right!

Around November of 2000, Forbes was arrested, expected to appear before a 'Chambre d'Accusation' court in Reunion where authorities on the French-owned island were said to have launched a legal process for his extradition, but this never happened. It was later also reported that his assets in South Africa had been sold.

This is not a matter David, or anyone in the family likes to discuss, but we have recounted it here because it does serve to illustrate the emotions stirred up by the high-intensity sport we all adore, and the frightening depths individuals in the racing industry can sink to. David, unfairly, became the victim of one heinous act of wholly misplaced anger and ensuing attempt at revenge.

CHAPTER 47

South Africa's Gambling Act of 1965 prohibited all forms of gambling except horseracing, perhaps the single most important reason for the massive growth and popularity of our sport throughout the 1960s, 70s and 80s.

Things changed after the first democratic election in 1994. Come 1996, the National Gambling Act legalised gambling establishments and the National Lottery. The Lotto was marketed with big bells and whistles on National TV and high-profile casinos sprung up all over the place, most of them linked to major hotel groups.

Spoilt for choice and novelty, gamblers started experimenting with the new 'easy ways to riches', massive numbers of individuals got hooked and, sadly but predictably, horseracing suffered. The defection of betting clients to other forms of gambling was first and glaringly noticed at the different race tracks where crowds started dwindling and gate fees were soon dropped for free entry to all. The age restriction of 18 was lifted to allow families onto the course with their kids, and hoping to foster love and appreciation for horses among youngsters.

The introduction of night racing at Newmarket in the second half of the 1996 caused excitement among old and new racing fans, with a turnout of more than 7 000 for the opening night on September 29. The evening's main race was won by our old friend Mike de Kock's Irish Ranger, ridden by jockey Greg Cheyne. A record R8-million was wagered on the nine-race programme but that would be the biggest handle and largest crowd to attend the Alberton track until it was closed in 2007.

Believe it, David, the wounded iron man, made it to the first night meeting just a month after he was shot. He'd recovered to an extent that he could attend his string's morning gallops within three weeks after his operations and he wanted to be at South Africa's first meeting under lights.

Those midweek night races were popular into the 2000s, though we all noticed a steady decline in racegoers and turnover. Newmarket, in its prime, hosted flourishing bookmakers, pubs and food stalls around the track on the ground level. They closed down, one by one, as the attendance figures fell. I think Rafael, the super schwarma chef, stuck it out to the bitter end, but he was the only one.

On-course bookmakers were also dealt heavy blows in this time. With fewer and fewer customers on course, most moved to premises away from the racetrack. Others gave up. My mate, Raymond Rhodes, tried his hand at bookmaking when he retired from riding in the mid-90s and he operated a betting stand near the Newmarket member's entrance. He shouldn't have done that, burnt his fingers and closed his shop, but that's a story for another day.

The huge floodlights and eventual complaints from nearby residents were a talking point and in time became a bug bear for racing's authorities. With betting turnovers on the decline and the cost of running the four Highveld race tracks increasing, there was talk of this venue being on the chopping block as early as 1999.

THOROUGHLY!

In April 1997, South African racing and breeding received a well-needed boost when SA trainer Alec Laird's SA-bred London News (Bush Telegraph) won the QEII Cup under SA-born Douglas Whyte. Alec paved the way for a number of our trainers who ventured overseas in the 2000s, and our bloodstock was in demand for a while.

David, the shooting setback notwithstanding, took his first Trainers' Title in his first full season with 114 winners and over R6-million in gross earnings in 1996/7. Two of my former assistants finished in the Top 6. Mike de Kock was second and Michael Clements, who had moved to Zimbabwe, took sixth place.

David's big-race wins included his first Durban July in 1997 with Super Quality (Elliodor), a 15.1-hand horse with a heart that filled his frame. He won the Cape, Computaform and SA Derby in the same year and will always be remembered in racing history as the horse who gave Michael Roberts the July winner he had desperately sought to win for the best part of 30 years.

Even when 'Muis' reached the pinnacle of his career winning the UK title in 1992, he told the media that the 'July' remained his life's ambition. He was in South Africa, visiting for a short period, when David offered him the ride on Super Quality and, aged 43, he finally achieved his dream on a memorable and emotional day.

Ironically, Super Quality was owned and raced in the silks of my former best friend, Paddy Hinton, who moved over to David's yard after our disagreement over Tracy's Element. I guess some things aren't meant to be. Muis, and David for that matter, were destined to win this great race. I wasn't. David, in fact, won it again in 1998 with Classic Flag (Allied Flag), a tremendous training feat with a horse of the same small size as Super Quality and perhaps an even bigger heart. Classic Flag was owned by Prof Willie Herbst and ridden by Anthony Delpech, who started a super winning run with David and would join him in Hong Kong several years later.

The statistics show that I saddled only 26 winners between 1995 and 1998, when I was ambling along, downcast and not exactly motivated. I couldn't find a decent horse to get me excited in this time and it seemed as if my career was indeed doomed to a rather dreary end.

I retired for a second time at the end of 1998 and turned my attention to the things old, forgotten horsemen were supposed to do.

CHAPTER 48

Maureen and I spent some quality time relaxing, or in my case trying to relax, at my Rooispruit Farm in the Karoo in 1996 and parts of 1997. There was breeding stock coming through from our resident stallion, Bel Byou, and some of them looked promising.

At home, in Johannesburg, I did a bit of gardening and had time for afternoon tea, but how much gardening can one do? And how many episodes of 'Oprah' can one watch before they drive you delirious? My green thumb felt like it was getting some arthritis, and television got boring, though the death of Diana, Princess Of Wales, shocked the world in August 1997. I didn't enjoy my life at home. I needed to be with my horses.

Perhaps, I should have stuck it out with the handful of runners in my single barn and not given up for six months. The interruption put me back for longer than that, in business terms, because horses that would have come to me migrated to new, up-and-coming stables, a number of owners left racing and I was out of the limelight for the first time in decades. I took myself out of the natural flow of the game and paid the price of having to start virtually from scratch.

But in the second half of 1997, I came back anyway, like I did from my sheep farming adventure in 1967. I got my single barn cleaned out and ready for work again. I renewed my owners/trainers licence, raced a dozen or so of my own runners and then took out an open licence again when, approaching the turn of the century, I was offered a few outside horses to train. There was a demand for my services again.

Racing on the Highveld was preparing for crucial changes. Jabu Moleketi, the Finance Minister for Gauteng, began pushing for the corporatisation of the sport in the province. The major turf clubs were registered as non-profit section 21 companies that belonged to their members — racehorse owners, trainers and lovers of the sport.

It was said that, due to severe financial distress to the racing clubs, they approached the Gauteng provincial government for relief in the form of reduced Tote tax rates. As a pre-condition to reducing the Tote tax rates, the Gauteng government was said to have insisted upon corporatisation, the introduction of appropriate, broadly based black economic empowerment and that the company obtained a listing on the Johannesburg Stock Exchange (JSE).

It was further advanced that corporatisation and listing on the JSE was a requisite in order to ensure proper corporate governance, true transparency and accountability and to enable meaningful black empowerment at shareholder level.

In 1997, Gauteng signed a memorandum of understanding with the racing industry, including representatives of the three major Gauteng turf clubs. The most significant stipulation was that that racing and betting in the province would in future be managed by one corporation, Phumelela Gaming and Leisure Ltd. The Racing Association

(RA) was established to represent owners and members of the three Gauteng turf clubs, Turffontein, Gosforth Park and Newmarket, and members of the Gauteng Racehorse Owners' Association joined the RA.

Members were asked to dispose of their assets to Phumelela, certain pledges were made to them regarding facilities, racing opportunities and stakes. Brian Mehl, the spokesman for the proposed company and who subsequently became CEO of Phumelela, at meetings leading up to corporatisation, promised that the ethos of horseracing would be maintained; facilities would be kept in good condition and where necessary extended and more racing opportunities would be created for the horses.

This, as my fellow trainer and late colleague Ian Jayes wrote in Sporting Post, was the start of 'one long, cold winter of discontent', and what would transpire over the next decade (and thereafter) was "the ugly face of capitalism".

I, and any number of others, saw storms brewing on the horizon. We were opposed to the sudden and wide extent of the changes, the shift of controlling power to a select few and other potential ramifications of corporate management. But as we see so often in politics and business money talks, palms are greased and laws that suit the power-wielders are steamrolled into place in front of God and everyone. Life goes on with new structures in place before you wipe your eyes.

In focusing on running their businesses, the majority of trainers, owners and other individuals working in racing just didn't have the time, coherence or the money to oppose the procedures that had been set in motion. Racing is a 24/7 business that requires the full attention of those who make a living from it. For some, the new leadership presented a vision that safeguarded the sport and secured a future and carried an element of the new, so it had to be supported or at least given a chance.

A stakes agreement finalised in August 1999 stipulated the amount Phumelela was required to pay to owners if their horses win a place in a race, and linked to totalisator turnover. This, in the years to come, proved to be one of the biggest bones of contention.

I laboured my way through to the year 2000 with mainly two good racing prospects, Cholula and Mardi Gras, who won 16 races between them. They gave me a much-needed lift, and I regained my composure and belief in myself.

Cholula was a daughter of, yes, Hobnob, bred by the Orfords at Bosworth Farm. She was a big, late maturing full-sister to a top colt named Topa Inca, who'd won the Dingaans and the Derby in 1990. They kept her in the paddock due to her backwardness and sent her to me as a three-year-old on a lease agreement. As I'd hoped but not quite expected, she turned out to be a magnificent stayer.

I couldn't follow my customary route to the SA Oaks, she just came in too late and I aimed her successfully at features for older fillies and mares. Cholula was in the same mould as my six previous SA Oaks winners. It's a pity her name will never be on the honour roll but she was special in many other ways. She won 11 of 25 starts, including the G2 Gerald Rosenberg and two Listed stakes races, just missed a place to El Picha in the 1999 Summer Cup and was good enough to race in the 2000 Durban July when El Picha won the race for the second time.

Mardi Gras was a beautiful colt by Danehill owned by Ms Vivian Pratt, another pleasant UK-based owner introduced to me by Tony Ruffel. Vivian had helped us in the 1980s to source our stallion Bel Byou and she was well known in British racing circles. She had lovely white and dark pink silks and Mardi Gras carried them to victory five times. He was below top class, not good enough to race in the major features or to go to stud, but he did manage a B Division win in Weichong Marwing's hands near the end of 1998 and Vivian was happy with what we'd achieved with him.

CHAPTER 49

The turn of the century gave us an indication of what was to come in the next two decades, with the media fuelling global fears to fever pitch in their projection of the Y2K Bug, also called Year 2000 Bug or Millennium Bug. This was a problem in the coding of computerised systems with the potential to create havoc in computers and computer networks around the world when the clocks turned at midnight on 31 December, 1999.

But like I'd seen with a variety of major news items, including the predictions, every year from 1932 to present, that the world was about to end, Y2K was a scare that went exactly nowhere. Fake news has grown steadily ever since and is being mass-produced today to persuade people to shift perspectives. Fake news itself is perhaps a bigger threat to civil society than Global Warming, Covid and Monkeypox!

So where were you when the corks popped and the fireworks went off on 1 January, 2000? I was in my Glenvista abode, wondering where my next meal would come from. I was contemplating what would happen to traditional horsemanship in the new era of veterinary assistance, swimming pools, treadmills and heart rate monitors designed to make thoroughbred training a science, not an art.

Jokes aside, I was pleased with developments and looking forward to getting some new runners on the track. I'd had calls from former patrons and my old mates including Peter Dimakogiannis, Dr Colin Hyams and Larry Nestadt were keen to throw me a few bones. During the course of 2000, I'd also learnt that leading owner and mining magnate Graham Beck was about to send me some young horses.

I'd met Beck back in the 1970s when he was racing with Syd Laird, who was in the process of buying The Curragh at Newmarket when I moved to the Western Cape. We'd only seen each other a few times since then, but there was a mutual respect and the relationship was amicable. I was really chuffed with the first group of his runners that arrived at my yard, including Cheetah Express and Glittering (Badger Land), Elda Ribetti (Jallad), Nautilus (Western Winter) and Rhythmically (Joshua Dancer).

Cheetah Express was a smart filly, but she was unsound and we couldn't get her to her full potential. She liked the handling of lightweight jockey Jason Jago, who partnered her in two of her four wins. We fancied her in the G2 SA Fillies Classic and she finished close up in fifth, but had to be retired after that.

The best of that Beck bunch was Rhythmically, a really smart horse with a good turn of foot and a nice action. His favourite jockey was Louis Nhlapo, an underrated rider who worked for me for a while. Louis was originally a graduate of James Maree's School For Work Riders, set up by the new Racing Trust but mainly with encouragement from Mary Slack. James had set up a four-month curriculum for work riders and later devised an advanced course to further hone the skills of those work riders who showed above-average talent. If anything from the Phumelela takeover deserved kudos, it was the School For Work Riders, still being managed successfully today.

I gave Louis a few chances and he used them all well, winning three, for example, on Rhythmically. He was also on the mark with a Dolpour filly Nettle, who took a year to win her Maiden in my silks but then let loose and won a further four, keeping the pot boiling. Louis, for a lack of support from other stables, had to retire early. He became a stipendiary steward with the National Horseracing Authority (NHA) based in Johannesburg where I believe he is still doing well.

I think I could have won a Listed race or even a small Graded feature with Rhythmically, but Beck received an offer he couldn't refuse from a Mauritian buyer and sold the colt on in 2002. He raced there between 2003 and 2007 where he won seven of 21 races including the Duke Of York Cup (twice) and all their other major features. He became a racing legend on the island where he was ridden most of the time by the evergreen Jeff Lloyd.

My star of the show, however, was my Rooispruit-bred chestnut filly Fading Light, an athletic daughter of Bel Byou and Fresh Breeze, a mare I'd won five races with in 1983 and 1984. Fading Light was a granddaughter of Malagasy, the first winner owned by Paddy and Maura Hinton, only better.

Fading Light was 'proper', with good pace and staying ability. While I initially thought of her as another SA Oaks prospect, she was a natural athlete good enough to compete in the classics over shorter. She was fond of jockey Corne Orffer and the pair completed an early Juvenile double in March 2001 before capturing April's G3 Pretty Polly Stakes over 1400m from Corne Spies' super-fast and later exported, Fun Fly.

In October 2001, we entered her for the G2 Spring Fillies Stakes in which we had to bump a few of Mike de Kock's useful Oppenheimer-owned fillies. Fading Light rose to the task and, after a battle with Carolina Cherry and Chinchuna, got the upperhand under Anthony Delpech to win by three-quarters from the former, a massive black filly who'd later become a super broodmare.

We took Fading Light to Cape Town for the G1 Fillies Guineas but in hindsight should've stayed at home. She'd drawn 14/16 and this was her first Cape run around the left-handed bend. That was just too much to overcome. She wasn't disgraced, just three lengths behind the winner Sports Chestnut. Her big moment came in February 2002's G1 Empress Club Stakes over 1600m where she took on the likes of Gary Player's top filly Raining Roses and Mary Slack's Velvet Green. Again, having to jump from a wide draw, Piere Strydom used her gate speed to get across and kept her galloping to secure the prize.

Fading Light was beaten in the Triple Tiara 1600, the G2 Fillies Classic, the G2 Oaks and the G1 Garden Province Stakes, but she raced in an era of star fillies including Ipi Tombe, Kournikova, Monyela, Escoleta Fitz and Crimson Palace – a depth of talent I haven't seen among fillies again since. She made me proud and reignited my ambition to win races at the highest level.

Bel Byou also produced an eight-time winner in Nobleman, trained by Louis Goosen. Interestingly, Nobleman was the winner of a Maiden Juvenile Plate in January 2000 in which David Ferraris' Celtic Grove (Fort Wood) was backed to favourite and ran unplaced on his debut. Celtic Grove turned out to be one of David's best. He won the Horse Of The Year Title in 2001.

The sad story of 2001 was the closure of Gosforth Park, even before the bell tolled for neighbouring Newmarket. Phumelela was in a hurry to get some cash in the bank ahead of their listing on the JSE in 2002. The charming old 'speed' track with its beautiful grandstand, all-glass fronts and plush reception rooms was sold in 2002 to Gosforth Park Properties for R18.5-million. It was turned into the Wesbank Raceway, with motorsport champion Peter Lindenberg as Chief Executive, and was subsequently taken over by a property developer.

GALLERY
PART 2

Smugglers Den, hard as nails. (Photo: H.F. Kenny).

Demon King (Cecil van As), with Peter Dimakogiannis and I.

Crown Pearl (Raymond Rhodes) winning at Gosforth Park.

Crown Pearl with part-owner Harry Rootenberg and Mrs Rootenberg.

David Ferraris and Mike de Kock as assistants in my stable, sipping champagne on the job. I should've kicked them both out.

Rakeen as a three-year-old at John Gosden's Stanley House at Newmarket, UK. (John Crofts Photography)

Rakeen 'walks' his first start in South Africa, Jeff Lloyd up. (H.F. Kenny).

Rakeen with happy connections: (from the left) Ivan Friedlander, Larry Nestadt, Guy Landon, Greg Blank and Anton Proctor (behind Greg).

Rakeen, playful in the winner's enclosure.

Maureen Ferraris, Weichong Marwing and Michael Clements with me at Gosforth Park, 1990.

A popular win on 1989 OK Gold Bowl day at Turffontein for the 'explosive' Miss Averof and Weichong Marwing. (H.F. Kenny)

Vigliotto wins the OK Gold Bowl in front of a 32,000-plus crowd, under a top ride from Marwing. (H.F. Kenny)

Turffontein officials with happy connections of Miss Averof, Vigliotto and General Blake: (From the left) Marwing, Meg and Colin Dunn, John Alexander, Shaun Cambouris, Hilda Podlas, Emmanuel Cambouris. (H.F. Kenny).

Hilda Podlas in a TV interview with Gordon Hood, post Gold Bowl. (H.F. Kenny).

St Just, small powerful chestnut. (H.F. Kenny).

The Monk (Marwing) winning the SA Derby at Turffontein, 1990.

Tracy's Element after the Gold Medallion at Scottsville with Maura, Paddy Hinton and I.

Tracy's Element (Marwing) wins the 1990 G1 SA Fillies Sprint.

With Jeff Lloyd and Paddy Hinton at Scottsville.

Sizzling Sun (Marwing) in the winner's arena with Des Scott and I following the 1994 Administrator's Handicap.

Trainer Of The Year Award, 1992.

Travel North (Willy Figueroa) with Carol and Kim Latilla, SA Derby 1995.

Sabina Park (Bernard Fayd'Herbe) wins the 2004 SA Oaks.

Overarching (Fayd'Herbe) in command in the 2005 Horse Chestnut Stakes. (H.F. Kenny)

*Raising the G1 Horse Chestnut trophy, with Dave Mollett looking on.
(H.F. Kenny)*

The 2013 Triple Tiara in a JC Photos Montage, Cherry On The Top.

Muzi Yeni and Romany Prince, my 2500th winner on 12 March, 2016. (JC Photos)

With Paul Peter at the TBA Sales Complex, 2020.

With my grandson Luke and son David, 2022.

CHAPTER 50

Maureen died of cancer in January 2003. I cannot describe in words what she'd meant to me in our marriage of 16 years and, again, I am adding this detail for purposes of perspective and timeline. Suffice to say, this was a setback that broke my heart, but I had to fight on without her.

The cliché goes that 'change is the only constant' and we all have life stories to back this up, but this was another period fraught with unexpected events that almost got my head spinning.

David was at the Magic Millions Sale in Australia when Maureen passed away and soon after his return he received, and accepted, an offer to train in the massively booming racing jurisdiction in Hong Kong. This was his opportunity of a lifetime, not only for its international scope and opportunity to work with some of the best horses and jockeys, but with the South African Rand in free fall it was a financial no-brainer.

That he'd won four National titles in a highly competitive local industry and that his friend Mike de Kock had broken through racing in Dubai in 2003, gave David the needed confidence to pursue this own fortunes. We had to make plans to wind down his Turffontein operation.

David's assistant, John Buckler, had built up a good relationship with their patrons and it was decided to split the horses between us. John had a start for his own business, he got about 20 and the remaining 40 came to me. I moved back into my old office with a string that was new to me. It felt as if I'd never left. Back in my old regimen with a competitive string helped me to focus again and eased the pain of dealing with my dear wife's passing.

There were several runners in David's bunch that had come to the end of their careers, but I did inherit a handful of promising racers and a few well-bred, unraced ones. Peter Dimakogiannis' Simply Salmon (Western Winter), had won seven, including the Listed Wolf Power Handicap and he had more to come. Rubirosa (Rakeen) was a useful staying filly on the upgrade.

David had bought Bishops Rock (Redoute's Choice) for owner Anthony Peter in Australia, also Silverpoint (Woodman) for a group including Colin Hyams and Serengeti Sunrise (Flying Spur) for a syndicate that included big-game hunter Andre de Kock and Sandy Evans who were both based near the Serengeti region in Tanzania.

My youngest new patron was up-and-coming attorney Michael de Broglio, a big thinker who was busy making a name for himself in legal circles. He was introduced to me by Alec Hogg, the astute media entrepreneur, founder of the popular Racing Digest Magazine in 1989 and the Moneyweb Group in the 2000s.

Alec and I got Michael enthusiastic about racing, the bug bit him properly and he attended the National Sale with us for the acquisition of his first horse, Sabina Park, by Sportsworld. She was a faultless filly with some class about her, but being unfashionably bred she was sold for just R55,000. Michael was chuffed with his investment, even more so when Sabina Park won her March 2003 debut by 5,25-lengths in the hands of veteran heavyweight jockey Rhys van Wyk. He had ridden many winners for David and stayed on to avail me of his services.

Sabina Park was a staying type and that she could win a sprint so easily, and in a good time, was encouraging to all of us. She won over 1400m just a month later and then stormed home by 2,25-lengths in April's 2003 G2 SA Fillies Nursery, raced over 1400m that year. This was a wonderful achievement for a rookie owner and Sabina Park had a good career ahead of her. Michael was over the moon, started a website for Sabina Park fans and we bought him another 'cheapie', Bold Achiever, by Kilconnel, who showed early promise on the work tracks.

There was more momentum in process. I received a surprise call from Graham Beck one morning and he said: "Ormond, my sympathies on your wife's death. I know what it feels like. I lost my son in 1995." I remembered that Clive Beck was killed in a car accident at the tender age of 35 and Beck added: "You will get through this, Rhona and I are thinking of you." Then, he said: "I have a consignment of fillies being shipped in from America next week. I want you to come down to Highlands and pick the ones you want. Let's have some fun!"

Beck owned Gainesway Farm in Kentucky, USA, where the former South African star galloper Wolf Power served his stud career, and of course the successful Highlands Farm Stud in Robertson, Western Cape, a regular among South Africa's leading breeders.

There were some purple-breds in Beck's imported group of 12 fillies, never a guarantee of success, but I was impressed by the physical conformation of most and I chose 10 to come to Johannesburg. Amazingly, they won us 44 races between them in the next four years!

With all my previous assistants having moved on and the stable needing more hands, I was lucky to find Sharon Strydom to join me following her long spell with James Maree at Eikenhof. Sharon (now Kotzen) knows thoroughbreds inside out and with her vast experience and work ethic, she became a pillar of strength in the yard for the next decade and more.

First off the mark, and the best of the Beck fillies overall, was Overarching (USA) by Arch. She was not too big in stature but a magnificent, strong and robust filly with a big chest. The media professors wrote that she looked pregnant when she came to the track. She wasn't ever in foal but they were right for once - she did have a somewhat awkward appearance due to her build. She was all class, however, and could run like the wind.

Being American-bred, Overarching was six months younger at competition level than her Southern Hemisphere rivals but she was made to race and came to hand quick. Rhys van Wyk partnered Overarching in her first run, a Newmarket 1200m early in July 2003. He'll remember it well because it was something that the term 'armchair ride' was not an apt description for. Overarching hardly came out of a canter in what was a 10-length success. Rhys didn't move a muscle, and the filly couldn't blow out a candle after the race.

Rhys' known strengths came in handy elsewhere. Owner/breeder, Ian McCrae, and partners, brought us a lovely Ceasour colt, Flavius, who was a talented sprinter but pulled like a dentist and wasted valuable energy trying to displace his riders' arms from their shoulders. Rhys got him to behave and they won three races before other top notch jockeys Mark Khan, Piere Strydom and Weichong Marwing also managed to get the better of him for winning rides. Flavius settled down somewhat and was another successful export to Mauritius where he won five races, including a minor feature.

Rhys, Weichong and Piere also took turns on another Beck owned filly, Riviersonderend, who started her career alongside Overarching and while she wasn't of the same quality, turned into a bit of an 'ATM' as a stayer. She was a beautiful filly with three shades of grey in her coat. We were fortunate, throughout 2003, to find weak fields for Riviersonderend to race in. She won her Maiden over 1600m, an E Division Race over 2000m, two D Divisions over 2000m and a C Division contest over 1800m; then landed the G3 Roland's Song Stakes over 1800m at Newmarket under visiting jockey Luca Sorrentino before the handicapper caught up with her – seven wins from 18 starts and a lovely filly to train.

I was looking for a stable jockey at the time and Sorrentino impressed me with several winners and a good strike rate. He was an Italian who rocked up at the track one morning asking for rides, much like Willy Figueroa, and also battled to speak English. Luca returned to Italy promising to come back as my retained jockey, but never did. I heard he'd run into 'female trouble' at home and never heard from him again. Google shows him as having last ridden at the Equestrian Club in Qatar in 2016.

CHAPTER 51

Are we getting a bit horse-heavy at this juncture in my recounting the details of my journey? I've been asked to reveal more stories about my interactions with owners to keep the balance right as we approach the final furlong of this tell-all. I didn't realise those were so interesting, but it got me thinking of my father Ernest, and Noel Fowles, a good friend from my youth.

On the few occasions when Noel and I were about to go out for a beer or a visit somewhere, my father used to say with a grin, "Noel, stay close to Ormond, you know he likes to take a swipe at people!" – and we'd laugh and go on.

I think I gradually moved down a few notches on the bad temper scale from 1986, when I married Maureen. Her kind and forgiving nature had a good influence on me and she was at my side with advice when things flared up and I needed to calm down. Also, when looking at things happening around the world, like the evils committed at the World Trade Centre in September 2001, I realised that life could be taken away unexpectedly and that every living moment should be treasured. Maureen's absence hasn't changed that view. I am a more relaxed man today than I was all those years ago.

When I reached 70 years of age in 2002, and after I was training on my own for a while with my short retirement in between, I guess not many felt like messing with the old guy too much. The new generation of owners knew all about me. When they brought me new horses, I was generally left alone to do my job.

In 2003, I even received a horse from the Herholdt family. I hadn't seen J.P. 'Zwei' Herholdt since late in 1976 after we'd had our unexpected meeting on the bridge in the middle of nowhere and I'd briefly thought my final hour was upon me. Luckily, I wasn't about to see him again. Zwei was said to be ill, out of the public eye and his horses were raced in partnership with his son, Eric, who was easy to deal with as a spokesman and accounts payer.

Their horse was a smart black colt named Western Heat who won three in a row but injured himself and had to be retired. That was a pity, he was a nice horse. But the family did find another good one in Kings Gambit, who won four of six for Lance Wiid before being sold and exported to England. J.P. Herholdt passed away in 2008.

A relationship that didn't end all that well was the one I'd tried to build with Michael de Broglio, the young legal eagle. He was on a high following Sabina Park's SA Nursery win and when she took a step up to 1800m and won again, we decided to aim her at the 2004 SA Oaks. His other filly, Bold Achiever, was a decent runner too. She won her debut over 1000m and looked like she was destined for bigger things.

Sabina Park (3-1) was third in the betting market for the G1 SA Oaks on 8 May, 2004. Angelina was the firm favourite at 7-10 with Rakara at 5-2 and the trio dominated the race too. Sabina Park had their measure with 250m to run and she surged ahead for a 3.5-length win.

Bernard Fayd'Herbe held her reins. This was my seventh win in the SA Oaks.

Sabina Park was a little below her best in her next few starts. This can happen to fillies after tough preps into a race like the Oaks, but there were many races left for her at four and I wasn't concerned. Bold Achiever also won again over 1400m and I thought all was hunky-dory until Michael announced out of the blue that he was keen on racing her in Dubai. He wished to move the filly to Mike de Kock, whom I think at that stage had taken occupancy of the Dubai throne alongside Sheikh Mohammed.

I don't think I raised my voice like I would have done before, just politely requested Michael to send a float for her and to ensure that there was room on the float, as well, for Bold Achiever. I was annoyed and disappointed that he was so keen to leave my stable after we had opened the door to the industry for him and found him a pair of good racers.

He noted in a Sporting Post interview in 2015, "…if my first two (horses) had been disasters, one might view the whole thing differently, but good horses help feed the addiction." Sabina Park picked up a few niggles and never won another race, but Michael retained her, kept her at stud and she produced the 2015 Summer Cup winner, Master Sabina.

Michael stayed fully involved in racing as an owner and breeder and did very well, while his professional career took off spectacularly. He also served on the Racing Association. I am told he lives in the United States these days and still has ties to our industry. I am happy that we brought a regular, important contributor into the game and sorry that my stable lost him early. But this is a game where loyalty often outweighs other factors. If owners want to leave, who am I to stop them?

I got to train Rubirosa for big-time owner and breeder Mike Rattray, my first for him and his wife Norma, and inherited from David. She was a lovely filly by Rakeen raised at his Lammerskraal Stud in the Western Cape and I raced her 10 times for four wins and six places in 2003 and 2004. She won the 2004 Listed Spook Express Handicap in the hands of Piere Strydom and placed in the G3 Queen Palm at Scottsville but a surprise call from Sally Jordaan at Lammerskraal threw a spanner in the works. They felt that Rubirosa's physical appearance was not what they wanted it to be. She was too 'light' and they wanted her to return to the farm.

I arranged a float for Rubirosa and asked them to load two other unraced Rattray-owned runners on the same truck. As her trainer, and closest to her, I felt that Rubirosa's condition was just about spot-on for this stage of her career and training programme. If this was an indication of disagreements to follow, I wanted no part of it.

CHAPTER 52

I'd like to touch individually on three of my top runners from the early 2000s in Overarching, Bishops Rock and Silverpoint.

Overarching was amazing in that her career stretched over three-and-a-half seasons from 2003 to 2006, and she won races in all those years. There were some nice pickings for her after her runaway debut win at Newmarket, including an E Division Sprint in which she defeated subsequent Listed winner Come Thunder by 2,75-lengths; a 1400m C Division contest in which she came home three lengths clear, and an Advanced Plate over a mile in which she got home by a length.

Although she saw out the 1600m without any apparent fuss, both Rhys van Wyk and Weichong Marwing felt that Overarching was best up to 1400m and that the G1 SA Fillies Sprint over 1200m would be a good first feature target. This was a step up in class – the Scottsville voodoo and always-powerful opposition has made this a standard-setting event. She was still three years old, an additional six months behind her older rivals with a hard task at weight-for-age. But the filly with the big barrel took no prisoners and Marwing rode her home to a wonderful 1,5-length win over Zolaroyale and Tycoon Rosita.

This victory, against the odds, was the deciding factor in Overarching's winning an Equus Award for Champion Older Sprinter (Female), and she was only three. Graham Beck was very pleased and phoned me a few times to chat about her success. I told him that she had much more to offer. We gave Overarching a three-month break, but she was a true champion and knew what she had to do in her preparation for her next race, the Listed Nomads over 1400m at Turffontein. She walked it by three, unextended!

Overarching was twice beaten over a mile next – first in the G2 Ipi Tombe Stakes (by Royal Approval) and then in the G2 November Handicap (Swartland). Although there were excuses, she gave credence to Van Wyk's and Marwing's view that she was best up to 1400m.

I brought her back to 1200m for one more race in December – the G3 Jo'burg Sprint in which Luca Sorrentino got her up to win by a quarter of a length from Hurricane Queen and a few other hard-galloping sprinters including Vega, Come Thunder and War Lord. This was a classy performance because there was a lot of pace in a race that was better than G3 level, and she beat them fair and square in an open contest. Trainer Buddy Maroun repeatedly stated in the press that Vega was one of the best, if not the best sprinter he'd trained, and that included his 22-time winning sprinting sensation, Golden Loom.

Considering the shape she was in, and that I wasn't convinced she didn't see out a mile, we took Overarching to Kenilworth for a go at the G1 Majorca Stakes. She finished in midfield to Shadow Dancing, first time on the left-hand bend and having to travel to Cape Town.

This was a race that answered no questions, but I wanted them answered. There were lean pickings on the sprinting calendar and with a filly as talented as Overarching we had to keep trying her over further to maximise her earning potential.

The G1 Empress Club Stakes over 1600m came next, and Overarching turned in a decent showing in third to Jamaica, a powerful front-runner and a formidable miler. She appeared one-paced, but she wasn't. The big mare, Jamaica, had a high cruising speed and was hard to pass when she was in front. I accepted that our filly couldn't make an impression on the older star on the day.

On Weight-For-Age Terms, receiving a sex allowance of 2,5kg, I believed it was worthwhile giving Overarching another try over a mile in the Horse Chestnut Stakes on 9 April, 2005. She was the only filly in a race against some accomplished males, but in her work she'd reached the peak of her powers. I engaged senior rider Bernard Fayd'Herbe, riding the crest of the wave at this time, to get the best possible assistance from the saddle and it was the right decision.

We had a confident jockey on a confident horse. Bernard rode a perfect race, pushed her along from the draw into midfield and near the rail. With 350m to run, Overarching moved up smartly, assumed control and won going away from Royal Mariner and Tyson. I'm glad we persisted with Overarching over the classic trip, it paid off handsomely when the right race came along at the right time.

Overarching and Bernard followed up just two weeks later in the G3 Camellia Stakes when she gave a field of fillies and mares weight, and a hiding over 1160m. A month later, still in top form, we really thought we had a second G1 SA Fillies Sprint in the bag but, as often happens at Scottsville, an upset came about. Overarching did everything but win. The race looked over as a contest, but 25-1 shot Far De Vie ran up late and nosed Overarching out of it, right on the line.

Overarching won one more of her next nine runs before we retired her to stud. She didn't go off the boil, rather had to contend with a new generation of stars including Ilha Da Vitoria and National Colour, who both became legends in their own right.

Our then six-year-old mare did post one more noteworthy victory in the 2006 G2 Hawaii Stakes on 4 March. She fought off the accomplished younger horse, National Spirit, who'd go on to win the G2 Drill Hall Stakes and the G1 Gold Challenge for Dominic Zaki in the same season. She returned to Highlands having won 11 of 28 starts, including two G1s. Sadly, like Pretty Border, she incurred a freak injury at stud and died after having produced only two runners.

Bishops Rock was not the best runner I'd trained, but he carries significance because he was the first import to South Africa sired by Redoute's Choice (Danehill), the stallion who'd go on to achieve high acclaim and was Champion sire of Australia in 2006, 2010 and 2014.

David bought Bishops Rock for Anthony Peter in Sydney just before he departed for Hong Kong in 2003. By the time we entered him for a Maiden Juvenile Plate in February, 2004, his sire had already produced a few stars in his homeland including Snitzel, Stratum, Miss Finland and Nadeem.

There were a few cheeky guys in the media who found this information on the internet. Bishops Rock was touted unbeatable on the eve of the race and when they opened the betting he was quoted at 5-10! He won the race by six lengths and was immediately hailed to be the next superstar, but this was not an opinion that emanated from me or from Anthony, for that matter.

Bishops Rock was always going to be just a solid, hard-knocking handicapper who won his way through the divisions up to G2 level, when he prevailed by a short-head from Lion Tamer in the Astrapak 1900 at Greyville under a strong Fayd'Herbe ride. That was as good as he was, but he heralded an era that made South African racing stronger via his racing progeny, two of which are successful stallions here today.

Another good sort bought by David at the Magic Millions Sale in Australia was Silverpoint, by Woodman, a handsome and talented chestnut horse who had pace and stayed well, like the good ones tend to do. He raced for David, Dr Colin Hyams and partners and won three times as a two-year-old, but was an unlucky type who got beaten into the places in all of the G2 SA Nursery, the Dingaans, the Gauteng Guineas and the G1 SA Classic, where he found interference before running second to Jam Alley.

Silverpoint's big day came in the 2005 G2 SA Derby, which happened to be staged on 30 April 2005, at the time of the National Yearling Sale. David was in South Africa buying horses and was able to attend the race while Pam held the fort in Hong Kong.

Silverpoint, ridden by Brett Smith finally got it right. He turned the tables on Jam Alley and others, beating Pavlovich and Oracle West for a deserved top-level win. The South China Morning Post reported on this, calling 2004/5 David's 'Season Of Dreams'. My son had struck gold with a wonderful horse called Vengeance Of Rain, bought from Australian magnate Lloyd Williams to race for Hong Kong owners. Given to David to train, the son of Zabeel had won the G1 Hong Kong Cup and the prestigious G1 QEII Cup just before David jetted out to the South African sale. Vengeance Of Rain had literally put him on the map in 2005, and there was more to come.

The Derby was Silverpoint's last win for me. We took him to Durban for the Daily News, a prep for the 2005 Durban July, and he finished in midfield. Then, on July day, we had him tuned to a tee, Anthony Delpech flew in from Hong Kong to take the ride and we had a little flutter at 20-1.

Guess what? He finished second, beaten half a length by another 20-1 chance, Dunford. Unlucky? In a way, yes, but I only say that because the year older Dunford was masterfully placed into the July by trainer Mike Bass. He came in off 52kg with a win in an Advanced Plate and a fifth in the Astrapak 1900 to his credit, by historic records not good enough to win it. But he did, and we ran second. And that was the way the cookie crumbled!

Silverpoint was sold to dissolve the partnership not long after this. I bid up to R1-million to retain him, but Mike Azzie and his partners went higher and secured the horse for the remainder of his racing career.

The 2004/5 season was a good and profitable one for the stable. I was right back on the boil with 73 winners, and our runners were competitive. Parade Magazine's Nicci Garner reported: "Many comebacks fail abysmally, but Ormond Ferraris wasted no time in getting back to business, finishing 10th on the national trainers' log (fourth in the Central Provinces) when his runners earned R3,3-million and his win-place strike rate was a high 60,45%. On a runners-to-earnings scale, he has beaten his compatriots hands-down with his horses earning a high R15,824 per race, indicating that when Ferraris sends a horse to the racetrack, they mean business!"

CHAPTER 53

A media release in December 2005 stated: "Following extensive consultations with relevant stakeholders... the Free State Gambling and Racing Board has granted Phumelela permission for the immediate closure of Bloemfontein Racecourse. The race meetings held at Bloemfontein will in future be staged at Vaal Racecourse in the Free State and at Flamingo Park Racecourse in the Northern Cape."

Extensive consultations? No, arguably just a hit-and-run for the management and shareholders of Phumelela. Bloemfontein Racecourse was purchased for R3.5-million in 1998 and sold for R32-million nine years later. Racing in the centre was popular and well supported by stables from all over the country. They raced mostly on Thursdays and about 26 race meetings a year were held at the track before its closure. I didn't race there, but many of my colleagues took their uncompetitive Highveld runners to the track and kept the fires burning in weaker company.

Phumelela announced that a multi-million rand refurbishment of Flamingo Park in Kimberley was in its final stages. The racing surface had been upgraded and 160 stables had been constructed on course to accommodate the three trainers previously based at Bloemfontein.

Phumelela felt that the refurbishment of Flamingo Park and the closure of Bloemfontein served their objective to establish a single racing centre in the central regions of South Africa with a resident horse population capable of sustaining an annual racing programme. Turffontein, Newmarket, Arlington and Fairview escaped the axe at this time.

The night meetings at Newmarket, not near as well attended as the first few in 1997, were still popular at this time, and while we had been expecting a final call on its fate, those who weren't 'in the know' were taken aback by Phumelela's 2005 annual report, which stated that Newmarket had been sold for R22-million to a property developer.

Phumelela reached a deal with the new owners that it would continue to lease Newmarket for an agreed upon monthly fee, to stage a maximum of 36 race meetings a year until 31 May 2012. However, in 2006, the Newmarket owners paid Phumelela R40-million to terminate the lease agreement. In February 2007, racing ceased and Newmarket was demolished to great dissatisfaction and tears from the racing public and most trainers.

The Alberton Record commented: "'The night Newmarket racehorses died', was the phrase used to describe the very last night race. This track held a special place in the hearts of the people of Alberton and punters of the Gauteng province. Since Newmarket was so geographically central to the extension of Alberton, the horseracing connection played an important part in the development of the town. The racecourse has, therefore, stayed close to the hearts of the town folk, providing much more than a simple opportunity to bet on the horses.'"

The land was undeveloped for several years and one of the most beautiful racetracks in the country lay in woeful ruins until a major wholesaler erected its warehouses around what used to be the 100m-mark. Today, there is a big shopping centre that serves most of Alberton and surrounds, but any racing fan with heart strings can feel how they're pulled when driving by the old Newmarket entrance on Ring Road. And one can't help but get some bitterness in your mouth too. Did this track really have to go?

Night racing was to proceed at Turffontein using the Newmarket flood lights which had to be moved and erected at the Johannesburg track. I, and any number of other trainers, were against the moving of lights and we voiced our dissatisfaction. There were also outcries from a number of families living in the suburbs of Springfield and Turffontein, adjacent to the course. The complaints centred around noise and the sharpness of the lights. Phumelela investigated the issue by appointing an expert using a sound level meter and, as expected, his findings had little or no impact on their decision.

One day, I joined a group of trainers alongside business mogul Markus Jooste, representing the Racing Association, and a few of his colleagues to inspect the areas where the lights would be placed. We spoke to Jooste, pleaded with him to re-consider racing under lights not only for the extra labour it would cost us, but also for safety. The area around the course had turned into a slum and people were getting mugged and murdered every week, with drug dealers and prostitutes moving in like rats taking occupancy of a deserted old house.

Jooste walked with us on the back end of the track in the area where Turffontein's wooden stables were built to accommodate trainers. I said: "The noise and lights here will disturb the sleeping horses. And also down the straight, there will be commotions near the main stables when horses are resting!" He agreed with us, said that he and the RA would be looking at solutions.

Nothing really came of our concerns. Phumelela advertised night racing with the same vigour they sold Bloemfontein and Newmarket.

"The revitalisation of Turffontein is consistent with the resurgence of the Jo'burg CBD," was one comment that came from CEO, Jim Tennant. Wonder where he got that one from?

While all of this was going on I was informed of the death of my erstwhile best friend, Paddy Hinton, in his retirement town, Somerset West. This is the paragraph in which I'd probably be expected to express regret for not making an attempt to reconcile after our fallout. But I'm not going to. What happened between us was unfortunate, but it happened in the course of our lives as participants in an industry that shaped us into what we were at that time. I prefer to reminisce about the many years of joy and friendship we shared, and let the rest be.

In October 2007, to the backdrop of what was developing into racing's equivalent of 'state capture', a group of concerned owners and trainers held a meeting in which various issues were tabled. The meeting was arranged and fronted by prominent owner Larry Wainstein, and matters discussed included:

-The lack of information about Phumelela's future.

-The closure of race tracks.

-The moving of the lights from Newmarket to Turffontein and the impact this would have on the animals' performance. The lack of input from the stakeholders based at Turffontein on this issue.

- The stakes we raced for in comparison to the cost of horses and up keep, which continually increased and not in proportion to stake increases.

-The perception that Phumelela's only concern was their share price.

-The concern that the Racing Association was not taking decisions in the interest of Owners and every decision Phumelela made, the perception is that RA agreed, which was felt is not in the best interest of Racing.

-Decisions were made to ensure the share price increased and not to improve or change for the betterment of Racing.

Wainstein asked for a proxy to call an urgent meeting with the Racing Association, so that a vote of no confidence could be put forward in RA Directors Jooste and Chris van Niekerk, who also held directorships of Phumelela and were trustees of the Racing Trust. The objective was to elect a new RA Board able to stand up to Phumelela and make decisions in the interests of owners, trainers and racing.

The outcome of this was that the RA Board turned Larry Wainstein to their corner and ensured that he and three other RA members standing on the same ticket were elected as directors of the RA to the exclusion of other candidates. Wainstein became Chairman of the Racing Association and later CEO, a position he held until January 2020. In his 12 years at the helm, the RA stood accused of nepotism; under-handed deals; stifling the press and actively pursuing some of its members via collaboration with the National Horseracing Authority; rewarding others who towed the line and, in the end, doing zero for the racehorse owners it was supposed to serve.

In this period, Markus Jooste, who was quite open about his ambitions to control racing's entire 'supply chain' like he controlled the furniture supply chain at Steinhoff, became the most powerful man in South African racing. His actions provoked indifference.

In the course of his dominating reign, Jooste got a large proportion of trainers to either support him or stay neutral in the governance debates by spreading his horses among many trainers. I was also sent a horse, it arrived on a float from Klawervlei Stud one afternoon. I wasn't impressed because this colt had one hoof that pointed east, and the other pointed west. I put him on the float and sent him straight back to Klawervlei. I wouldn't have taken him into my stable, anyway.

CHAPTER 54

The year 2007 saw the rise of Apple's Steve Jobs, who launched the iPhone, the frontrunner of the smart phone that rules the lives of the majority of the world's population today. Jobs became a media tycoon while I trained horses with powerful names, including Herod The Great (Tara's Halls), Trojan (Al Mufti) and Natural Selection (Western Winter).

The latter, a workmanlike chestnut owned by Peter Dimakogiannis, produced the run of his life in joint-fourth with Pocket Power in the 2007 Durban July, beaten (as my horses traditionally were in this great race), by less than half a length! If I could transpose a smart phone's emoji onto this page, I'd pick the little crying man. Not only for myself. My assistant, Sharon Strydom, recalled how she and jockey Marthinus Mienie sat alone near the Greyville Jockeys Room shedding a tear together after the race that day.

Sharon loved Natural Selection and had travelled with him to away centres a few times; Marthinus was a heavyweight rider (the best available jock I could find for the race) who had to shed about 4kg to ride the horse for us. He did, and came mighty close to an unlikely win.

This period in history also produced the massive stock market crash that took place on September 29, 2008, with the fall of Dow Jones Industrial Average. The crash began in the US and later spread to Europe and the rest of the globe.

It was said that white-collar crime lay at the root of the economic collapse. I am not qualified to comment on that but I do recall that a number of America's big bankers were named. Their massive bonuses were said to have given them an incentive to take the kinds of risks that caused the meltdown.

While those high-profile bankers gave America a bad name, the one 'Yank' I dealt with between 2006 and 2010 was a man as forthright and honourable as you'd find anywhere in the world. Former racing scribe and later horse syndication specialist, Barry Irwin, was sometimes maligned in his homeland for his outspoken views against drug abuse and other contentious issues in racing. In South Africa, he came under fire from the pro-Markus Jooste crowd for speaking out against nepotism and the capture of racing by the elite. In my book, the Team Valor President was a pleasure to deal with, a straight-shooter, a shrewd judge of horseflesh and a man who paid his bills on time.

Our relationship came about when Barry acquired a filly in my stable called She's On Fire. She was a talented daughter of Jet Master who won some good early races for Gavin Lerena, Willy Figueroa and Piere Strydom, riding for UK-based owner Anna Doyle.

Barry spotted her finishing fourth in the G1 Empress Club Stakes in March 2007 to his own filly, Little Miss Magic, and bought her privately from bloodstock agent Peter Doyle with a long-term view of developing her pedigree in the broodmare paddock. She incurred a knee injury, had to undergo two operations and Sharon and I had to nurse her along to get her to a fair level of fitness.

It took almost a year to get She's On Fire back to good health, but Barry was patient and it paid off. She went to the Vaal in January 2008 for a second place in a pipe-opener and then came within a length-and-quarter of yet another Irwin-owned filly, Stratos, in the 2008 renewal of the G1 Empress Club Stakes. She remained sound, improved and on 29 March put daylight between herself and G1 Fillies Classic winner Zaitoon in the G2 Gerald Rosenberg over 2000m. She was eased down eight lengths to the good by Barry's favourite South African jockey, Weichong Marwing. She was naughty and full of fire, really. Barry and his wife, Kathleen Irwin, were on course that day, but the filly played up so badly we had to take her away without the US couple getting a chance to lead her along on the rope.

With Marwing booked for another trainer, we asked Sean Cormack to ride She's On Fire in the G1 Gommagomma Challenge over 2000m at Turffontein, a R3,5-million race sponsored by a subsidiary of Markus Jooste's Steinhoff. She took second place from an 11-draw, beaten two-and-a-half lengths by Eddington on the day.

Barry felt she could have won. His Team Valor website reported: "(Irwin) is convinced the mare could have won the 10-furlong fixture if Weichong Marwing would have been available, as he most likely would have made use of the mare's prodigious stamina by pressing the pace of the wire-to-wire longshot winner Eddington. She's On Fire was sent off as the favourite after being listed as high as 16-1 earlier in the week by bookies.

"Veteran trainer Ormond Ferraris said, 'She's On Fire ran a nice race on Saturday. Pity we did not get first. However, we did pick up a nice second stake ($92,900). I have nominated her to run in the Durban July. I have spoken with (Weichong) Marwing and he has not at this stage committed himself to a ride. However, he did advise that it would all depend on the draw.'"

She's On Fire qualified for the July with an authoritative win in the G3 Jubilee Handicap and when she drew Number 10 out of 20 for the big race, Weichong took the ride on 5 July 2008. But this field was just too strong for her. She ran among the midfielders, beaten five lengths by dead-heating stars Pocket Power and Dancer's Daughter.

Barry's filly Gypsy's Warning, however, was one that went all the way to the top. This one was another Scott Bros-bred by Mogok out of Gypsy Queen that caught Barry's roving eye when she won the G1 2008 Thekwini Stakes over 1600m at Clairwood Park for owner Rob Griffiths and trainer Duncan Howells. Barry bought a share from the owner, who retained a share himself and she was transferred to me in September of that year.

We won two quick races with her, including the G3 Acacia Handicap over 1600m, where Piere Strydom did duty, followed by a third place in the Empress Club, where the grey racing machine Dancer's Daughter packed too many guns. But Gypsy's Warning was a filly of mettle and she made fast progress into the 2009 G1 SA Fillies Classic on 28 March 2009. Strydom booted her home to a two-length win over Mike de Kock's Zirconeum, a filly who was beaten just three-quarters in the 2009 Durban July a few months later.

This time, Barry bypassed the July as he had an overseas campaign mapped out for Gypsy's Warning. We gave the filly a farewell run in the G1 Woolavington at Greyville, where a 14/16 draw put us on the backfoot and Zirconeum got her revenge.

Exported to the United States right after the Woolavington, Gypsy's Warning was sent to the barn of Graham Motion and picked up right where she left off with a gutsy victory in the 2010 G3 Eatontown Stakes at Monmouth over Breeders' Cup winner Maram.

Gypsy's Warning placed third in a pair of G1 events, The Beverly D and the Yellow Ribbon, both times beaten less than two lengths. She then finished off 2010 with a rousing win in the G1 Matriarch at Hollywood Park, becoming the first South African-bred runner to win a US G1 race since Team Valor's former campaigner Crimson Palace turned the trick six years earlier in the 2004 Beverly D. Gypsy's Warning was sold as a broodmare prospect at Keeneland in November of 2011 for more than a million dollars.

CHAPTER 55

Here are a few final tales of the terrible variety before we get to the concluding and a more satisfying period of my career.

Remember diamond dealer F.P. 'Boet' Oosthuizen, my friend and patron from Wolmaransstad, the gentleman who was at my side when I almost collapsed in a nervous heap during the running of the 1976 SA Oaks? Well, Boet was badly injured when a heavy gate at the entrance to his home malfunctioned and fell on him in January, 2008. I remember passing through that very gate when Boet and wife Elsabé invited Maureen and I to his home in 2002. Boet pulled me aside after a cup of tea and home-baked bread and said, "Kom hier (Come here), come and check this diamond!"

He took me to a room inside his house, opened a safe and produced a massive, sparkling purple diamond, one of a kind. It must've been worth millions and I said, "Boet, are you selling it? Wow!"

He said, "No, hell, I'm keeping it!"

Boet seemed to suggest there were a few more 'big ones' lying around his farm. When I heard of his and his wife's death on their farm at the end of 2008, I suspected foul play. But in speaking to Boet's family recently I discovered there was none of the kind.

After the accident at his gate, Boet wasn't as mobile as he used to be, he battled to walk. On 20 July 2008, a massive fire broke out in his house. Boet struggled to get the then also ill Elsabé out of the house, and to safety, but failed. He narrowly escaped the harrowing flames, crawling away in time, but his partner succumbed to the flames. Boet, overcome by grief and illness, passed away in December 2008. He was a true gem of an individual, and his family still deals in the precious stone today.

I personally escaped serious injury in my own home in March 2009 when I was attacked and robbed in my Johannesburg townhouse one morning at 5 am. I'd left at 3:45 to go to my stables, but returned unusually early because I had a trip to my Karoo farm planned. My son, Paul, was due to pick me up at 5:30.

I'd unlocked my front door and was halfway inside when a tall, skinny man grabbed me around my neck and tried to strangle me. He shouted, "Want money, want money!" and then a struggle ensued and we rolled and wrestled on the floor with my little dog barking away. Some notes I had withdrawn for our trip fell from my pocket while we grappled. My assailant broke loose, grabbed the cash, jumped over a neighbouring wall and disappeared.

The robber entered the house through a sliding security door, which he'd bashed open violently. He must have been watching me for a while because he knew my movements. Aged 77 at the time, I was proud to have landed a few punches in our brawl. Many of my friends and acquaintances had been mugged or attacked over the years, but this was the first time something like this had happened to me. I was truly shocked.

Another owner and friend, Andre de Kock from Serengeti Sunrise fame, was killed in the Maswa Game Reserve adjacent to Serengeti in Kenya in February 2011 while he was hunting with clients. He'd stopped to retrieve a blue bag discarded in the veld. It was filled with ammunition and belonged to poachers, who were actually right there hiding behind the bushes where they'd savagely taken the tusks off an elephant. They fired on the group with AK-47s, killing Andre and wounding one of his fellow hunters.

On 5 March 2011, my long-time, on-and-off stable jockey, Tobie van Booma, died in a car crash at the relatively young age of 55. I've written a lot about Tobie in this book – complimentary and not so complimentary. All I can say in conclusion is that Tobie played a significant role in my career. Ours was a business and a personal relationship and despite the many headaches he gave me, I was very fond of the young boy I employed in 1970 and the man I worked with for large parts of 30 years after that. May he rest in peace.

On the racing front, an incident that came to mind involved Peter Dimakogiannis's gelding Santa, a lovely chestnut by National Emblem who'd won us eight races between April 2006 and March 2011, with two Listed and two G3 successes among them. He was also touched off twice in the G2 Gold Bowl and finished fourth in the then G1 Canon Gold Cup.

Santa suffered a bout of colic not long after running in a plated race on 12 March, 2011. It was so bad, the big guy was in a terrible amount of pain, so Sharon I decided to hook up a float and rush him to a veterinary clinic. The veterinarian himself was unable to get to us in time. On the highway, on the way to the clinic, Sharon got stuck in a massive traffic jam on one of Johannesburg's poorly maintained and badly managed highways. She tried to drive around cars with her hazard lights on when she was stopped by an officer from the JMPD (Johannesburg Traffic Department), who threatened to arrest her.

When Sharon explained that she had a very sick horse in the float that needed emergency attention, the officer paused for a moment and said, "But it's just a horse, not a human". She pleaded with him to help her through the worst of the bottleneck – it was possible using the emergency lane, but he refused and waved her off. Sharon turned back, frantically searching for a different route, but to no avail. On the drive back to the stables, Santa must have suffered severely. He died shortly after being offloaded back at Turffontein where a vet, by then, was waiting to help.

Mother Africa - a strange old continent we were born to. I've just reviewed this chapter by candlelight as South Africa has entered Stage 6 'Loadshedding' and there is no electricity, countrywide. Only God knows what awaits our children and grandchildren who remain in this sadly deteriorating place we call home.

CHAPTER 56

Barring the incident with Santa, Peter Dimakogiannis was perhaps the luckiest owner in my stable from the time he joined me in the late 1970s until I called it a day in 2019. His other good performer at this time was the pitch-black Snowdon, another offspring of Western Winter. He was a good, strong sprinter who did everything but hit the big time, placing in G1s, 2s and 3s but not getting as much as a Listed win to his name. But he was typical of a horse that was any owner's dream – nine wins and 19 places between 2010 and 2015 and earnings of near R1,25-million.

Not that a weak spell was ever going to stop Peter from buying his customary two or three horses per year – but I wish I'd had a horse like Snowdon for every owner that ever joined my yard – a type that keeps interest going for years with good wins and cash flow. Every person investing in this sometimes frustrating sport deserves at least one good horse. Many give up after a few tries – there have been stories of owners going a lifetime without a winner. Recently, I saw an interview with a chap in Durban who landed his first winner after 25 years of ownership. Thoroughbred racing is as cruel as it can be rewarding.

Barry Irwin, a lucky owner on four continents, continued his support of my stable until he started trimming his investments due to being disillusioned with where the sport was heading in South Africa. His pair of runners alongside She's On Fire and Gypsy's Warning were Trojan and Success Counts (Count Du Bois), raced in partnership with filmmaker Anant Singh and his wife Vanashree. Trojan bagged six wins and the filly Success Counts won three including the G3 Starling Stakes in November 2010, in which one of few jockeys available was Mauritian-born apprentice Nooresh Juglall. The kid rode a perfect race and I took a liking to him.

Other notables in the yard were Captain Haddock (Spectrum), S'il Vous Plait (Silvano), Sharp Design (National Emblem) and Knock on Wood (Muhtafal).

Captain Haddock was the last horse sent to me by Graham Beck just before his death in July 2010. He was a son of Highlands's stallion Spectrum and the first foal of Overarching. Spectrum never made it as a stallion, in later years he had more success as a sire of broodmares. This wonderful mare upgraded him and Captain Haddock won six times. My regrets in this respect were that I never got to train for Mr Beck a lot earlier than the 2000s and that Overarching, as noted, suffered an early death in a freak accident after delivering her second foal. I will always have special memories of the man and the mare.

S'il Vout Plais, owned by Vivian Pratt, was a stayer much in the Santa mould. He won plenty of handicaps but couldn't quite crack it at the top level with places up to G3. He did, however, pay nine visits to the winner's enclosure between May 2011 and September 2015 and banked just short of R900,000.

Sharp Design was a nifty little sprinter owned by Ronnie Burg. His dam, the seven-time winner Sharp Ledge, passed on her own above average speed to this offspring, whose career record showed 10 wins and 11 places from just 23 starts. Ronnie and his friends enjoyed a lot of thrills with this horse. He won four in a row between October and December 2012 to pay for Ronnie's end-of-year holidays. Sharp Design's biggest prize was the G3 Tommy Hotspur Handicap on 12 February 2013, following which the Sporting Post reported under the headline: 'Uncle Ormond's Ferrari', "Ormond Ferraris' speed demon Sharp Design ran his opposition ragged to grab the biggest prize of his glittering career to date."

Nooresh commented in the post-race interview: "It was a wise move by Mr Ferraris to put the blinkers on. Last time, Sharp Design didn't travel and didn't want to load either. But he came out tonight like a machine. That's the way we know him."

Knock On Wood was a gelding that rose through the divisions quickly after his debut in November 2010, though didn't get to the very top. He raced for David and I, in David's orange-and-white silks inherited from his grandfather, Ernest, and progressed to a MR90 Handicap within six months. He went off the boil in late 2011 and the first half 2012, but regained his zest in July to win the 2012 KZN Breeders at Greyville under Bernard Fay'd Herbe, who kept his good strike rate for us.

It was the same with young Nooresh Juglall, who used every chance we gave him to the best of his ability, and partnered Knock On Wood to his biggest success in the G3 2013 London News Handicap. His best run, however, came in the G1 2013 Champions Challenge, where Nooresh got into the irons again and Knock On Wood managed a workmanlike second at level weights to Heavy Metal, punching above his weight.

Knock On Wood was one of our favourites in the yard because of his truly amazing temperament. He was a gentle, laid-back horse who seemed almost human at times, and had a relationship with his groom Simphiwe Magida unlike any horse we'd seen before. Knock On Wood was to Simphiwe what a puppy dog would be to a loving young owner – playful and loving but also respectful and loyal. He enjoyed his work duties on the track and loved being groomed.

Simphiwe could've slept next to him in his stable at night with his arms around him. Maybe he did. They were a pair we'd watch in amazement from time to time, and when Knock On Wood was retired in December 2014 a group of us gathered around the float to see him off. Simphiwe was in tears, Sharon too, and I had to swallow the lumps in my throat as the then eight-year-old gelding stepped onto the float like a lamb, on his groom's command.

Meanwhile, the selling of racecourses continued unabated. KZN's racing operator Gold Circle, while not a Listed company like their Johannesburg counterparts Phumelela, in May 2012 sold Clairwood, 'The Garden Course' to Capital Property Fund for R420-million, which subsequently leased it back to Gold Circle for a period of two years. The course was originally opened in 1921. While most racing purists were against the sale, the funds were ringfenced and provided a backstop when Gold Circle was approaching a crash in 2020.

Arlington's final horse race was run in 2013 and was preceded by Phumelela's last-ditch attempts to offload the property to the Nelson Mandela Bay Municipality and Africa Race Group (ARG).

The latter resulted in a protracted legal battle, which ultimately led the Public Protector to investigate former Steinhoff CEO Markus Jooste as a key shareholder in Phumelela Gaming and Leisure. Costly court battles and dwindling revenue led Phumelela to enter voluntary business rescue in May 2020.

Arlington Racecourse in Gqeberha (formerly Port Elizabeth) was sold at auction for R25.7-million to a Durban-based consortium. The land was expected to be developed into a residential area, while proceeds from the sale was put towards Phumelela Gaming and Leisure's business rescue, a closely guarded process that started in 2020 and is still ongoing. Executives are said to have signed non-disclosure agreements with the Business Rescue Practioner, John Evans, and while rumours of dirty tricks within Phumelela were rife, nothing has been officially revealed. Evans supplied his expert services for reportedly in the region of R50,000 per day and at this writing, two years later, is still at it, wrapping the rescue.

In 2019, Phumelela dispelled the last remnants of its plundering reign by closing Kimberley Racecourse. "The decision is based purely on commercial factors," a statement from the company read. A financial analysis conducted on Kimberley Racing in isolation from the other racecourses, indicated it was losing around R23.5-million a year. It has the lowest TAB turnover of any of the local race meetings at around R3-million. It is also one of the least cost-effective meetings to stage as we have to bring in people like stipes and judges from other centres."

One has to wonder if the wrong calculations were applied when they announced with the sale of easy-accessible and punter-friendly Bloemfontein Racecourse in 2005 that it was their objective to establish a single racing centre in the central regions of South Africa with a resident horse population capable of sustaining an annual racing programme.

Whatever suits, at whatever time. The way of all the world's corporate penny pinchers.

CHAPTER 57

They say that trainers don't find top horses, they find you! I've found many a good one on my own in my time as a trainer, but perhaps I'll agree with that statement in reference to one filly as we go into the last two chapters of my memoirs.

Midway through 2011, I received a call one morning from my friend, the late Anne Upton, exchanging pleasantries and catching up on a few trivial matters. She asked if I knew someone who'd be able to take over as Stud Manager at Bridget Oppenheimer's Mauritzfontein Stud in Kimberley.

Anne explained: "Gavin Schafer has left the farm and Mrs O needs someone urgently to fill his position, but it has to be a person of calibre, it's a big job!"

The first name that came into my head was Guy Murdoch, a man of specialist knowledge and experience I'd dealt with for many years. Guy was in charge of Gary Player's farm near Colesberg in The Karoo region and I couldn't think of anyone more suitable to manage South Africa's major breeding operation.

I didn't give the matter much more thought when the conversation with Anne ended, but several weeks after that I took a surprise call from another lady. It was Bridget Oppenheimer and she said: "Ormond Ferraris, good day to you, this is Mrs Oppenheimer." I just briefly thought this was a joke, but there was absolutely no reason why anybody would try to prank me. And nobody could fake Mrs O's unique accent so perfectly so I knew, this was her, all right.

"Yes, Mrs Oppenheimer, what can I do for you?"

"Well, yes, I phoned to say thank you very much for recommending Guy Murdoch as Stud Manager at Mauritzfontein. I am very pleased with him and I am grateful to you. I would like to send you two fillies. They are well bred. I believe you will enjoy training them. Is that in order?"

"Perfectly so, Mrs O!"

"That's marvellous. Please get in touch with Guy and arrange to have them collected. Thank you indeed!"

Soon on their way to me were Erin, a half-sister by Fort Wood to G1 Cape Guineas winner Flight Alert, and Cherry On The Top, a Mauritzfontein bred out of one of the farm's promising broodmares Carolina Cherry (Fort Wood) from a service by Wilgerbosdrift's stallion Tiger Ridge, owned by Mrs O's daughter Mary Slack.

I liked both fillies a lot and it was evident that Mrs O didn't send me any rejects. Both fillies had class about them and Cherry On The Top, in particular, impressed me in her work from the first day she set foot on the training track.

I'd learnt from my farrier, Renier van Rooyen, whose services were also in regular demand at Mauritzfontein, that Cherry On The Top had been earmarked for a big career not long after she was born. She had troublesome feet, however, her hooves weren't as straight as they should've been and, since she was three weeks old, Renier had been trimming them periodically to keep her balanced.

Renier, Sharon and I kept a close eye on those hooves. A part of Cherry On The Top's success was owing to Renier keeping her feet healthy overall by correcting her hooves. Left unchecked, she'd be prone to cutting herself and risking serious injury. The master farrier visited us twice a week and Cherry On The Top was invariably his first call.

Erin had a few niggles herself, nothing we couldn't handle, and while I initially expected her to be the first of the pair to race, it was Cherry On The Top who came to hand the quickest, showing a lot of pace and getting herself into competitive shape like many top horses do.

Mrs O placed frequent calls to inquire about the progress of her fillies and it was always a pleasure to talk to her. She wasn't smug, pompous or condescending and she never dictated anything. I knew that she liked to have the best available jockeys on her runners so we booked high-riding Robbie Fradd to ride the Cherry in her first run, a Maiden Juvenile Plate over 1450m at Turffontein on 3 April, 2012. There were only eight rivals to beat and she came home 'smoking a pipe' – a big debut and a proud first up stable win for Mrs Oppenheimer, who was delighted.

Fradd never felt pressure in the race, just placed Cherry On The Top in the right position and allowed her to stride and finish off in his hands. Even though she wasn't near extended, he reported that she gave him the feel of a top filly, which was as much encouraging as it was validating what I had quietly suspected.

Similar sentiments were expressed by Anthony Delpech, who rode Cherry On The Top in a handicap over 1600m against older fillies and mares in her next start on 19 May when she gave most of them weight and a beating. Sherman Brown, too, was excited following his win on the filly on 7 July – a Juvenile Plate over 1600m in which punters started cottoning on to her ability and she went to post a strong odds-on favourite.

We aimed Cherry On The Top at her first feature, the G3 Starling Stakes over 1400m on 3 November 2012, but she suffered a rare off day and couldn't get into the hunt from a 16 draw, one-paced somewhere in the pack. We were all disappointed, but I knew she was much better than this and she proved herself in the G3 Fillies Mile on 1 December when she raced home two lengths clear in a good time, Sherman Brown doing the honours.

With everything back on track, Cherry On The Top was shaping as a Wilgerbosdrift Triple Tiara prospect for 2013 and we started gearing her work towards the first leg, the G2 Gauteng Fillies Guineas on 2 March, 2013. This came via another handicap success in a mile on the inside track at Turffontein in which I gave Nooresh Juglall a leg up. At this point, we had to monitor her work even more carefully to have her at her best for the three races which were a month apart, and staged over 1600m, 1800m and 2450m respectively.

Mrs Oppenheimer loved the idea of owning a Triple Tiara prospect. She invited me to lunch at her Blue Skies Residence on the family's Brenthurst Estate in Johannesburg. This happened mostly on Wednesdays for several months and before her health deteriorated. I can describe her home as a large country cottage marked by understated opulence, tastefully decorated and served by an assistant, a chef and butlers.

Mrs O didn't allow many individuals to get too close to her. Her wealth, coupled with her status and celebrity were natural barriers to familiarity with people outside of her family circle. But she enjoyed and appreciated compliments from all walks of life. Those fortunate enough to engage her in a conversation were privy to her pointed wit, her genuine concerns about the state of government and the politics of racing and her timely pouring of liquid refreshments to accompany good chatter. I enjoyed every visit thoroughly. Sometimes, she had other friends over, including Sally Reunert, whose company was a true delight, and I also got to meet her granddaughter, Jessica Slack, a sweet girl I've had a wonderful relationship with since.

I never got to engage with Mary Slack, really. Herself a pillar of the industry for decades, I guess we moved in different circles for most of our careers. She was another I would loved to have trained for, but it was a privilege that never transpired.

With Fradd, Delpech, Strydom and Fayd'Herbe elsewhere engaged I decided to stick with Nooresh for the Guineas. He'd been working hard in the yard, was a good listener and strong in a finish. He was duly composed in the race itself. Cherry On The Top was well placed from a wide draw, positioned to strike at the 400m-mark and she raced away to a 2,25-lengths win over Geoff Woodruff's Do You Remember, a smart home-bred owned by my former patron, Michael de Broglio.

Cherry On The Top was approaching her peak and I felt a strong sense of confidence going into the second leg, the SA Fillies Classic over 1800m. Do You Remember looked to be our only danger in the race. She'd already won over 1700m, took a place over 2200m and being by Silvano was a likely improver. But Cherry On The Top was supreme and commanding this time. Handily placed by Juglall, she powered well clear with 200m to run and left Do You Remember over five lengths adrift.

With seven SA Oaks to my name, one would have thought I'd take the approach to this one in my stride, but with a rare series title and a massive bonus cheque at stake, the build-up to this renewal was a trifle different and everything that could pose a worry, did so. Renier van Rooyen was called in for extra time on Cherry On The Top's hooves. Sharon and Nooresh were constantly around the filly, watching her every move with eagle eyes. Her final few breezes were taxing on our nerves. She was tough, fit as a fiddle but there was always a chance that she could hurt herself prepping.

My other minor concern, unjustified as it turned out, was that young Nooresh Juglall would bend under pressure. The jump from 1800m to 2450m would not be easy, even for a filly of Cherry On The Top's class. Nooresh would have to be patient with a focus on holding her together without restraining her natural inclination to burst clear. Despite our convictions, there was no guarantee that she would see out the testing distance. Perfect timing was key, coupled with a feel for how her rivals were travelling during the running of the race. The wily heavyweight, Bernard Fayd'Herbe, was booked for Do You Remember, who posed a major danger again. And the last thing I needed was to be beaten in such a prestigious race by a filly owned by a former patron.

When the time came to confirm jockey bookings, I decided to give Mrs O a call. I explained the worrying factors but also told her I felt we had to stay loyal to the young rider. She fully agreed, saying, "Don't worry, Juglall has done very well so far. He will give her a good ride. I agree, you should keep him on!"

Oaks Day, 27 April 2013, dawned quicker than expected. A traditional public holiday, this one fell on a Saturday and with a day added to the weekend, Turffontein hosted a nice turnout of racing fans. Not near the number of people the occasion deserved, but a decent crowd nonetheless. Mrs Oppenheimer was there with daughter Mary, whose Wilgerbosdrift Farm sponsored the Tiara and Jessica, her granddaughter, representing three generations of the Oppenheimer family.

The three ladies came to the parade ring to welcome Cherry On The Top, who was in prime condition. I felt confident when Nooresh left us to mount her and she cantered down smoothly with her ears pricked. This was a big moment for all of us. The ladies and Guy Murdoch stayed on in the parade ring to watch the race on the big screen.

Everything went right. Sometimes it didn't. This time, when things had to fall into place just one more time, they did. Cherry On The Top stole the show. She hugged the running rail for most of the journey, placed five lengths off a good clip set by outsiders Moikavano, Rue Di Rivoli and Princess Line.

Moikavano raised the white flag going through the 450m-mark, allowing Princess Line and Sky to move in with Do You Remember also starting to make up ground. All eyes were on Cherry On The Top but Nooresh was waiting, as we'd planned, to make his move as late as possible. He finally let her go about 250m out and she responded instantly. She took over with authority and the race was over as a contest despite another game effort from Do You Remember in second, ahead of Jet Belle.

Cherry On The Top was the second filly in history, after the star Igugu, to win the Triple Tiara and her Oaks success was a joy and a relief for all of us. She was named Equus Champion Three-Year-Old Filly for 2012/2013 and completed her career with nine wins and 5 places, a bankroll of R2,1-million and a R1-million bonus cheque for her Triple Tiara championship. *(There is a beautiful Andrew Bon video on Youtube with a race replay and scenes of Mrs O enjoying the race, throwing her hands in the air and sharing the joy with her family, worth watching).*

After all that, I'm sure readers are expecting me to say it and why not? Winning the Triple Tiara for Bridget Oppenheimer in 2013 was a perfect pinnacle to my career. Yes, indeed, the Cherry On The Top of it all!

CHAPTER 58

There are some interesting things in the news today, 25 September 2022. There were surprise wins by political parties in Sweden and Italy who are opposed to their children being taught by men in high-heeled shoes. This is the way the world tends to balance itself after a heavy tilt in one direction or the other. I've seen these ups-and-downs so many times in my 90 years on planet earth – in my personal life and in racing - and I hope you've enjoyed reading about my journey. I'm going to wrap it all now with another series of closing ups and down. Then, I will pour myself a tot of whiskey and retire to bed.

Not long after Cherry On The Top's Oaks win, Mrs Oppenheimer fell ill and sadly passed away on 23 October 2013. I am forever grateful for the opportunity to have trained a Triple Tiara winner for her.

Here's the tail of this story. Five years later, in 2018, Jessica (now Jell), sent me Summer Pudding to train, another smart filly from the same family as Cherry On The Top. She was coming along the right way and I'd identified her as a fresh Triple Tiara prospect when circumstances led me to retire. Transferred to my neighbour Paul Peter,

Summer Pudding became a star filly too and won the Triple Tiara herself in 2019, followed by the G1 Woolavington and the G1 Summer Cup.

On Saturday, 12 March 2016, I saddled my 2,500th career winner when Romany Prince (Kahal, Muzi Yeni) won the Listed Drum Star Handicap at Turffontein. Quite appropriately, he was owned by my staunch and long-time patron, Peter Dimakogiannis. "Ferraris's 2500 winners have been achieved at close to 40 per season, a remarkable feat considering he has never had a string of more than 60," reported The Citizen. Peter retired to Greece in 2021.

The Trainers Benevolent Fund, close to my heart and in my administrative control since the 1970s, lost its funding from the National Horseracing Authority in July 2016. I found this most upsetting since a few months prior to this I'd had a meeting with the NHA's CEO, Lyndon Barends, in which he pledged his support and wanted to merge all existing benevolent funds into one fund for our benefit. But the NHA suddenly decided to abolish their Rule 95.4 which held that, 'Twenty Percent of all fines imposed and deposits forfeited shall be transferred from the general funds of the NHA to the funds of the Trainers' and Riders' Benevolent Fund.' A significant loss for us there.

In May 2017, I received a Lifetime Membership from the National Horseracing Authority for being a colour holder for 30 consecutive years. Lyndon Barends sent me a certificate, a Life Member Badge and a congratulatory letter. He was quite a famous guy, Lyndon, travelled a lot and reportedly served horseracing well by having a fitness centre installed at the NHA. I was never sure if it was a centre for physical fitness or mental fitness, but I doubt it was the latter. In September 2018, the NHA announced that Lyndon had resigned after he was provisionally sequestrated in the Western Cape High Court, with Firstrand Bank claiming in legal papers that he was insolvent.

After the demise of Phumelela in 2020, the Racing Association decided to cut their own contribution to the Benevolent Fund from R10,000 per month to R6,000 per month. Our fund is still helping where we can. Most recently funds were paid out to the benefit of the late Stanley Ferreira, Romeo Francis and Terry Lowe, but the new administrator Jeff Shill reports that our reserve stash won't last forever. When next you feel like a charity donation, please give Jeff a ring at the Tawny Syndicate.

On March 2020, it was announced that the Listed Oaks Trial over 2000m at Turffontein would carry my name, 'in recognition of achievements'. The first Listed Ormond Ferraris Oaks Trial was run on 14 March 2020 and a further two thereafter. When I depart these shores, I will make sure to see who wins that race every year and I'll be watching you, too. Remember to raise an annual glass on good times, exciting winners and the future of the great Sport Of Kings.

I have to tell of two more passings, I know there have been many mentioned so far but I've had a lengthy innings and have seen more than my share of good people come and go. Dear to my heart was my assistant, Judy van der Merwe, who died of cancer at the tender age of 56, in 2021. Another shock came when Nooresh Juglall, who'd become champion jockey of Mauritius, died in a freak accident on the track at Champ De Mars when a horse fell on top of him. How fleeting life is, even for those who've been here longer than normal.

My grandson, Luke Ferraris, joined the South Africa Jockeys Academy in 2017 and he proved to be the naturally talented rider we always believed he'd become. Luke was only 16 when he won a race on Autumn Rain over 1200m at Scottsville on 23 June, 2018. Autumn Rain was owned by his father David and raced in the silks formerly used by my own father, Ernest. Father, son and grandfather were on course and it was a memorable day for us.

In that same month, I was informed about a grooms' strike at the Randjesfontein Training Centre which came close to erupting in violence against the trainers based at the centre. It was reported that, stoked up by workers' unions and the Economic Freedom Fighters (EFF), grooms armed themselves and started destroying property, while assistant trainers were threatened with death if they refused to join the strike. The strikers also threatened to open the barns and let the horses loose. The trainers themselves, and those left of their staff, fed and watered all their horses. Mike de Kock was quoted as saying: "To have been confronted by 300 weapon-wielding, threatening grooms left a bitter taste in my mouth. When members of my family and staff, and my horses are threatened with death and harm, what am I to do? From now on, we'll be living in fear and uncertainty every day."

I felt for Mike and his fellow-trainers because a storm was brewing at our Turffontein base too and the situation was volatile. We could feel it. I fully understood the plight of our grooms, who found it hard to make a living in a period of serious economic decline, but while most of us paid them more than the minimum required wages, the South African Rand is not a currency that stretches far and the exorbitant cost of feed and transport prevented us from paying them what they were worth.

Then came the day, 4 May 2019, Champions Day at Turffontein, and we were told a day before that our grooms had scheduled an early meeting. I arranged with my 20 grooms to come to work at 3 am on Saturday – an hour earlier than usual – so they could attend their meeting which was scheduled for 5 am. I wanted them to do the bedding, and to feed and water the horses. Just a few came along at 3 am but they soon disappeared leaving me and my head lad, John Sibeko, to get by on our own.

About 50 grooms from around the barns at Turffontein started protesting on the track. They walked on to the course after the second race and refused to leave, delaying proceedings for the best part of an hour.

I'd started feeling distressed and it got so bad that I had to be taken to a clinic for treatment and observation. This was it. I'd had enough. I decided to give up training once and for all and The Racing Post quoted me as saying: "I would love to pay the grooms what they want – big salaries – but it is simply not possible. The costs of feeding and training horses today are astronomical and stakes have not increased in proportion to the high expenses. The few millionaires in racing can afford it but I fear for the middle man, the smaller owner."

On Monday, 6 May 2019, I handed in my licence. I informed my patrons of my decision and arranged for my horses to be transferred to other stables. I took a final walk through the barns I'd occupied at Turffontein for 40 years.

Finally, I cleared my office, locked the door and drove the hell home.

THE END.

COVER IMAGE

Ormond Ferraris with Wagga Wagga
at the Vaal, 1977.

(Painting by Alan Kluckow).

TRIBUTES TO ORMOND FERRARIS

David Ferraris

"My dad taught me everything I know. He was a strong stable master and ran his yard like a military academy and taught me to do the same – stable management has to be a trainer's Number One priority. You win your races from the stable.

"He has a soft side which was never really revealed to the public but of course one we knew about. I recall a day at The Curragh, our old Newmarket stables in Alberton. There was a huge rainstorm and all the rabbit holes were flooded.

"He loved those bunnies so much he went out in the pouring rain and dug down with his hands in the burrows to pull all the baby bunnies out so they wouldn't drown. So while much of his success was a result of his strict stable regimes and horsemanship, he couldn't have achieved what he did without caring deeply for the animals he worked with. That is the truly human side we all love about him."

Michael Clements

"In 1991, Lynn and Dickie Roberts spoke with Ormond about an Assistant Trainer position for me - and following their recommendation I got the job, working alongside David Ferraris as one of Ormond's Assistant Trainers. David soon went off to train in Cape Town in his own right and I maintained the Assistant Trainer position with Ormond.

"I was with Ormond from 1991 to 1993, with three barns of 60 horses at Turffontein. During this period, his yard grew from strength to strength with his biggest support at the time coming from Paddy Hinton. Ormond's domination in the Classics is what stands out in my memory – 'Only fit horses win races' repeats over and over in my mind when I recall Ormond today.

"Whilst I was with Ormond, he won his first Trainers Championship. The look-and-learn knowledge I picked up from him assisted me in the art of getting horses 'fit' to win races, by balancing their training programs and nutrition, along with keeping them sound. This all placed me in good stead to win two of my own Trainers Championships in Zimbabwe in the late 90s, along with being Champion Trainer in Singapore in 2020. I currently lead the Trainers log here in 2021.

"In the Ferraris yard it was all about all about dedication, hard work and honesty - qualities that he influences everyone with."

Mike de Kock

"There are two incidents I recall from a truly memorable time as assistant to Ormond Ferraris. In March 1984, he had a juvenile filly called Battle Vixen which was showing us the world in work. She was very fast and he was lining her up for a 1000m debut at Newmarket. He decided to put jockey Mark Nel on her back first time out. Mark was not one of the boom jockeys of the time, but rode a lot of work and was more than capable of bringing a horse home when the money was down. With Mark on, instead of Raymond Rhodes or Tobie van Booma, the stable would be able to secure better odds on her winning her first start.

"Battle Vixen opened at 16-1 and the money poured on. We considered her a racing certainty, and more money came until she was eventually odds-on favourite at 8-10. She saddled well, cantered down well and all she had to do was reproduce her track work to win. Well, Battle Vixen did that, showing all her speed and natural ability and going clear. But there was one in the race with her that was a little better! Brian Amery's grey filly Espiritu, ridden by Derek Martin, got up in the last stride to beat us.

"Mr Ferraris was devastated. He went pale after the race, just stood still on the grandstand swallowing lumps in his throat. David Ferraris and I walked down to the second box to receive Battle Vixen and Nel, who really didn't do anything wrong and was as disappointed as we were. Minutes later, Mr Ferraris arrived, looking sombre. He hung over the low wall at the second box and told us: 'That's me, I'm out. That's enough. I've lost my cash. I have nothing left. Please find yourselves other jobs. I can't pay you at the end of the month. Make sure Battle Vixen and the others get back home safely. Cheers!' He walked off towards the Newmarket gates and disappeared.

"At 4:30 the next morning, when we got to the stables, Mr Ferraris was already there, making tea. He'd been there since 4 am. We got paid, on time, at month-end."

———

"There was another funny incident at Turffontein early in 1985. David and I were helping Mr Ferraris to saddle Venator in his saddling stable at the back of the parade ring. This was another one strongly fancied to win and we wanted to have our money on after the canterdown. He was, maybe, around 2-1 or 5-2.

Just then, on the blower, came the announcement, "Venator, all the money coming for this one, now 7-10!"

"Mr Ferraris stopped saddling, stood still for a moment, then held his arms over his chest and exclaimed, 'Rhodes, fucking Raymond, he stole my price again. Christ!' He collapsed against the stable wall, moaning loudly and faking a heart attack, but got up a few seconds later to walk with the horse into the parade ring."

———

"I had a good, hard grounding under Ormond Ferraris. He was a hard taskmaster and a stern person, but a supremely knowledgeable horseman. He gave me my big break – the opportunity to learn from a champion trainer with a championship yard."

Jeff Shill

"In the many years working for the Tawny Syndicate who raced horses with Ormond Ferraris, I never got to know the man well until just recently when he handed over the Trainers Benevolent Fund to me. In our meetings since I discovered what a pleasant and funny individual he actually is. There are two funny stories I do remember.

"One concerns Rakeen, the expensive Northern Dancer colt we imported from John Gosden and had persistent niggles. Soon after he was put in training, Larry Nestadt phoned Mr Ferraris and asked if he could come to the morning gallops to see Rakeen work. On the agreed day, Larry arrived at Turffontein at 5 am and shortly after that Mr Ferraris worked Rakeen against a two-time winner. This was not an impressive piece of work at all. The average handicapper got the better of Rakeen and Mr Ferraris said: 'Larry, we could be in trouble. Rakeen doesn't look too good.' We all know how good Rakeen became in time. Larry never attended a morning breeze-up again.

"Then there was the Mr Prospector stallion, Krusenstern, imported for his pedigree with the possibility of a racing career. Mr Ferraris reported after the first few gallops, 'Guys, this horse is very slow, he won't win a race, seriously.' When we took him to stud, unraced, he said: 'If Krusenstern sires a winner, I will run around Turffontein naked!'

"Well, Krusenstern was no star at stud, but he did produce a few winners including The Decagon, a G3 placed, multiple winner trained by David Ferraris.

"I think now is the right time to remind Mr Ferraris of his promise."

Sharon Kotzen (Strydom)

"It was a pleasure and an honour to have been a part of the Ormond Ferraris team for 14 years. He is my mentor and is still always there for me, advising and guiding when needed. He has my utmost respect and is a true legend.

"Lessons taught well include:

1. Routine
2. Check each horse before you work them
3. Feed only the best quality. Winning starts in the manger

"Mr Ferraris is always spoken about as being hard, but has a really soft heart and is always the first person to go more than a mile to help anyone out. He and Judy van der Merwe became like family."

Barry Irwin

"I have had horses trained all over the globe for the last six decades and no horses owned/managed by me ever looked better than those conditioned by Mr O. Ferraris. And… I don't ever recall getting a vet bill unless an accident occurred. That should just about say it all."

Kieron Geoghegan

"I am Kieron Geoghegan, Ormond Ferraris's nephew, and I have a few fond memories to share.

"Let me mention Ormond's liking for cars first. He enjoyed driving good motor vehicles and I remember when he was dating Norma he had a little truck (bakkie) he used at work and a Morris 1000 which he later sold to my mother, Ethne. I learnt to drive that when I was about eight years old. Other cars that come to mind was a silver Chev Malibu and a Chrysler GM Valiant. When training at the Vaal, he had a Merc 380SEC and he drove Mercedes cars for a long time before moving to BMW 530s. He's back in a C-Class Merc these days.

"Ormond's always had two speeds. One was stop, the other was as fast as whatever the car he was driving could go. I think he has slowed his top speed down just a bit in recent years. He was an excellent driver, still is, but terrifying if you were afraid of speed. I loved taking a ride with him. He was always up for a race.

"When Ormond decided to become a sheep farmer in June 1966, my mom Ethne, my dad Brendan and I drove down to Kimberley to visit him and Norma and their three boys. A few days after we arrived, Ormond suffered blood poisoning from sheep dip and the pain got so bad that my dad had to take him to Kimberley Hospital one night. He came back with both hands and lower arms bandaged and couldn't use his hands at all.

"When my parents had to return to Johannesburg, I asked if I could stay on for a while to help my uncle and they agreed. Perhaps I should've gone back home, because that was a bloody cold winter with temperatures below zero and I was a small guy.

"The first morning, Ormond woke me at 4 am and we left the house to start the daily chores. I was in short pants and my young bones were freezing. We walked up to his Chev 100 LDV.3 which had the column straight six-gear shift and he threw me the keys. 'You drive, I can't,' he commanded. It was pitch dark and we had all the farm hands on the back of the truck. We were headed out to let the sheep out of the kraals in the paddocks and break the ice on the sheep water troughs.

"I just manage to depress the clutch by pulling myself down on the steering wheel. The truck stalled first time, but Ormond exclaimed, 'fucking drive properly!' and I learnt immediately and we pulled away. We had to pass through all the farm gates and he devised a technique so the truck wouldn't stall. I would slow down and Ormond would shout at one of the hands to jump off, dash for the gate and open it. We'd drive through and the worker would have to close the gate again and then sprint like an Olympic athlete to get back on because Ormond was in a hurry to get going. By the end of the morning run, I was a perfect driver of a C100 and you might remember they were big vehicles!

"All Ormond said to me at the end of the morning run, was 'Christ, at least you are not bloody stalling the truck!'"

———

"The drought was terrible and water was a massive issue. I used to break the ice on the sheep troughs with my bare hands, alongside the others. When Ormond said, 'Break It!', you broke it.

"Another of the rituals was to check for lame sheep when they were brought in to kraals. There were problems with ticks in their cloven hooves. The solution for this was to get the lame sheep into the kraal corner, grab the back leg and flip it onto its back to check the lame leg.

"I am not sure if you know how big and feisty a Merino ram can be. I had an encounter with one. After several attempts, the herder for that paddock couldn't wrestle the ram to the ground. Ormond, still bandaged to the elbow, ordered me in. 'Just get in there and show him how to do it. Go!' I hit the ground running and with a flying dive I managed to grab the sheep's thick wool on its backside. He then dragged me around in my shorts, and in the kraal filled with 'Duwweltjie' thorns that stung me on my stomach and legs.

"'Grab his bloody leg!' Ormond shouted. 'Don't let go!' I was more petrified of letting go than being dragged. Eventually, with the help of the herder, we got the big Merino onto its back so we could check the lame leg.

"Ormond said: 'Christ, you can bugger around!'"

———

"The drought caused problems of a various nature. One of the farm dams fed by a windmill had a blocked exit valve. We couldn't pipe the water to the troughs so the valve had to be cleared.

"Ormond ordered the farm labourers to get into the big concrete dam, find the exit valve with their bare feet and then clear it. There was a thick layer of mud at the bottom of the dam and about three feet of water. But no coercion or shouting could get them in. In frustration he asked me to do it. I wasn't at all perturbed. I was a very good swimmer and there was only three feet of water. I stripped to my underwear and climbed down the ladder.

"The water was freezing. I proceeded through about six inches of mud and the next moment yelped and jumped four feet up with an agonising stinging in my foot. The staff were hysterical with laughter. 'Stop buggering around and clear the valve!' said Ormond. I was stung another two or three times with the staff now helpless with laughter as they watched. Again, I ploughed on, found the valve, cleared it and with chattering teeth swam back to the ladder, like Mark

Spitz. When I got out, blue and freezing, the staff told me that they were water scorpion stings.

"'Oh, bullshit,'" said Ormond.

———

"This was a great and defining time in my life. Ormond taught me that there is nothing that you cannot do when pushed and he gave me great confidence in myself by pushing me so hard. I never, however, felt threatened by him and always knew that he wouldn't change. We lived near his stables at Turffontein, so I'd often climb over the wall and visit him. We had long chats, also into my later years. He was kind and good to me throughout. My mother was much the same as Ormond. Ethne was driven to be the best at what she did and she, too, reached remarkable heights in her ballet career."

Renier van Rooyen

"I worked as a farrier in the Ormond Ferraris stable, on and off, from 1975 to 2019 and I'd like to share a few memories, firstly of the man himself. He was very strict, hell-bent on routine, grumpy and finicky at times. He didn't tolerate nonsense or laziness and when members of staff got something wrong, they knew about it.

"I believe that his rigorous discipline and stern demeanour lay at the heart of his success and I was working for him in the years David Ferraris and Mike de Kock were assistant trainers. He was hard on them, also on jockeys like Tobie van Booma and Weichong Marwing, but his toughness provided the foundations for their own great careers.

"Mr Ferraris demanded excellence from his staff, because he surrounded himself with the best workers he could find and rewarded them well. He expected loyalty too, kept stable info close to his chest.

"This reminds me of a funny incident. There was a period in the late 1970s when I had an apprentice farrier working for me, who came to work in his car, a green Volkswagen Beetle. 'I hate green, it's unlucky,' mumbled Mr Ferraris, so my appie started parking his car elsewhere and out of sight. The youngster saved up a few Rands and in time had his car re-sprayed. Its new colour was yellow. The car looked as bright as a fresh lemon and he was confident enough to park it near the Ferraris stable again. 'What's going on here,' asked the boss when he saw the yellow Beetle. He called me aside. 'Has that youngster come into money? I see he's driving a new car? What are you guys up to?'

"For all his barking at the staff, sometimes a bad temper and a sullen face, Mr Ferraris is a man with a big heart and his grumpiness was just a screen for the good that lies beneath. He actually likes people and I was witness to many a time when he went out of his way to help and assist colleagues in need. He started and managed the Benevolent Fund out of a deep care and respect for his fellow horsemen, and there were other times he just helped them from his own pocket so friends could survive another week in this merciless sport. Often, too, his dry sense of humour showed.

"I was privileged to have worked with his Triple Tiara winner Cherry On The Top from the time she was about three weeks old, throughout her career to when she won the Triple Tiara. Not many get that opportunity and I was also lucky to have had assistance from Sharon Strydom and two top grooms, Patrick and Alpheus, who watched her like hawks with the master Mr Ferraris overseeing the lot.

"She grew quick and became a big filly. She was a bit weak behind, brushed herself all the time with an injury possible every time. So I had to look carefully after her feet. She had big hooves, we had to keep her balanced. Things got better when she got stronger, but we never let up. There was always a chance that she could hurt herself and that was just not going to happen under our watch. From the day she came in, Mr Ferraris liked her, identified her as a potentially top filly and made her a priority. He was fussy around her, very attentive and careful.

"I have to say, however, that when Mr Ferraris asked a question from an expert, he gave his trust and cooperation to that person. He worked very rarely with veterinarians, but when there was an emergency and they gave their advice, he did not interfere and let them do their jobs. Same with me, as a master farrier. The few times he needed my advice, he listened, accepted it and let me carry on with his full support.

"Good times, they were!"

Charl Pretorius

"Mr Ferraris was as much an inspiration to racing fans as he was to his training colleagues. When I was about eight years old, in 1976, I was already an avid racing junkie. My hours spent studying race cards and being transfixed to anything about racing on television annoyed my family, especially my younger brother. I'd often ride an imaginary horse on the couch with a stick in my hand, shouting, 'Ferraris, Cavé!, 'Ferraris, Cavé!' They were at their best as a jockey/trainer combination and horses like Pretty Border and Wagga Wagga were household names. I had doors slammed on me, and was told to put a lid on it.

'Who is Ferraris and Cavé?', I was asked by members of my family and visiting friends. I told them.

"I had an uncle who showed an interest in my racing activities. He took me to Turffontein one day in August 1982, when I was 14 years old. Youngsters under 18 weren't allowed on the track. But I snuck in, I was tall and was allowed through the turnstiles. We'd come to see the sprinter King Of Jazz.

"My uncle dared me to approach Mr Ferraris and ask him if King Of Jazz would win. I followed the trainer from the parade ring to the escalator that led up to the grandstand. I stepped on, just behind him. He was dressed in a grey suit and a hat, with a pair of binoculars over his shoulder. I looked up at this tall, much-admired man and said, 'Hi sir, can King Of Jazz win?'

"Mr Ferraris saw that I was a young guy probably not allowed on the track, seemed bemused and paused a while. He may have frowned. Then he said, 'He's fit, boetie. Ta.' We told everyone who wanted to hear that we had 'inside info'. We backed King Of Jazz and he won.

"Forward another eight years to November 1989, when I was 22 and working as a junior racing reporter for Beeld in Johannesburg. The press brigade was formidable: Robert Garner, Etienne Louw, Francois Wolfaardt, Geoff Sinclair, Andre van der Kooi, Eddie Balshaw, Jeff Zerbst, Chris Oberholzer and Graeme Hawkins. There was a silent rule: New guys on the block had to prove themselves by interviewing the hard-nosed trainers after their favourites had lost.

"One day at Newmarket, the Ferraris-trained Fearless Spirit, everyone's banker, got beaten under a length for the third time in succession. I was commandeered to go from the press room to the jockeys room to await Mr Ferraris for a comment. When he walked along by, I mustered the courage and mumbled, 'Mr Ferraris? Fearless Spirit, any comment?'

Again, he gave me a strange look, paused briefly and said, 'No comment, Boet. Ta', and walked off. I was told I was very lucky not to get sworn at!

"In May 1992, David Ferraris arranged for me to visit the stable to interview his father for a Business Day profile. I arrived, as arranged, at 5 am, and watched his first and second string at work. He didn't say a word. At about 9 am, when I asked David if I could go ahead and do the interview, he said that something had come up. Mr Ferraris couldn't see me. I had to return the following morning, at the crack of dawn. The next day he was silent, again, but come 9 am he invited me into his office, poured me a cup of Rooibos tea and we got chatting. It was an honour and an adventure, and the interview was well received by readers. We've been on good speaking terms ever since that article was published on 14 May, 1992.

"To have assisted Mr Ferraris in the writing of this book now, at 55, was a rare and unexpected privilege for which I am thankful. The man has been a part of my life as far back as I can remember – first as a racing idol I read about in the press and saw on television; then as a constant subject for media articles; a friendly acquaintance and now as a friend. Fifty years after I first heard his name and he was my celebrity racing hero, we collaborated on a book we are both proud of. For me, an event that would never have crossed my mind in any childhood dream. Thank you very much for that, Mr Ferraris. Ta!"

SOURCES

In our research for this book, we had to rely on several undated articles from the racing pages of The SA Racehorse, The Star, The Citizen, Sunday Express, Sunday Times, Business Day, Beeld, Parade Magazine and Cape Argus. We tried to match these, in most cases, to horse names and race dates supplied by the ARO website *(www.aro.co.za)*. Some may be inaccurate, give or take a day. We attribute all undated references to these various publications. Writers' names were noted when quoted. In researching the historic Stipendiary Boards and information about Alan Forbes (Chapters 34 and 43), the National Horseracing Authority was helpful.

OTHER SOURCES USED:

Chapters 1-5
South African History Online (www.sahistory.org.za)

Chapter 6
Trove: (www.trove.nla.gov.au)

Chapter 7
Papers Past (https: natlib.govt.nz)
The Spectator Archive
Time Magazine, May 1, 1950 *(GOLD: Judgment Day)*

Chapter 48
Sporting Post 25 August 2011 *(Phumela responds to Ian Jayes)*
Sporting Post 30 January 2012 *(Horse racing at odds with itself)*

Chapter 56
Business Insider (April 2021)
Iol.co.za (Jul 2013)
The Racing Record